FIELD GUIDE TO
FYNBOS
FAUNA

Cliff Dorse • Suretha Dorse

Published by Struik Nature
(an imprint of Penguin Random House South Africa (Pty) Ltd)
Reg. No. 1953/000441/07
The Estuaries No. 4, Oxbow Crescent, Century Avenue, Century City, 7441
PO Box 1144, Cape Town, 8000 South Africa

Visit **www.struiknature.co.za** and join the Struik Nature Club for
updates, news, events and special offers.

First published in 2023
1 3 5 7 9 10 8 6 4 2

Publisher: Pippa Parker
Managing editor: Roelien Theron
Editor: Heléne Booyens
Concept designer: Neil Bester
Designer: Emily Vosloo
Typesetter: Deirdre Geldenhuys
Proofreader: Emsie du Plessis

Reproduction by Studio Repro
Printed and bound by ABC Press

ISBN 978 1 77584 739 7 (Print)
ISBN 978 1 77584 740 3 (ePub)

ACKNOWLEDGEMENTS

We endeavour to spend as much time as we possibly can in natural habitat, especially within the Fynbos Biome. We are honoured to have spent many hours in the field with our friends and colleagues, many of which are leaders in their respective fields. We thank you all for sharing your knowledge and time so generously with us. These individuals and many others also advised us regarding the content and development of this book. To these people we would also like to express our sincerest gratitude.

We were heartened by the overwhelming generosity of people who were willing to contribute images. Many of these images are of extremely rarely encountered animals and the book would be much poorer without them. The following is a collated list of the people who contributed their photos and or time to assist with this publication: Adam Buckham, Adam Riley, Albert Froneman, Alta Oosthuizen, Alvin Cope, Andrew Turner, Anton Pauw, Ara Monadjem, Bernard DuPont, Cathy Withers-Clarke, Chris and Mathilde Stuart, David Jacobs, Dennis Cope, Dominic Rollinson, Elana Kellerman, Guy Palmer, Henry de Lange, Howard Langley, Jacques Theron, Jacques van der Merwe, Jenny Javis, John Graham, Jonathan Bell, Justin Rhys Nicolau, Kevin Shaw, Krystal Tolley, Kyle Finn, Luke Verburgt, Magriet Brink, Margaret Hardaker, Marius Burger, Matthew Prophet, Mike Buckham, Mike Fabricius, Natio van Rooyen, Owen Wittridge, Patrick Rollinson, Peter Ryan, Peter Taylor, Rob Tarr, Roger de la Harpe, Sam Hockey, Stefan Theron, Tony Rebelo, Trevor Hardaker, Trevor Morgan and Werner Conradie.

South and southern Africa have the most amazing assortment of field guides – perhaps the best available for any region in the world. This is testament to our amazing biodiversity, the nature-loving public and the wonderful experts in the respective fields who write the various guides. The fact that most of these field guides are produced by Struik Nature (Penguin Random House) is not a coincidence. The professional team have mastered the production of the field guide and we are privileged to have produced this publication with them. We would especially like to thank Heléne Booyens, Pippa Parker, Emily Vosloo and Neil Bester for all their expertise and patience with us and in producing this work.

We would like to acknowledge and thank all the authors that produced the valuable books, scientific papers and online resources that assisted us throughout our careers thus far and also helped shape this book. It would additionally be seriously amiss if we failed to acknowledge the wonderful resource that is iNaturalist (https://www.inaturalist.org). Our huge appreciation to everyone who contributes to it. It provides easily accessible data of where species have been recorded and, very importantly, allowed us to review various colour forms or patterns that occur within the Fynbos Biome. Everyone is urged to use platforms such as iNaturalist to get identifications and to log valuable data. Citizen science at its best!

And finally, we would like to thank all the passionate individuals, especially our fellow career conservators, out there doing their best to conserve the incredible Fynbos Biome. Thank you for your dedication and persistence, often in the face of extreme pressure and adversity.

Cliff and Suretha Dorse

CONTENTS

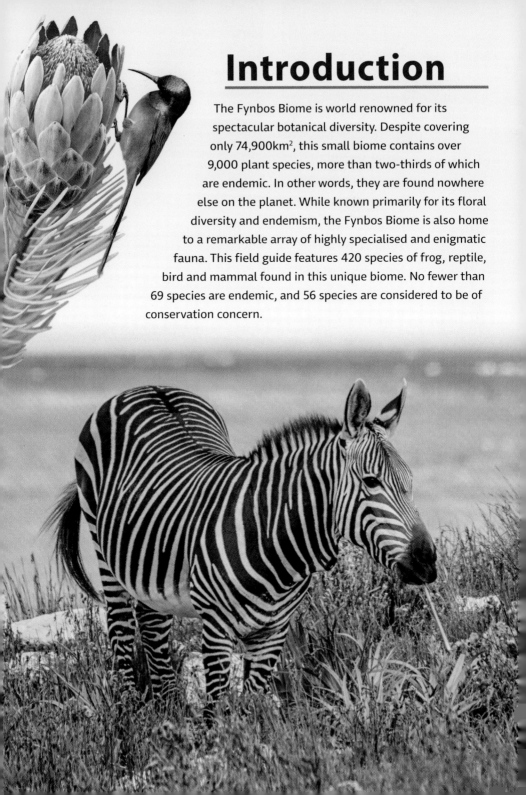

Introduction

The Fynbos Biome is world renowned for its spectacular botanical diversity. Despite covering only 74,900km², this small biome contains over 9,000 plant species, more than two-thirds of which are endemic. In other words, they are found nowhere else on the planet. While known primarily for its floral diversity and endemism, the Fynbos Biome is also home to a remarkable array of highly specialised and enigmatic fauna. This field guide features 420 species of frog, reptile, bird and mammal found in this unique biome. No fewer than 69 species are endemic, and 56 species are considered to be of conservation concern.

Sand Rain Frog calling from vegetation

Male Cape Rockjumper, an iconic endemic species

ANIMALS OF THE FYNBOS

This field guide covers four animal groups:

FROGS Of the 54 frog species that occur in the Fynbos Biome, over half are found nowhere else. This level of endemism is comparable to that of the Biome flora. Of all the animal groups in the region, frogs are the most sensitive to threats such as climate change owing to the small distribution ranges and the specific habitat requirements of many species. There are 16 species of conservation concern.

REPTILES A total of 113 reptile species occurs in the region: 34 snake, 73 lizard, five tortoise and one terrapin species. The Fynbos Biome endemics comprise one snake species and 23 lizard species. The majority of these endemic and range-restricted species are confined to mountainous areas. Many species restricted to the highly transformed lowlands, such as Geometric Tortoise and Southern Adder, are highly threatened.

BIRDS This book includes 162 bird species associated with Fynbos habitats. It excludes species that occur only in non-Fynbos Biome habitats and transformed areas in the region, as well as rare vagrants (see page 266 for the full list). Eight species are Fynbos Biome endemics. At present, 16 species are of conservation concern, most of which are raptors. Sadly, several species that were once widespread in the Fynbos Biome are now locally extinct.

MAMMALS Africa is famed for its mammals, especially large, diurnal species that are readily seen. In contrast, most of the 91 mammal species found in the Fynbos Biome are nocturnal, secretive and seldom observed. Rodents are the most diverse, with 27 species. Carnivores (18 species), bats (13 species) and hoofed mammals (13 species) follow. Close to a fifth of Fynbos mammals are of conservation concern. Several species of large mammal were historically eradicated from the region, although some have been reintroduced (see page 14).

Armadillo Lizard in defensive posture

Karoo Round-eared Sengi, the Biome's smallest sengi

The iconic King Protea (*Protea cynaroides*), the national flower of South Africa

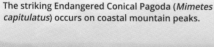

A Klipspringer in Boland Granite Fynbos

WHAT IS FYNBOS?

Fynbos is an evergreen, hard-leaved, fire-prone shrubland, generally characterised by the presence of restios, ericoid and proteoid shrubs. The term 'Fynbos' is derived from the Dutch word 'fijn-bosch', which means fine or narrow-leaved bush.

The climate within the Fynbos Biome is Mediterranean, with predominantly winter rainfall in the western parts of the region, while further east the rainfall is less restricted to winter months and summer rainfall events are common. The rainfall ranges from approximately 300mm to over 3,000mm per annum. This large range in precipitation, coupled with a complex mosaic of different topography, soil types, nutrient availability and disturbance regimes, creates diverse ecological niches for plants and animals. As such, Fynbos is extremely species diverse, with many plant species having limited distribution ranges.

FYNBOS IN CONTEXT

All terrestrial vegetation on Earth can be divided into six floristic kingdoms. These kingdoms are the largest classification unit for flowering plants, and can comprise various floristic regions. The **Cape Floristic Kingdom** is by far the smallest of the six floral kingdoms and contains only one region, namely the **Cape Floristic Region** (CFR). This region was originally defined as an area covering some 90,800km². It formed a distinctive and clearly delineated area at

The striking Endangered Conical Pagoda (*Mimetes capitulatus*) occurs on coastal mountain peaks.

the south-western tip of Africa, contained predominantly in the Western Cape Province. The CFR followed the Cape Fold Mountains and the relatively narrow coastal belt from the Northern Cape town of Nieuwoudtville to Grahamstown in the Eastern Cape.

More recently, the CFR was further defined to consist of the original core CFR (as above) as well as the Succulent Karoo Biome. This region is referred to as the **Greater CFR** and incorporates the **Succulent Karoo** vegetation from near Willowmore in the Eastern Cape, and extends into southern Namibia just to the north of Lüderitz. This inclusion increases the Greater CFR to an area exceeding 189,600km². When

referring to the CFR in this book, it implies the Greater CFR, unless otherwise specified.

The CFR contains four biomes, namely Fynbos, Succulent Karoo, Albany Thicket and Afrotemperate Forest. The **Fynbos Biome** is the most distinctive of these and covers some 74,900km². It consists of three major vegetation complexes, namely **Fynbos Heathland** (also called True Fynbos, and referred to as Fynbos in the species accounts), **Renosterveld** and **Strandveld Thicket**.

Each of these major vegetation complexes is further divided into vegetation types, which represent plant communities with similar floristic composition and vegetation structure.

COMPOSITION OF THE CAPE FLORISTIC KINGDOM

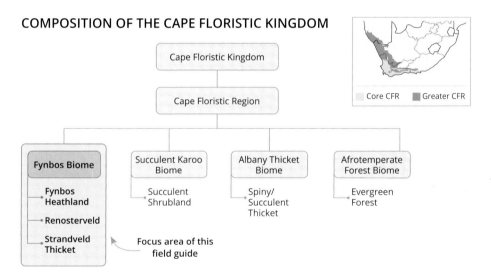

GLOBAL SIGNIFICANCE

In recognition of the global significance of the CFR, specific Protected Areas were declared a World Heritage Site by the United Nations Educational, Scientific and Cultural Organization (UNESCO) in 2004. This status emphasises the international importance of the CFR, deeming it as critical heritage, relevant to every person on the planet. The CFR is also one of 36 Global Biodiversity Hotspots recognised by Conservation International. These terrestrial regions, which collectively comprise only about 2.4% of the Earth's surface area, were identified based on their biological diversity (at least 1,500 endemic plant species) as well as the threat to their long-term survival (having lost at least 70% of the historical indigenous vegetation cover). The CFR contains more than 11,423 plant species and close to 78% of these are endemic. It has been referred to as the world's 'hottest hotspot' for plant diversity and endemism.

The CFR is also notable for high levels of endemism among reptiles, amphibians, insects and freshwater fishes.

VEGETATION COMPLEXES

The Fynbos Biome comprises three vegetation complexes, which are in turn divided into various vegetation types. These vegetation types are synonymous with ecosystem or habitat types and are the vegetation community classification unit used for biodiversity planning.

1 Fynbos Heathland (67% of Biome)

True Fynbos plant communities are restricted to nutrient-poor, acidic, sandy soils or limestone substrates. Where the rainfall is above 600mm per annum, Fynbos also occurs on granite and shale clay soils. It characteristically contains restios, ericas and protea species and is generally described as a species-rich shrubland. Fire is a critical driving force, and the fire return interval can be anything from 8–30 years.

2 Renosterveld (29% of Biome)

Renosterveld plant communities are present on nutrient-rich, fine-grained shale or granitic soils, where the rainfall is 300–600mm per annum. The dominant growth form is small-leaved, low-growing evergreen shrubs, particularly of the Asteraceae family. Restios, proteas and ericas are absent or very poorly represented. There is an abundance of grasses, geophytes and annuals. Renosterveld is a fire-prone shrubland, but would historically also have had more influence from indigenous grazing animals. The natural fire frequency interval is estimated to be 10–15 years. Renosterveld contains exceptional levels of species diversity and endemism. Due to its association with fertile soils, this vegetation complex has been greatly transformed by agricultural activities.

3 Strandveld (4% of Biome)

Strandveld is restricted to deep, well-drained, marine-derived alkaline sands along the coast. The rainfall is usually 200–400mm per annum. It is a shrubland with sparse to moderate plant cover, including restios, large broad-leaved shrubs and small trees, interspersed with a diversity of annuals and bulbs. Strandveld has a larger proportion of berry-producing shrubs than Fynbos and Renosterveld. In general, Strandveld is less fire-prone than Fynbos and Renosterveld, but the wetter dune troughs may burn more frequently than the drier thicket-dominated dune ridges.

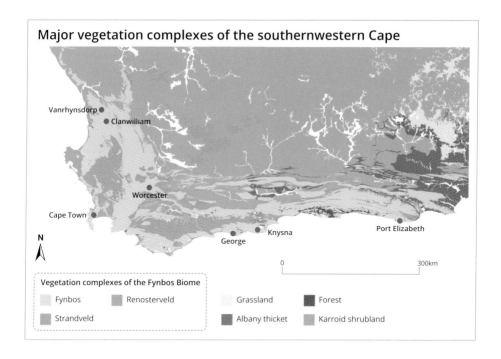

Major vegetation complexes of the southernwestern Cape

Vanrhynsdorp
Clanwilliam
Worcester
Cape Town
George
Knysna
Port Elizabeth

N

0   300km

Vegetation complexes of the Fynbos Biome

- Fynbos
- Renosterveld
- Strandveld
- Grassland
- Albany thicket
- Forest
- Karroid shrubland

FUNCTIONAL ECOLOGY

The various vegetation or ecosystem types within the Fynbos Biome provide habitats for a diverse array of fauna species. While an ecosystem is a community of biotic and abiotic components, habitat, simply put, is where an organism lives within that community. Some species can be considered **generalists** and are able to survive in a diverse range of vegetation types. Others, the **specialists**, are selective with regards to one or more ecological attributes and have smaller, sometimes tiny, global ranges or are confined to a specific vegetation type.

The faunal component of an ecosystem fulfils a critical role in maintaining the system. Each species fulfils a specific niche. There is a complex network of interactions that maintains the health of an ecosystem. Should one component disappear, the balance is disrupted. These imbalances create knock-on effects that may require significant management intervention to restore or maintain a measure of the original functioning ecosystem. Some specialist interactions cannot be artificially re-created and those ecosystem imbalances cannot be corrected once lost.

The Clicking Stream Frog is a habitat generalist, found in diverse habitats, including transformed areas.

The Banded Stream Frog is a habitat specialist, restricted to mountain Fynbos.

Cape White-eye pollinating aloe flowers

Pygmy Hairy-footed Gerbil pollinating a pincushion

Some 30% of the CFR's plant species are adapted to the dispersal of their seed by ants (myrmecochory).

Faunal functions

Thanks to a growing body of knowledge compiled by researchers, conservators and citizen science, we are discovering more and more about the fascinating and highly specialised fauna associated with Fynbos. In addition to the role of herbivory, animals influence plant communities and habitats in various ways.

POLLINATION The Fynbos Biome is home to a multitude of fascinating specialist pollinators and pollination strategies. While insects are the most specialised of all pollinators (see box below), many plant species rely on bird and mammals to fulfil this function. Bird pollination is common, with many plant species being adapted to attract and be pollinated by birds. Examples include Orange-breasted Sunbirds, specifically attracted to ericas, while Malachite Sunbirds favour the large red and orange tubular flowers of geophytes, and Cape Sugarbirds prefer proteas and pincushions. Mammals also perform this specialised function. Some ground proteas, such as the Clasping-leaf Sugarbush (*Protea amplexicaulis*), position their flowers at ground level and have a yeasty scent. This attracts various rodents that pollinate the flowers. Even genets and mongooses have been recorded visiting these ground proteas.

SEED DISPERSAL The seeds of some Fynbos plant species are dependent on animals to be distributed and planted. One such example involves scatter-hoarding rodents. Species such as the Cape Spiny Mouse store hard-shelled nuts underground. Some of this food stock is never eaten, ultimately forming a seedbank that is spurred to germinate by fire. Some rodent species such as mole-rats and Cape Porcupine

INSECT POLLINATORS

Notable specialised insect pollinators in the Fynbos Biome include oil-collecting bees (Melittidae), the sole pollinators of a wide range of orchids and annuals, as well as needle-nose flies (*Philoliche*) and tangle-veined flies (Nemestrinidae). The Meg-proboscid Tangle-veined Fly (*Moegistorhynchus longirostris*), pictured right, pollinates many long-tubed flowers with its extraordinary long proboscis.

also facilitate the spread of geophytes through vegetative dispersal. Certain geophytes have adapted to herbivory pressure by producing a multitude of bulblets, which are spread through the digging and burrowing of these rodents.

ECOSYSTEM ENGINEERS Certain faunal species fulfil a critical role in shaping and changing habitat. Termites, for example, store plant material underground, enriching the soil with nutrients. Centuries of this activity create large raised, circular patches, known as 'heuweltjies', within the landscape. Heuweltjies enable the establishment of bigger shrubs, in turn providing shelter for plants and animals.

Aardvark create numerous substantial burrows, which are utilised by a wide range of other species. Their vigorous digging activities also create disturbance patches that are favoured by a diverse community of annual plant species. Hippopotamuses, as another example, modify plant communities, distribute nutrients and create pathways that facilitate water movement. Numerous other species use these pathways as habitat and movement corridors.

Cape Mole-rats facilitate the spread of geophytes.

These circular patches are known as 'heuweltjies'.

Connectivity

Much of the natural vegetation of the Fynbos Biome has been fragmented by human activity, especially in the lowlands. Some sites are no longer viable for many of the fauna species that historically occurred there. The absence of specific species can have a number of repercussions and are particularly evident in the case of larger predators, which tend to disappear first. For example:

- The active persecution of snakes, such as the harmless Mole Snake, has contributed to the unchecked increase of rodent populations at some sites. The resultant overabundance can severely impact on plant communities. Habitat restoration is hampered, since the foraging activity of rodents decimates seed banks and seedling recruitment in degraded areas. Restoration efforts must therefore include management interventions that favour predator species in order to restore some balance.
- At some isolated sites where larger predators no longer persist, the small antelope populations can increase to the point where they severely impact on the ecological

Hippos beneficially shape their environment.

The loss of Mole Snakes from sites can lead to the proliferation of rodent populations.

A Red Hartebeest is released into a nature reserve.

Honey Badgers have large home ranges.

integrity of the remnant. Active fauna management is required to ensure populations are maintained at sustainable levels. Similarly, some actively reintroduced larger fauna may need to be managed to ensure that they do not exceed the carrying capacity of the veld. Some species have substantial home range requirements. Honey Badgers, for instance, have huge home ranges of up to 550km². Although the home range of this species is not yet defined within the Fynbos Biome specifically, it is safe to assume that no single protected area in the Biome is large enough to support a self-sustaining population.

For the ecological integrity of all sites and the persistence of fauna species, the most important factor is for protected areas to be as large as possible and to have some form of ecological connectivity. Some generalist species can persist in smaller remnants, and some are more adaptable to urban and isolated or degraded environments. However, the full complement of species within an ecosystem can only be conserved with sufficiently large, intact and connected protected areas.

THEN AND NOW: LARGE MAMMALS IN THE FYNBOS

Historically, many large mammal species occured in the Fynbos Biome. Early accounts report African Elephant (*Loxodonta africana*), Lion (*Panthera leo*), Spotted Hyaena (*Crocuta crocuta*), Serval (*Leptailurus serval*) and African Wild Dog (*Lycaon pictus*) in the vicinity of Cape Town. Even African Savanna Buffalo (*Syncerus caffer*) were reported as far east as Swellendam.

As Fynbos is generally nutrient poor with a low carrying capacity for large fauna, these animals occurred at lower densities and had large home ranges. Many of the larger herbivores probably moved long distances to take advantage of the flush of new growth following fires. These herds were decimated after the settlers arrived in the 17th century and most of the large fauna we see in the region's protected areas today were reintroduced following their local extinction.

The recent popularity of the game farming industry has resulted in an array of extra-limital game being introduced to the region, including Nyala (*Tragelaphus angasii*), Blue Wildebeest (*Connochaetes taurinus*), Springbok (*Antidorcas marsupialis*), Sable Antelope (*Hippotragus niger*) and even Giraffe (*Giraffa camelopardalis*). These species were never a component of the faunal assemblage of the Fynbos Biome and are often stocked to the detriment of the environment.

FYNBOS AND FIRE

The primary ecological driving force in the Fynbos Biome is fire. It is a popular misconception that fire 'destroys' Fynbos and is catastrophic to wildlife. In truth, Fynbos ecosystems become senescent and unproductive when fire is withheld for too long. Although some animals do perish during wildfires, indigenous species are adapted to natural fire cycles. Many individuals escape the fire by fleeing or by sheltering in underground or rocky refugia. Others re-emerge from underground egg clutches or recolonise the site from unburnt neighbouring areas. These species are dependent on a healthy and functioning ecosystem, which in turn is dependent on fire, to persist.

Ecological control burns are an essential management tool within the Fynbos Biome.

THREATS

The main threats to Fynbos Biome habitats are **transformation**, **degradation**, **fragmentation** and **climate change**. Where habitat remains intact, **direct persecution** and **harvesting** still pose a threat to certain animal species.

Transformation

Habitat loss through land transformation is the primary driver of species extinctions around the world. This is also the case in the Fynbos Biome, where 26% of the CFR has already been lost to agriculture and urban development. The lowlands have been most severely impacted, with 96% of lowland Renosterveld and 49% of lowland Fynbos habitats having been lost.

Montane Marsh Frogs are adapted to natural fire cycles and survive these events.

Habitat degradation

Degradation happens in a number of ways. Causes of degradation include:

The endangered Umbrella Lily (*Hessea cinamomea*) depends on fire to flower.

ALIEN INVASIVE SPECIES As the second biggest threat to biodiversity, unsurprisingly some 73% of the CFR is subject to alien plant invasion of varying degrees. Stands of alien species, such as woody alien trees and shrubs can become so dense that they outcompete and completely replace almost all indigenous species. This fundamental change to the plant communities and vegetation structure has a marked impact on the associated fauna. Most locally indigenous faunal species are not able to adapt to the changed environment and only generalist species, mainly thicket or forest

Pine invasion within Fynbos Biome habitats poses a significant risk in terms of fire and water security.

Atlantis Sand Fynbos cleared for development

Clearing thick stands of Port Jackson (*Acacia saligna*) requires significant effort and resources.

Alien clearing allows indigenous species to recover.

The alien Mallard Duck (*Anas platyrhynchos*) poses a threat to indigenous Yellow-billed Ducks.

species, can colonise such invaded areas. Secondary impacts of uncontrolled alien plant invasions include increased water usage, which threatens water security for biodiversity and humans. Similarly, increased fire frequency and intensity significantly impacts on ecosystems as well as threatening human life and infrastructure.

There are also many invasive faunal species that impact negatively on terrestrial and aquatic ecosystems by competing for resources with locally indigenous species occupying the same niches. Some introduced species also hybridise with indigenous ones, ultimately leading to the loss of our local species.

OVERGRAZING Fynbos is particularly susceptible to overgrazing as the nutrient-poor soils do not provide enough good fodder to sustain big herds. The new growth in young veld is most palatable, but this is the time when overgrazing and trampling can do significant damage. The result is a loss of vegetation cover, soil disturbances and ultimately the loss of certain species.

OVERHARVESTING Unsustainable plant harvesting for medicinal use and the cut flower industry can also degrade the habitat, especially where important structural elements or keystone species are targeted. Without careful management, species can be harvested into local extinction.

SOIL EROSION A loss of vegetation cover, soil disturbances and changes to hydrological processes lead to soil erosion. When the topsoil

Little Karoo Dwarf Chameleon

is lost, plant recruitment is significantly lower and less diverse since the seedbank is removed and niches for seedling establishment are reduced. Additionally, it creates windows for alien plant invasions. Erosion can also lead to sedimentation of downstream watercourses and the degradation of wetland habitats. Prevention is better than cure as it is difficult and expensive to halt and repair large-scale soil erosion.

GROUND WATER ABSTRACTION Water resources are under ever-increasing pressure as demand grows. The impact of large scale ground water abstraction is difficult to monitor and control, but the hydrology of natural areas can be severely affected.

Fragmentation
Fragmentation is the result of habitat loss and degradation, creating patches of remaining veld that are no longer connected to one another. These patches are generally small and have a large edge-to-area ratio. The edge effects of neighbouring land uses and activities impact on these remnants, decreasing their viability and increasing the cost and intensity of the conservation management required to sustain them. Small and isolated remnants cannot effectively protect and sustain all species and many will become locally extinct over time. This is particularly evident in the case of medium-sized to large fauna, which have large home ranges.

Climate change
The increase of greenhouse gases such as carbon dioxide and methane is changing the world's climate. There is still some uncertainty

Poor veld management can lead to significant erosion.

Large, intact conservation areas can support large game such as Eland.

A fragmented landscape

Montane Marsh Frogs are sensitive to climate change.

Leopard eradiction can cause proliferation of Caracal.

Hyrax populations surge when predators are removed.

as to the exact impact of these changes but predications are that the Fynbos Biome will become warmer with less predictable rainfall. Theoretically the western areas will become drier while the eastern areas might see an increase in precipitation, with more frequently occurring and severe floods and droughts. One of the main concerns for the biodiversity of the Fynbos Biome is the impact on organisms that have adapted to specialised and specific habitat conditions. These organisms will not be able to adapt to such relatively quick changes to their environment and will therefore not survive.

While reducing global carbon emissions is the primary focus against climate change, conserving as much habitat as possible and ensuring that natural remnants are as large and connected as possible is also critically important.

Direct persecution

Some animals are perceived as a nuisance to humans. Perhaps the most well-known example is the controlling of carnivores in livestock farming areas. While predator management is understandably practised to protect livestock, the indiscriminate killing of predators is often ineffective and can even aggravate the situation when natural predator-prey relationships are disrupted. For example, eradicating Leopard in an area may cause a proliferation in smaller carnivores, such as Caracal, which ultimately have a much larger negative impact on farmers. Similarly, the persecution of birds of prey, such as Verreaux's Eagle, can cause overpopulation of their Rock Hyrax prey, reducing the amount of browsing available to livestock.

Perceived nuisance animals also include species such as Aardvark and Cape Porcupine,

which burrow under jackal-proof fences. Aardvark occasionally dig their large burrows into dam walls and in the middle of gravel roads.

Non-selective control techniques, such as setting traps and using poison, are problematic as they often don't kill the targeted animal and can result in significant collateral damage. The impact of poison on vulture colonies are a well-known example. Fortunately, there are some innovative projects designed to reduce the conflict between humans and potential damage causing animals.

The poaching of small game is also prevalent in some Fynbos Biome areas. Snares are the most commonly used method of poaching, which is unselective and can stay set for months or even years. Worryingly, there is also an increasing trend of illegal hunting with dogs. This often takes the form of gambling, where bets are made on which dog will make the kill and the pay-out varies according to what species is killed.

CONSERVATION

The importance of our environment, and the need to protect it, is well established and a legal requirement in South Africa. Besides the ethical consideration that every species on Earth has the same right to be here as humans, the motivation to conserve our natural heritage is also based on the value biodiversity has for humans. This includes aspects such as ecosystem services (i.e. clean water and air), tourism, consumptive value, aesthetic value as well as social, spiritual, educational and bequest value. In essence, we are dependent on biodiversity.

The biological significance of the CFR is indisputable. It is considered one of the most

Angulate Tortoise

special places for plant diversity and endemism in the world. The urgency for adequate conservation is clearly depicted by 2020 statistics showing 3,427 plant taxa from the Fynbos Biome of conservation concern. With 91.7% of these taxa endemic to the region, they can only be protected and saved here.

Conservation efforts in the Fynbos Biome have long been skewed towards the mountainous areas. This was primarily to protect critical water catchment areas. The largely privately owned lowlands were considered to be important for agricultural activities and urban development. Unfortunately, these lowland areas contain vastly different biodiversity. As such, a conservation crisis has resulted, with the lowland systems being heavily transformed and shockingly under-conserved. Urgent action is required if we are to save some of the remaining lowland biodiversity.

Many species of large mammal that used to occur in the Fynbos Biome are now locally extinct, and a few species and subspecies are globally extinct. These include the Blue Buck (*Hippotragus leucophaeus*) and Cape Lion (*Panthera leo melanochaita*). Blue Buck was a

Fynbos endemic and already restricted to the Overberg by the 17th century. It then became the first large African mammal to officially become extinct in the 18th century as a result of hunting and competition for grazing with livestock.

Conservation initiatives have fortunately had some success in preventing further global and local extinctions and conservators continue to work tirelessly to prevent more. A great example of how conservation efforts prevented the extinction of a Fynbos endemic involves the Bontebok (*Damaliscus pygargus pygargus*). Bontebok were naturally restricted to the Renosterveld areas around Bredasdorp and Mossel Bay, Western Cape Province. The population declined to 22 individuals owing to hunting and habitat loss. Thanks to the efforts of Bredasdorp farming families, they were saved from extinction. They however remain at risk due to the long-term impacts of the restricted gene pool, limited remaining natural habitat, indiscriminate game movement and hybridisation with Blesbok (*Damaliscus pygargus phillipsi*).

ENJOY RESPONSIBLY

Always consider your individual impact on the animal and the environment it depends on. Interactions with these wonderful creatures should aim to do as little damage to them and their surroundings as possible. Take these precautions:

- Respect and adhere to the legislative restrictions involved in capturing, handling and moving of wildlife.
- Avoid directly handling animals.
- Limit all negative impacts on sensitive habitats – actively searching for certain species can be destructive to their habitat, e.g. breaking off exfoliated rock sheets; entering sensitive areas such as recently burnt veld or peat wetlands; and moving rocks.
- Take a precautionary approach with regards to the sharing of localities of sensitive, threatened or collectable species on social media. This information can unintentionally aid poachers and the illegal wildlife trade.

The endemic Bontebok was saved from extinction.

HOW TO USE THIS BOOK

This field guide comprises four chapters: **frogs**, **reptiles**, **birds** and **mammals**. Each section starts with an overview of the local species diversity, including life history and viewing guidelines, as well as illustrations of key identification features. The individual species descriptions include characteristic features, habitat preference, call (where applicable), conservation status and level of endemism.

Family account

Genus account

Common name

Scientific name

Picture number

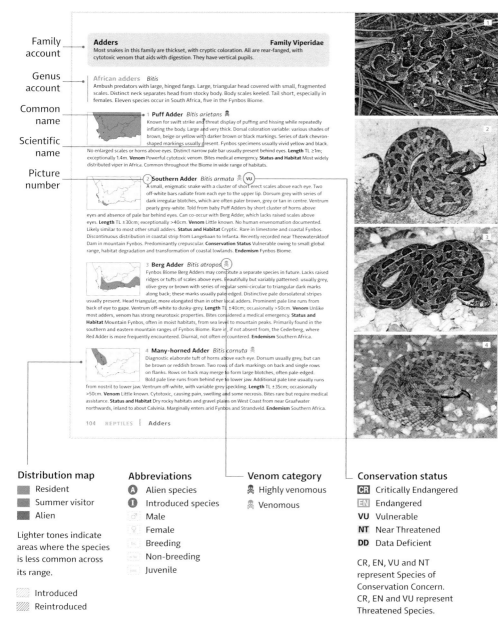

Adders   **Family Viperidae**
Most snakes in this family are thickset, with cryptic coloration. All are rear-fanged, with cytotoxic venom that aids with digestion. They have vertical pupils.

African adders *Bitis*
Ambush predators with large, hinged fangs. Large, triangular head covered with small, fragmented scales. Distinct neck separates head from stocky body. Body scales keeled. Tail short, especially in females. Eleven species occur in South Africa, five in the Fynbos Biome.

1 Puff Adder *Bitis arietans* 🐍
Known for swift strike and threat display of puffing and hissing while repeatedly inflating the body. Large and very thick. Dorsal coloration variable: various shades of brown, beige or yellow with darker brown or black markings. Series of dark chevron-shaped markings usually present. Fynbos specimens usually vivid yellow and black. No enlarged scales or horns above eyes. Distinct narrow pale bar usually present behind eyes. **Length** TL ≥1m; exceptionally 1.4m. **Venom** Powerful cytotoxic venom. Bites medical emergency. **Status and Habitat** Most widely distributed viper in Africa. Common throughout the Biome in wide range of habitats.

2 Southern Adder *Bitis armata* 🐍 VU
A small, enigmatic snake with a cluster of short erect scales above each eye. Two off-white bars radiate from each eye to the upper lip. Dorsum grey with series of dark irregular blotches, which are often paler brown, grey or tan in centre. Ventrum pearly grey-white. Told from baby Puff Adders by short cluster of horns above eyes and absence of pale bar behind eyes. **Length** TL ±30cm; exceptionally >40cm. **Venom** Little known. No human envenomation documented. Likely similar to most other small adders. **Status and Habitat** Cryptic. Rare in limestone and coastal Fynbos. Discontinuous distribution in coastal strip from Langebaan to Infanta. Recently recorded near Theewaterskloof Dam in mountain Fynbos. Predominantly crepuscular. **Conservation Status** Vulnerable owing to small global range, habitat degradation and transformation of coastal lowlands. **Endemism** Fynbos Biome.

3 Berg Adder *Bitis atropos* 🐍
Fynbos Biome Berg Adders may constitute a separate species in future. Lacks raised ridges or tufts of scales above eyes. Beautifully but variably patterned: usually grey, olive-grey or brown with series of regular semi-circular to triangular dark marks along back; these marks usually pale-edged. Distinctive pale dorsolateral stripes usually present. Head triangular, more elongated than in other local adders. Prominent pale line runs from back of eye to gape. Ventrum off-white to dusky-grey. **Length** TL ±40cm; occasionally >50cm. **Venom** Unlike most adders, venom has strong neurotoxic properties. Bites considered a medical emergency. **Status and Habitat** Mountain Fynbos, often in moist habitats, from sea level to mountain peaks. Primarily found in the southern and eastern mountain ranges of Fynbos Biome. Rare in, if not absent from, the Cederberg, where Red Adder is more frequently encountered. Diurnal, not often encountered. **Endemism** Southern Africa.

4 Many-horned Adder *Bitis cornuta* 🐍
Diagnostic elaborate tuft of horns above each eye. Dorsum usually grey, but can be brown or reddish brown. Two rows of dark markings on back and single rows on flanks. Rows on back may merge to form large blotches, often pale-edged. Bold pale line runs from behind eye to lower jaw. Additional pale line usually runs from nostril to lower jaw. Ventrum off-white, with variable grey speckling. **Length** TL ±35cm; occasionally >50cm. **Venom** Little known. Cytotoxic, causing pain, swelling and some necrosis. Bites rare but require medical assistance. **Status and Habitat** Dry rocky habitats and gravel plains on West Coast from near Graafwater northwards, inland to about Calvinia. Marginally enters arid Fynbos and Strandveld. **Endemism** Southern Africa.

104   REPTILES | Adders

Distribution map
▪ Resident
▪ Summer visitor
▪ Alien

Lighter tones indicate areas where the species is less common across its range.

▨ Introduced
▨ Reintroduced

Abbreviations
Ⓐ Alien species
Ⓘ Introduced species
♂ Male
♀ Female
Breeding
Non-breeding
Juvenile

Venom category
🐍 Highly venomous
🐍 Venomous

Conservation status
CR Critically Endangered
EN Endangered
VU Vulnerable
NT Near Threatened
DD Data Deficient

CR, EN, VU and NT represent Species of Conservation Concern. CR, EN and VU represent Threatened Species.

Frogs

Six frog families occur in the Fynbos Biome, namely rain frogs (Brevicipitidae), toads (Bufonidae), ghost frogs (Heleophrynidae), reed frogs (Hyperoliidae), platannas (Pipidae) and African common frogs (Pyxicephalidae). A total of 54 species have been recorded. The Guttural Toad (*Sclerophrys gutturalis*) is not locally indigenous to the Biome but has been introduced into the southern suburbs of Cape Town.

ENDEMISM

Relative to the reptiles, mammals and birds found in the Fynbos Biome, frogs exhibit exceptionally high levels of endemism. This is primarily due to the low dispersal abilities of most amphibians and to the mountainous topography of the region. Almost 60% of the frog species in the Fynbos Biome are found nowhere else, and three-quarters of these are endemic to the Cape Floristic Region (CFR).

Frog genera endemic to the Fynbos Biome	
Genus	**Number of species**
Moss frogs (*Arthroleptella*)	10
Mountain toadlets (*Capensibufo*)	5
Micro Frog (*Microbatrachella*)	1
Montane Marsh Frog (*Poyntonia*)	1

Note: Ghost frogs (*Heleophryne* spp.) also inhabit Southern Afrotemperate Forest patches within the Biome and are considered core CFR endemics rather than true Fynbos endemics.

While the majority of frogs call, there are exceptions. Rose's Mountain Toadlet appears to be mute.

Clicking Stream Frogs occur in a wide array of colours and markings.

CONSERVATION CONCERN

Significantly, almost 30% of the frog species recorded in the Fynbos Biome is of conservation concern. The main threats to Fynbos Biome amphibians are habitat loss and invasion by alien vegetation. Several species have extremely small global distribution ranges, making them particularly vulnerable. In addition, the Fynbos Biome will likely be significantly affected by the long-term impacts of global climate change. Of all the Fynbos Biome fauna, frogs are likely to be the most negatively impacted due to their small distribution ranges and the specific habitat requirements of many species.

LIFE HISTORY

All Fynbos Biome frogs are dependent on at least some moisture. Most species have aquatic tadpoles and require standing water for some part of the year. Even the rain frogs, which are unable to swim and whose tadpoles develop in underground nests, are dependent on moisture from rainfall or coastal fogs to be active on land. As such, the peak season for frog activity in the Fynbos Biome is from midwinter to early summer. While all frogs have a well-defined breeding season related to seasonal rainfall, many are opportunistic and will take advantage of unseasonal rainfall events to breed. Males call to attract females during the breeding season. As calling is the primary method of attracting and selecting a mate, there can be substantial variation in coloration and patterns within the same population of some species.

FROGGING IN THE FYNBOS

Many frogs are cryptic and difficult to observe. Their unique calls advertise their presence, however, and most can be identified by call alone. If a frog is located or photographed without its call being heard, note the following:
- Extent of webbing between the fingers and toes
- Shape of the pupil (vertical or horizontal)
- Presence and shape of parotoid glands
- Presence and size of tympanum
- Coloration and patterning of the dorsal and ventral surfaces (though colour can be extremely variable in some species)
- Location (many species have a limited distribution)

Frog species of conservation concern		
Critically Endangered (CR)		
1	Rose's Mountain Toadlet	Capensibufo rosei
2	Table Mountain Ghost Frog	Heleophryne rosei
3	Rough Moss Frog	Arthroleptella rugosa
4	Northern Moss Frog	Arthroleptella subvoce
5	Micro Frog	Microbatrachella capensis
Endangered (EN)		
6	Western Leopard Toad	Sclerophrys pantherina
7	Hewitt's Ghost Frog	Heleophryne hewitti
8	Knysna Leaf-folding Frog	Afrixalus knysnae
9	Cape Platanna	Xenopus gilli
Near Threatened (NT)		
10	Landdroskop Moss Frog	Arthroleptella landdrosia
11	Drewes's Moss Frog	Arthroleptella drewesii
12	Cape Peninsula Moss Frog	Arthroleptella lightfooti
13	Cape Rain Frog	Breviceps gibbosus
14	Cape Caco	Cacosternum capense
15	Flat Caco	Cacosternum platys
16	Montane Marsh Frog	Poyntonia paludicola
Data Deficient (DD)		
17	Moonlight Mountain Toadlet	Capensibufo selenophos
18	Deception Peak Mountain Toadlet	Capensibufo deceptus
19	Landdroskop Mountain Toadlet	Capensibufo magistratus

Identification features

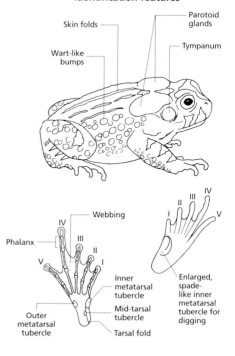

23

Rain frogs   Family Brevicipitidae

A small family, endemic to Africa. A single genus of 20 species occurs in South Africa; six species are found in the Fynbos Biome. Largely fossorial, these specialised frogs are seldom observed.

Rain frogs *Breviceps*

Small, rotund frogs with short legs and a grumpy expression. They walk or run instead of hopping. Most have no traces of webbing and lack a visible tympanum. Rain frogs spend long periods underground; they use enlarged, spade-like metatarsal tubercles to dig backwards into soil. They emerge in rainy or misty conditions to forage on the surface. If threatened, they inflate their body, secrete a milky substance through the skin and may give an alarm call. The males' forelimbs are too short to clasp the larger females during amplexus. Instead, they 'glue' themselves to their partner's back with adhesive secretions (see top left picture). The pair then dig down to deposit their eggs in an underground chamber. Lacking a free-swimming tadpole phase, young do not require standing water. Rain frogs are best identified by distribution and call. Males call from concealed positions on the ground or in vegetation.

1 Strawberry Rain Frog *Breviceps acutirostris*

A medium-sized rain frog with no obvious face mask. Upperparts markedly granular; coloration ranges from light beige to red, with dark bumps. Underparts finely rough, black to plum, with cream spots. **Length** 40mm. **Call** Short, insect-like, trilling whistle, repeated in quick succession. **Habitat** High-rainfall areas of mountain Fynbos and Afrotemperate Forests between Hottentots Holland and Langeberg ranges. Overlaps with Plain Rain Frog in the east of its range. **Endemism** CFR (in South Africa).

2 Plain Rain Frog *Breviceps fuscus*

A medium-sized rain frog with no face mask. Upperparts rough, evenly dark and uniform, ranging in colour from light brown to dark charcoal. Dark spots occasionally visible. Underparts smooth and usually uniformly dark. **Length** 50mm. **Call** Mournful, drawn-out, high-pitched whistle repeated at regular intervals. **Habitat** Endemic to mountain Fynbos and Afrotemperate Forests, from around Swellendam to Kareedouw Pass, Eastern Cape. Co-occurs with Cape Mountain Rain Frog (most of its range) and Strawberry Rain Frog (around Grootvadersbosch). **Endemism** CFR (in South Africa).

3 Cape Rain Frog *Breviceps gibbosus* NT

The largest rain frog. Dark mark extends from eye towards arm. Upper- and underparts rough. Upperparts variable shades of brown, often with darker spots and cream markings along either side of spine. Underparts pale with darker blotches. **Length** 80mm. **Call** Frequently repeated long, reverberating melodious whistle. Most guttural of the rain frog calls. **Habitat** Confined to lowlands from Citrusdal south to Cape Town. Prefers fine-grained soils but also found in Cape Flats Sand Fynbos. Can persist in suburban gardens and stands of invasive pine trees. **Endemism** Fynbos Biome. **Conservation status** Near Threatened owing to habitat destruction and fragmentation by agriculture and urbanisation. Regularly eaten by Hadeda Ibis, which recently colonised the Fynbos Biome.

Cape Mountain Rain Frogs in amplexus

1 Cape Mountain Rain Frog *Breviceps montanus*

A small rain frog with a distinctive dark mask running from the eye to the top of the arm. Similar to Sand Rain Frog. Upper- and underparts rough. Upperparts range from beige to dark brown, with reddish to orange hue and variable dark marbling. Paler patches alongside spine may fuse to form indistinct vertebral band. Underparts pale with darker markings. **Length** 31mm. **Call** Series of short, high-pitched whistles. **Habitat** Mountain Fynbos from north of Clanwilliam to Outeniqua Mountains; occurs from near sea level to high mountain peaks. **Endemism** Fynbos Biome.

2 Namaqua Rain Frog *Breviceps namaquensis*

A medium-sized rain frog with a dark mark extending from the eye towards the arm. Fleshy webbing present on feet. Upperparts granular or smooth; coloration varies from brown to yellow, with large dark brown to black irregularly shaped markings. Pale patches form rough bands along spine and upper flanks. Underparts smooth and pale, some showing translucent patches. **Length** 45mm. **Call** Repetitive, clear, slow, medium-pitched whistle. **Habitat** Coastal sand from Blaauwberg to Orange River, at least as far inland as Vanrhynsdorp. Co-occurs with Sand Rain Frog in the south. **Endemism** South Africa.

3 Sand Rain Frog *Breviceps rosei*

Two subspecies known. A small rain frog with a dark mask running from below the eye to the top of the arm. Upper- and underparts fairly rough. Upperparts irregularly patterned with pale beige, dark brown and orange. Thin, pale vertebral line may be present (mostly in *B. r. vansoni*) with paler patches forming paired half-circle patterns edged in black on either side. Underparts pale with some darker flecking. **Length** 36mm. **Call** A quick high-pitched whistle repeated at short, regular intervals (reputedly slower in *B. r. vansoni*). **Habitat** Sandy soils in Strandveld and coastal Fynbos from Lambert's Bay to Gouritsmond. *B. r. rosei* north from False Bay; *B. r. vansoni* east from Kleinmond. **Endemism** Fynbos Biome.

Toads   Family Bufonidae

Toads are well known and distinctive in appearance. Just as owls are a type of bird, toads are a type of frog. They are differentiated from other frogs in that they lay their eggs in well-defined strings and have paired toxin-producing parotoid glands on the neck and upper back. Three genera occur in the region.

Mountain toadlets *Capensibufo*

One of the most enigmatic and interesting frog genera in South Africa. Mountain toadlets are small, attenuated toads with attractive colour patterns, horizontal pupils and no webbing. Five species are known – three described as recently as 2017. All are endemic to the Fynbos Biome and allopatric, and most have extremely limited distribution ranges. Three species have no advertisement calls and the call of one species is undescribed. Annual breeding congregations occur at small, temporary, well-vegetated wetlands in mountain Fynbos.

4 Deception Peak Mountain Toadlet *Capensibufo deceptus* DD

A relatively large mountain toadlet. Upperparts smooth with numerous raised warts; coloration dark reddish brown with pale vertebral stripe containing thin white line. Parotoid glands linear; not expanded at any point. Visible tympanum distinguishes this species from all others except Tradouw Mountain Toadlet. Underparts plain, pale grey or lightly speckled. **Length** 38mm. **Call** Unknown; expected to have advertisement call owing to presence of tympanum. **Habitat** Hawequas Sandstone Fynbos below Deception Peak in DuToits Mountain. **Endemism** Fynbos Biome. **Conservation Status** Data Deficient as recently described.

B. rosei vansoni   B. rosei rosei

Western Leopard Toads in amplexus. Note the egg strings.

1 Landdroskop Mountain Toadlet *Capensibufo magistratus* DD

Upperparts smooth, with numerous raised warts; coloration a mosaic of pale grey, brown and dark brown, often with pale or orange vertebral stripe. Parotoid glands expanded centrally. No tympanum visible. Underparts dark with white spots, or white with irregular dark marks. **Length** 26mm. **Call** No advertisement call, but can emit distress call. **Habitat** Mountain Fynbos in Hawekwas Mountains, Hottentots Holland, Groenland, Kogelberg and Riviersonderend mountains. **Endemism** Fynbos Biome. **Conservation Status** Data Deficient as recently described and insufficiently known.

2 Rose's Mountain Toadlet *Capensibufo rosei* CR

Upperparts smooth, with numerous raised warts. Coloration varies from grey to dark brown with numerous dark blotches and occasional orange marking. Can appear very dark. Pale vertebral stripe seldom present. Parotoid glands expanded anteriorly. No tympanum visible. Underparts immaculate to lightly speckled. **Length** 28mm. **Call** None – completely silent. **Habitat** Endemic to Peninsula Mountain Fynbos. **Endemism** Fynbos Biome. **Conservation Status** Critically Endangered owing to extremely small geographic range and inexplicable disappearance from several historical sites.

3 Moonlight Mountain Toadlet *Capensibufo selenophos* DD

Upperparts smooth, with numerous raised warts; coloration grey to brown with dark spots. Orange vertebral band with thin pale vertebral stripe present. Parotoid glands expanded centrally. No tympanum visible. Underparts have white spots on darker background. **Length** 24mm. **Call** No advertisement call. **Habitat** Mountain Fynbos from Kleinrivier to Soetmuis mountains. **Endemism** Fynbos Biome. **Conservation Status** Data Deficient as recently described and insufficiently known.

4 Tradouw Mountain Toadlet *Capensibufo tradouwi*

Most widespread of the mountain toadlets and constituting at least two species. Upperparts smooth, with numerous raised red to brown warts; coloration varies from pale grey to dark brown with irregular markings. Pale vertebral stripe often present. Underparts white with variable grey markings. Parotoid glands expanded posteriorly, usually dull red. Visible tympanum separates this species from all others in genus, except for highly localised Deception Peak Mountain Toadlet. **Length** 38mm. **Call** Rasping croak. **Habitat** High-altitude mountain Fynbos from Matsikamma Mountains near Vanrhynsdorp to Misgund in Tsitsikamma Mountains. Breeding areas include rock pools or slow-flowing streams. **Endemism** Fynbos Biome.

Typical toads *Sclerophrys*

Robust, short-legged, large to very large frogs with a conspicuous tympanum and horizontal pupil. They have dry glandular skin and can spend many months far away from their breeding sites while foraging. Toads are explosive breeders, with males forming large choruses at breeding sites. Eight species occur in South Africa. Four species are found in the Fynbos Biome, one of which, the Guttural Toad, is introduced.

5 Raucous Toad *Sclerophrys capensis*

Upperparts rough, with numerous warts; coloration olive to brown with roughly symmetrical, irregular blotches. Parotoid glands large and prominent. No dark marks between eyes and snout, resulting in unmarked triangular area. Dark bar between eyes. Tympanum conspicuous, slightly smaller than eye. Underparts pale grey, unmarked. Limited fleshy webbing between toes. Juveniles usually colourful; snout and parotoid glands bright pink. **Length** 115mm. **Call** Harsh, repetitive, raucous quacks. **Habitat** Common and widespread, but absent from Cape Peninsula, Cape Flats and sandy West Coast. Found in natural and transformed habitats. **Endemism** Southern Africa.

1 Guttural Toad *Sclerophrys gutturalis* ①

Upperparts rough; coloration light to dark brown with roughly symmetrical, irregular blotches and numerous smaller irregular marks. Thin, pale vertebral line may be present. Distinct dark blotches on snout and behind eyes result in pale cross on top of head. Parotoid glands conspicuous. Variable red markings on back of thighs. Tympanum conspicuous; smaller than diameter of eye. Underparts pale grey, unmarked. Limited fleshy webbing between toes. **Length** 120mm. **Call** A frequently repeated, pulsed, guttural call, which accelerates slightly. **Habitat** Widespread summer-rainfall species irresponsibly introduced to the Constantia area in Cape Town.

2 Western Leopard Toad *Sclerophrys pantherina* EN

Beautiful and striking. Upperparts rough, covered with numerous warts, pale yellow with symmetrical dark red to brown blotches edged with black and yellow. Parotoid glands large, conspicuous, typically orange-brown. Top of snout usually without dark marks. Tympanum small but conspicuous. Underparts dull white to cream and unmarked, occasionally discoloured during breeding season. Prominent webbed fringe on toes. **Length** 150mm. **Call** Protracted snore. Males usually call from partially concealed positions during the day and from open water at night. **Habitat** Lowland of Agulhas Plain, Cape Flats and Cape Peninsula, including transformed habitats (gardens, agricultural areas or areas invaded with alien vegetation). Breeds in a variety of water bodies. **Endemism** Fynbos Biome. **Conservation status** Endangered. Much of its range has been developed into suburbia. Particularly vulnerable to road mortality, especially during breeding migrations.

3 Eastern Leopard Toad *Sclerophrys pardalis*

Very similar to Western Leopard Toad; may be lumped with this species in future, but distribution ranges exclusive. Upperparts rough, with numerous warts, dull yellow or with symmetrical dark red to brown blotches edged with black and yellow. Parotoid glands large and conspicuous. Top of snout usually without dark marks. Tympanum small but conspicuous. Underparts dull white, unmarked. Prominent webbed margin on toes. **Length** 150mm. **Call** Long snoring call similar to Western Leopard Toad, but somewhat deeper. **Habitat** Woodland, grassland, thickets, parks and gardens of the Eastern Cape. Potentially occurs in Fynbos habitats in the southern Cape. **Endemism** South Africa.

Van Dijk's toads *Vandijkophrynus*

Typically toad-like. Medium-sized, smaller than typical toads (*Sclerophrys*), with visible tympanum and horizontal pupils. Breeding is more subdued than in typical toads, and calling males are normally well-spaced at breeding sites. The relatively soft calls are uttered intermittently. Four species occur in South Africa, two of which are found in the Fynbos Biome.

4 Cape Sand Toad *Vandijkophrynus angusticeps*

Upperparts rough, pale grey to brown, heavily marked with irregularly shaped blotches. Pale vertebral stripe usually present. Parotoid glands large and conspicuous. Tympanum small, clearly defined. Underparts white, unmarked. No obvious webbing, but toes have webbed fringe. A key identification feature is the yellow upper feet. **Length** 60mm. **Call** Relatively soft protracted croak, uttered intermittently. **Habitat** Fynbos Biome endemic found in coastal lowlands and mountains. Breeds in temporary pools. Can persist in agricultural areas, but not suburbia. **Endemism** Fynbos Biome.

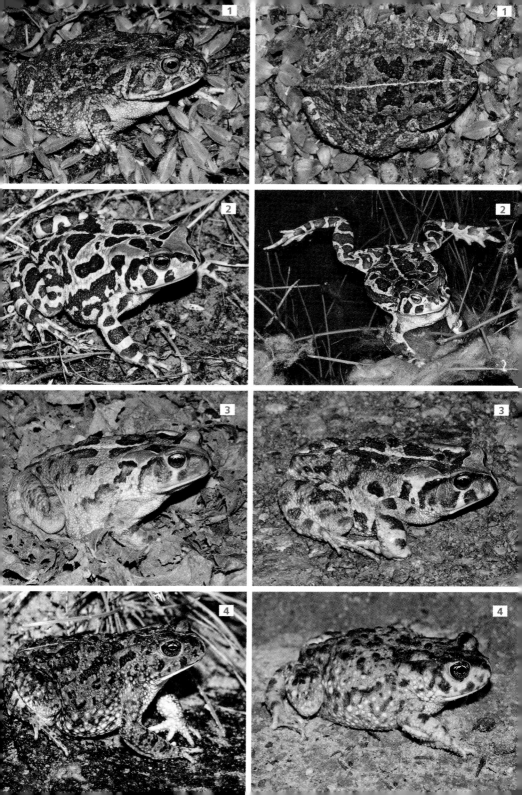

1 **Karoo Toad** *Vandijkophrynus gariepensis*

A Karoo species that enters the Fynbos Biome on the arid edges; not known to co-occur with Cape Sand Toad. Upperparts rough, covered with numerous round bumps; coloration extremely varied, usually brown to olive- or orange-brown with numerous irregular darker blotches. Markings usually bold, but can be faint. Parotoid glands large and prominent. Tympanum small, not conspicuous. Underparts pale grey to white, unmarked in adults and spotted black in subadults. No webbing. **Length** 90mm. **Call** Low protracted croak. Two calls produced in quick succession, with long intervals between bouts of calling. **Habitat** Widespread in South Africa, but marginal in Fynbos Biome. Breeds in a wide range of natural and human-made permanent or temporary water bodies. **Endemism** Southern Africa.

Ghost frogs   Family Heleophrynidae

A small, enigmatic family comprising two genera and seven species endemic to South Africa, Lesotho and Eswatini.

Ghost frogs   *Heleophryne*

These medium-sized, distinctive and attractive frogs are well adapted to fast-flowing, perennial mountain streams. Their flattened body enables them to utilise narrow rock crevices. Their elongated limbs with enlarged disc-shaped finger and toe tips make them adept at climbing. Extensive toe webbing allows them to swim strongly. Tadpoles have uniquely enlarged mouths to suck onto rocks in strong-flowing streams. Skin granular. Tympanum usually not visible. Prominent bulging eyes with vertical pupils; all but one species have a horizontal line through eye. No two species co-occur. Ghost frogs are dependent on clear, perennial streams as the tadpole phase is a year or longer. Six species occur in the Fynbos Biome.

2 **Cederberg Ghost Frog** *Heleophryne depressa*

Dorsal coloration varying shades of olive-green, marked with irregular, rounded, dark shapes that range from purple-brown to maroon. Markings form irregular dark bands on limbs. Underparts uniformly cream to yellow. **Length** 45mm. **Call** High-pitched, soft, whistle-like notes repeated irregularly. **Habitat** Found in clear mountain streams in Cederberg, Groot Winterhoek and Koue Bokkeveld mountains. **Endemism** Fynbos Biome.

3 **Hewitt's Ghost Frog** *Heleophryne hewitti* 🅴🅽

Dorsal coloration ranges from beige to shades of green, with lighter margins around varyingly shaped burgundy or brown blotches. Markings on limbs form irregular dark bands. Underside uniformly pale. **Length** 50mm. **Call** Single soft, high-pitched, clear, whistle-like *peep*, repeated relatively slowly. **Habitat** Only known to breed in five rivers in Elandsberg and Cockscomb mountain ranges in the Eastern Cape. Associated with clear, perennial streams within Fynbos vegetation. **Endemism** CFR (in South Africa). **Conservation Status** Endangered owing to ongoing degradation and fragmentation of its habitat, mainly by forestry activities.

4 **Eastern Ghost Frog** *Heleophryne orientalis*

Dorsal coloration ranges from tan to olive-green, with variable dark maroon or brown blotches. Blotches occasionally pale-edged. Underside uniformly pale. Markings on limbs form dark bands. **Length** 46mm. **Call** Single medium-pitched, clear knocking *ping* repeated at regular intervals, resembling the noise of a small hammer on an anvil. **Habitat** Clear, perennial mountain streams in central to eastern sections of Langeberg range to Gouritz River in the east. Found predominantly in Afrotemperate Forest patches. **Endemism** CFR (in South Africa).

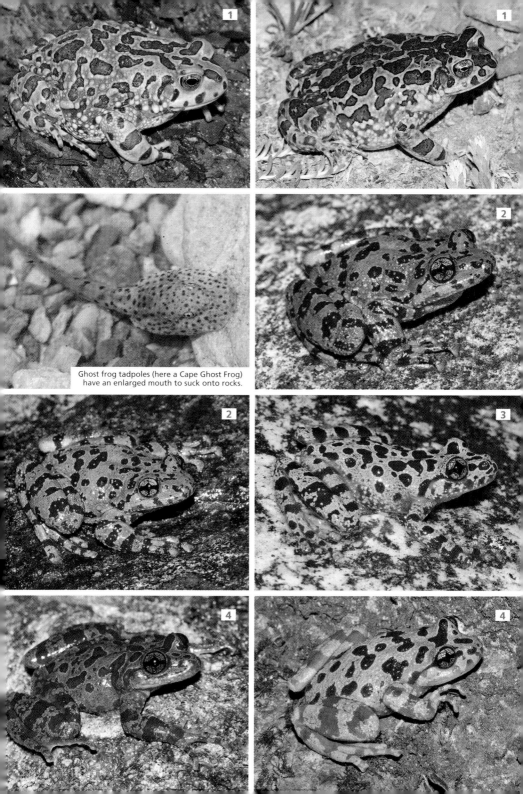

Ghost frog tadpoles (here a Cape Ghost Frog) have an enlarged mouth to suck onto rocks.

1 Cape Ghost Frog *Heleophryne purcelli*

Dorsal coloration ranges from yellowish brown to olive, green or bright green, marked with smaller, irregularly shaped, burgundy to brown spots, with no or limited pale edging. Ventral surface pale. Dark markings on limbs form rough bands. **Length** 56mm. **Call** A short *pick* note at regular intervals. Similar to that of Eastern Ghost Frog but higher-pitched and slightly faster. **Habitat** Perennial mountain streams of central to southern Cederberg Mountain range to Hottentots Holland and Kogelberg mountains, including Hex River Mountains and eastwards into western sections of Langeberg Mountains. **Endemism** CFR (in South Africa).

2 Southern Ghost Frog *Heleophryne regis*

Dorsal coloration varies from mustard-yellow to green with variable number of maroon to brown blotches of various sizes and shapes. Blotches seldom pale-edged. Markings on limbs form irregular bands. Underparts uniformly pale. **Length** 49mm. **Call** Quick, low-pitched, grating and croaking notes repeated at regular intervals. **Habitat** Clear, perennial streams in coastal mountain ranges of the Garden Route in the Western and Eastern Cape, from Outeniqua Mountains, including Tsitsikamma range, to Kareedouw Mountains. **Endemism** CFR (in South Africa).

3 Table Mountain Ghost Frog *Heleophryne rosei* **CR**

The largest ghost frog. Distribution and lack of a prominent horizontal line through eye sets it apart from other ghost frogs. Dorsal coloration pale green with intricate maroon, plum to brown blotches of varying size and shape, usually interconnected. This coloration creates a banded appearance on limbs. **Length** 63mm. **Call** Seldom heard. Medium to high-pitched, croak-like *pick* notes in quick succession. **Habitat** Breeds in a limited number of rocky mountain streams on Table Mountain. Occurs in upper sections of streams in Southern Afrotemperate Forest and Peninsula Sandstone Fynbos. **Endemism** CFR (in South Africa). **Conservation status** Critically Endangered owing to its highly restricted range and changes to the hydrology of the breeding streams.

Reed frogs   Family Hyperoliidae

Small to medium-sized frogs, most of which have bright coloration. Most species are arboreal. This large African family comprises 15 genera, three of which are found in the Fynbos Biome.

Leaf-folding frogs   *Afrixalus*

These frogs are similar to reed frogs (*Hyperolius*) but can easily be differentiated by a vertical pupil. Strong jumpers, with terminal discs on fingers and toes that aid climbing. Feet webbed. Tympanum not visible. They are known as leaf-folding frogs as they conceal their eggs in a folded leaf. Their alternative common name is 'spiny reed frog' owing to the presence of numerous small dermal spines (asperities). Five species occur in South Africa, one entering the Fynbos Biome.

4 Knysna Leaf-folding Frog *Afrixalus knysnae* **EN**

Dorsal coloration yellow to brown with variable intensity broad dark brown vertebral band and flanks. Small dermal spines present on dorsal surface, none present on white belly. Male has yellow throat. **Length** 25mm. **Call** Rapid chatter resembling an insect call. **Habitat** Coastal wetlands in Fynbos Biome and ecotonal Afrotemperate Forest in a small area of the southern Cape: Groenvlei in the west to Covie in the east. Has been recorded sheltering in Arum Lily (*Zantedeschia aethiopica*) flowers. **Endemism** CFR (in South Africa). **Conservation status** Endangered owing to habitat degradation and loss.

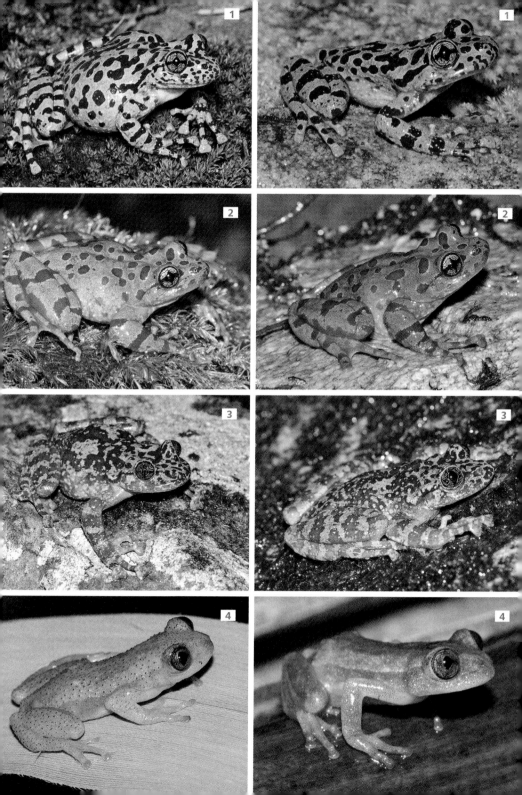

Reed frogs *Hyperolius*

Reed frogs are very colourful, with great variation between different populations, sexes and age groups. Some species even change colour between day and night. The horizontal pupil easily separates reed frogs from the similar leaf-folding frogs (*Afrixalus*). Adept climbers, they have terminal discs on their fingers and toes. There is some webbing between the digits. The tympanum is usually not visible. With well over 100 species, *Hyperolius* is the largest of the African frog genera. The taxonomic status of several species is unresolved. Two species occur in the Fynbos Biome.

1 Arum Lily Frog *Hyperolius horstockii*

Dorsal coloration cream to pale brown, with darker flanks edged with black and white lines. The upper white lines run from tip of snout to base of thighs. Ventral surface white and granular. Hidden areas of the limbs red. **Length** 45mm. **Call** Loud nasal bleat. Calling occurs at night. **Habitat** Endemic to coastal lowlands of Fynbos Biome. Historically, only known to occur east of Cape Town, but there are several recent records on the West Coast as far north as Langebaan. Breeds in wide variety of vleis, dams and slow-flowing rivers with emergent vegetation. While Arum Lily Frogs will indeed shelter in Arum Lily (*Zantedeschia aethiopica*) flowers during the day, they are in no way dependent on the presence of these flowers. **Endemism** Fynbos Biome.

2 Painted Reed Frog *Hyperolius marmoratus*

An extremely variable and taxonomically complex species with three distinctive subspecies in South Africa. Only one, *H. m. verrucosus*, naturally occurred along the east coast of the Fynbos Biome, as far west as Tsitsikamma. The species has been widely translocated, and is now established along the coastal strip west to Cape Town. The source of introduced populations derives from all three South African subspecies. Coloration extremely variable. Cellular adjustments can also reduce visible pigment in response to environmental stimuli, such as light, temperature, surrounds and emotional state (inset). Most Western Cape specimens have a dark brown back with variable white spots. Juveniles are shades of brown, a colour form also common in adults. Toes, fingers and hidden surfaces of limbs red. Ventral surface white or pink. **Length** 32mm. **Call** Short, high-pitched, loud and piercing whistle. **Habitat** Wide variety of natural and artificial wetlands, including rivers, vleis, marshes and detention ponds.

Rattling frogs *Semnodactylus*

Monotypic. The Rattling Frog is endemic to South Africa where it is widespread, occurring in both the Fynbos and Grassland biomes. Easily distinguished from all other Fynbos Biome amphibians by the peculiar arrangement of the digits on the hands. A large gap between the second and third finger results in two fingers pointing forwards and two backwards, which enables them to climb through thick grass easily. The Rattling Frog walks rather than jumps.

3 Rattling Frog *Semnodactylus wealii*

This beautiful frog has grey to yellowish upperparts and distinctive dark brown longitudinal stripes with paler centres. Tympanum not visible. Pupil vertical. Inner areas of legs, hands and feet yellow. Belly roughly granular with varying degree of dark markings. **Length** 44mm. **Call** Short harsh rattle. Calls very loud; choruses can be deafening. Calls mainly at night. **Habitat** Inhabits Fynbos, grasslands and agricultural pastures on the coastal lowlands east of Cape Town. Appears to have been extirpated from Cape Flats. Breeds in a variety of wetlands and marshes, including farm dams with some fringing vegetation. **Endemism** South Africa.

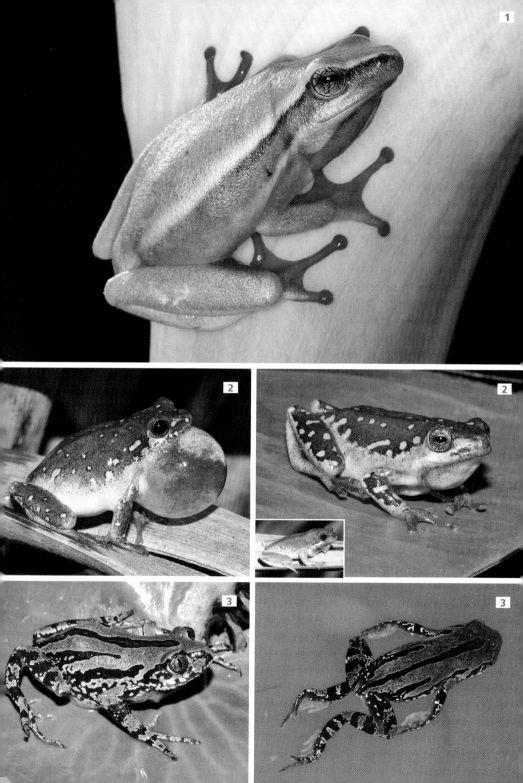

Clawed frogs
Family Pipidae
These primitive tongueless frogs are highly aquatic. Only the genus *Xenopus* occurs in South Africa.

Platannas / Clawed frogs   *Xenopus*
Highly distinctive African frogs. Body streamlined and flattened, adapted to entirely aquatic lifestyle. No tympanum, no tongue and no movable eyelids. Eyes with circular pupils. Hind legs large, powerful; feet with extensive webbing. Unique keratinised claws on three inner toes. Unwebbed hands used to guide food into mouth. Lateral sensory system on the head and flanks enable these frogs to detect vibrations in the water. The distinctive tadpoles superficially resemble small translucent catfish. Two of the three South African species occur in the Fynbos Biome.

1 Cape Platanna *Xenopus gilli* EN
Smaller than Common Platanna; no subocular tentacles; lateral line sense organs less conspicuous. Upperparts light yellow-brown with elongated dark brown patches roughly forming parallel longitudinal rows. Underside pale grey to black with golden-yellow vermiculations. **Length** 60mm. **Call** Difficult to hear, high-pitched metallic buzz, produced underwater during the day and night. **Habitat** Acidic, humic-stained lowland Fynbos wetlands on the Cape Peninsula, Cape Flats and coastal forelands of the Agulhas Plain. **Endemism** Fynbos Biome. **Conservation status** Endangered owing to habitat loss and degradation.

2 Common Platanna *Xenopus laevis*
Larger than Cape Platanna, with short subocular tentacles. Lateral line sense organs very conspicuous. Upperparts grey to dark brown, often with darker brown blotches which never form defined longitudinal rows. Underside uniformly pale grey, occasionally mottled with darker grey. **Length** 150mm. **Call** Both males and females produce a rhythmic undulating snoring call. Calls produced during the day or night from under water. **Habitat** Very adaptable, being found in almost all wetland types.

African common frogs
Family Pyxicephalidae
A large and diverse family of African frogs. Seven genera and 25 species are represented in the Fynbos Biome, 18 of which are endemic.

River frogs *Amietia*
Large frogs, strongly associated with permanent water. They have long, powerful legs and a significant amount of webbing on their feet, making them efficient jumpers and swimmers. The extensive webbing distinguishes them from stream frogs (*Strongylopus*). Pupils horizontal. Numerous broken longitudinal skin ridges present. Four of the six South African species occur in the Fynbos Biome. Some species occur in close proximity to one another. Calls and the extent of webbing between the toes are critical in differentiating between them.

3 Common River Frog *Amietia delalandii*
Dorsal coloration various shades of green or brown, with numerous irregular dark spots. Pale or green vertebral line may be present. Upper lip black, usually with row of small pale spots. Underparts white; throat occasionally with dark marbling. Tympanum large and conspicuous. Eyes extend beyond profile of head when viewed directly from above. Two of last phalanges on longest toe free of webbing. **Length** 90mm. **Call** Short series of rapid clicks, often followed by nasal croak. **Habitat** Widespread in the eastern summer-rainfall parts of South Africa, where it enters the far eastern parts of the Fynbos Biome. Inhabits natural and artificial wetland habitats.

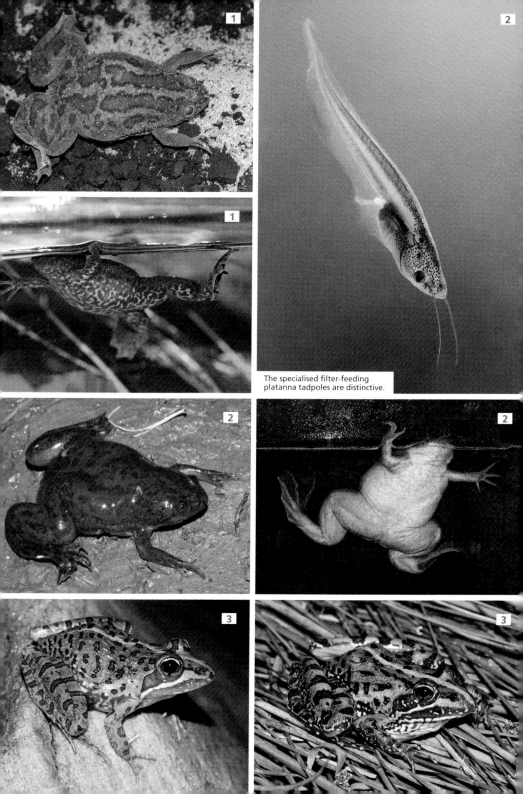

The specialised filter-feeding
platanna tadpoles are distinctive.

1 Cape River Frog *Amietia fuscigula*

One of the most frequently observed frogs in the Fynbos Biome. Dorsal coloration variable, ranging from light to dark brown or occasionally green with variety of irregular dark blotches. Pale vertebral line may be present. Underparts white with dark mottling on throat. Tympanum obvious, slightly smaller than diameter of eye. Only last phalange or half of last phalange on longest toe free of webbing. Eyes do not extend beyond profile of head when viewed directly from above. **Length** 125mm. **Call** Low guttural croaks. Series of clicks occasionally precedes the croaking call. Calls during the day and night. **Habitat** A wide diversity of permanent rivers, wetlands and artificial water bodies across the Fynbos Biome and in Afrotemperate Forest. **Endemism** CFR (in South Africa).

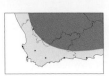

2 Poynton's River Frog *Amietia poyntoni*

Dorsal coloration shades of brown, olive or grey with irregular dark blotches. Pale vertebral line often present. Thin black line between nostril and eye. Underparts white, sometimes with extensive black marbling on throat. Tympanum distinctive, smaller than diameter of eye. Toes heavily webbed with variable number of phalanges free of webbing. Eyes do not extend beyond profile of head when viewed directly from above. Very similar to Cape River Frog but absent from much of the Fynbos Biome. **Length** 125mm. **Call** A very long series of rapid clicks followed by a few harsh croaks. Also croaks without the preceding clicking call. Calls during the day and night. **Habitat** Widespread through the interior of southern Africa including the Karoo. Fynbos Biome range unclear but likely to occur along the interior edges. Inhabits a variety of permanent natural and artificial water bodies. **Endemism** Southern Africa.

3 Van Dijk's River Frog *Amietia vandijki*

Dorsal coloration variable, usually dark to pale brown with variety of irregular dark blotches or small marks. Back can also be greenish grey in colour. Large pale mark sometimes present at centre of back. Underparts white. Tympanum present but partially obscured by fold of skin, which runs from behind eye to top of arm. Feet less heavily webbed than Cape River Frog; two or three phalanges of longest toe free of webbing. Eyes do not extend beyond profile of head when viewed directly from above. **Length** 60mm. **Call** Slow series of short clucks. **Habitat** The most range-restricted Fynbos Biome *Amietia* species, inhabiting streams and forested gorges in mountain Fynbos and afrotemperate forest in Swartberg and Langeberg mountain ranges. **Endemism** CFR (in South Africa).

Moss frogs *Arthroleptella*

Very small, cryptic frogs. Moss frogs occur in dense vegetation in moist habitats (seeps, wet cliffs, or edges of streams and vleis) in mountain Fynbos and occasionally in forested kloofs. They call during the day and lay their eggs in terrestrial nests, with no free-swimming tadpole stage. There is no webbing and the small tympanum is inconspicuous. Species are morphologically similar with a very wide diversity of colours and makings, the full variation of which is not captured in the accounts below. Call and distribution are critical in identifying the various species, many being allopatric. De Villiers's Moss Frog is the most widespread of all and occurs with or in close proximity to Landdroskop, Drewes's, Kogelberg and Drakenstein moss frogs. In all areas of overlap or potential overlap, De Villiers's Moss Frog is separated by its noticeably shorter call. While all moss frogs occur in fire-driven Fynbos ecosystems, their populations appear to be much reduced after fire events. This is particularly evident where the presence of alien invasive plants increases both the intensity and frequency of fire events. This genus comprises ten species and is endemic to the CFR.

1 Riviersonderend Moss Frog *Arthroleptella atermina* NE

Dorsal coloration extremely variable, ranging from light to dark brown or reddish brown with varying degrees of mottling and dark and orange markings. Pale or orange vertebral stripe may be present. Back notably rough in males. Throat and belly dark, becoming lighter towards vent. **Length** 20mm. **Call** A series of about four (range 2–12) clicks lasting roughly 0.5 seconds. **Habitat** Densely vegetated wet habitats in mountain Fynbos of Riviersonderend Mountains. **Endemism** Fynbos Biome. **Conservation status** Not Evaluated.

2 Bainskloof Moss Frog *Arthroleptella bicolor*

Dorsal coloration extremely variable, ranging from dark brown to orange-brown. Random scattered white spots or dark markings may be present. Pale vertebral line sometimes present. Most show distinct dark mark behind eye that runs to top of arm. Male's throat and belly dark with varying degrees of white mottling towards vent. Underparts of females white or pale grey with some mottling. **Length** 20mm. **Call** Irregular series of about five clicks lasting roughly 0.4 seconds. **Habitat** Densely vegetated wet habitats in mountain Fynbos in Limietberg and Waterval mountains. **Endemism** Fynbos Biome.

3 Drakenstein Moss Frog *Arthroleptella draconella* NE

Dorsal coloration extremely variable, ranging from orange to brown or grey with darker markings. Distinct dark mark behind eye runs to top of arm. Back smooth in females and with numerous raised glands in males. Forearms often orange. Throat and belly mottled dark to light grey. Finger and toe tips slightly swollen. **Length** 20mm. **Call** A relatively long series of about six clicks lasting roughly 0.7 seconds. **Habitat** Densely vegetated wet environments in mountain Fynbos in the Klein Drakenstein, Hawekwas and DuToits mountains. **Endemism** Fynbos Biome. **Conservation status** Not Evaluated.

4 Drewes's Moss Frog *Arthroleptella drewesii* NT

Dorsal coloration varies from almost black to light orange-brown with diffuse darker or orange markings. Dark mark runs from behind eye to top of arm. Male's belly and throat dark with varying degrees of white mottling. Underparts of female white. Finger and toe tips slightly swollen. **Length** 18mm. **Call** Relatively long call comprising series of about six clicks lasting roughly 0.8 seconds. **Habitat** Densely vegetated wet environments in mountain Fynbos in the Kleinrivier and Babilonstoring mountains. **Endemism** Fynbos Biome. **Conservation status** Near Threatened.

Moss frogs are tiny. This is an adult Cape Peninsula Moss Frog.

1 Kogelberg Moss Frog *Arthroleptella kogelbergensis* NE

Dorsal coloration varies from brown to orange-brown or grey with variable dark markings. Black mark runs from behind eye to top of arm. Pale vertebral stripe often present. Underparts black in male, sometimes with pale markings, especially towards vent. Underparts of female yellow. Tips of toes expanded. **Length** 20mm. **Call** Relatively long series of about seven clicks lasting roughly 0.84 seconds. **Habitat** Densely vegetated wet environments in mountain Fynbos in the Kogelberg Mountains. **Endemism** Fynbos Biome. **Conservation status** Not Evaluated. Potentially threatened owing to very small range and vulnerability to climate change.

2 Landdroskop Moss Frog *Arthroleptella landdrosia* NT

Dorsal coloration varies from brown to orange-brown, variably patterned with dark marks and white spots. There is a broad black line from behind the eye which runs to the top of the arm. A narrow pale vertebral stripe is often present. Male underparts black with some white markings. Reportedly paler below in females. **Length** 16mm. **Call** Long series of clicks lasting about 0.96 seconds. Call similar to that of Kogelberg Moss Frog but they do not co-occur. **Habitat** Restricted to Hottentots Holland Mountains in wet densely vegetated habitats. **Endemism** Fynbos Biome. **Conservation status** Near Threatened. Very small global range. Some populations negatively affected by too frequent fires.

3 Cape Peninsula Moss Frog *Arthroleptella lightfooti* NT

Dorsal coloration extremely variable, from pale to dark brown, black or orange, usually with array of darker brown or orange markings. Pale or orange vertebral stripe occasionally present. Broad black line runs from behind eye to top of arm. Male's throat and belly dark grey to black with some white markings. Underparts white in female. **Length** 20mm. **Call** A short high-pitched single chirp. **Habitat** Restricted to Cape Peninsula where it is the only moss frog. Occurs in densely vegetated wet habitats in mountain Fynbos and forested kloofs. **Endemism** Fynbos Biome. **Conservation status** Near Threatened.

4 Rough Moss Frog *Arthroleptella rugosa* CR

Dorsal coloration variable, ranging from brown to dark brown or orange-brown with numerous glandular bumps. Pale vertebral stripe may be present. Broad black line runs from behind eye to top of arm. Throat and belly black, sometimes with white vermiculations or spotting. **Length** 20mm. **Call** Short scratchy chirp unlike the other moss frogs. **Habitat** Densely vegetated wet seeps in mountain Fynbos on the Klein Swartberg, near Caledon, where it is the only moss frog. **Endemism** Fynbos Biome. **Conservation status** Critically Endangered. One of the most highly threatened vertebrates in the Fynbos Biome. Threatened by rampant alien plant invasion (notably pine trees) within its extremely small range.

5 Northern Moss Frog *Arthroleptella subvoce* CR

A tiny frog. Dorsal coloration mottled light to dark brown with darker markings. Pale vertebral stripe may be present. Broad black line runs from snout through eye to top of arm. Male's throat and belly coloration paler than in other moss frogs, being pale grey with darker speckles. **Length** 15mm. **Call** Somewhat softer and slower than other moss frogs. Call about 0.98 seconds, comprising several notes. **Habitat** The most northerly distributed moss frog and the only one in the Groot Winterhoek Mountains, where it is found in very few densely vegetated wet seeps. **Endemism** Fynbos Biome. **Conservation status** Critically Endangered. Very small range with few populations known. Some populations negatively affected by too frequent fires.

1 De Villiers's Moss Frog *Arthroleptella villiersi*

The most widespread of all moss frogs and very common in suitable habitat. Dorsal coloration extremely variable, ranging from almost black to brown to orange, with a varying degree of white and/or dark markings. Pale vertebral stripe may be present. Dark line runs from behind eye to top of arm. Throat and ventral surface dark, with or without white markings, which can be quite extensive. Females have large white patches on underparts. **Length** 20mm. **Call** A single short, high-pitched chirp. **Habitat** Densely vegetated wet environments in mountain Fynbos, both on the upper slopes and on low-lying areas. Found in Hottentots Holland, Kogelberg, Kleinrivier and Bredasdorp mountains. **Endemism** Fynbos Biome.

Cacos *Cacosternum*

Fairly small, slender-limbed frogs with distinctive dark blotches on underside. Pupils horizontal. No webbing. Tympanum not visible in most species. Sixteen species known, all from Africa, with five found in the Fynbos Biome. Regional species all breed in seasonal wetlands, from where most species call during the day and evening. The ranges of Flat, Southern and Klipheuwel cacos are currently not well defined and additional work is needed to clarify these.

2 Klipheuwel Caco *Cacosternum aggestum*

Dorsal coloration very variable, ranging from pale to dark grey or brown with scattered dark markings. Occasional metallic green markings are present, especially on the snout. Females often largely green in colour. A pale vertebral stripe is sometimes present. Some darker marks present on the ventral surface. **Length** 20mm. **Call** A rapid series of accelerating clicks often compared to a marble dropping in a glass bottle. Very similar to Southern and Flat cacos. **Habitat** Shallow temporary wetlands in the lowlands between Darling, Hermon and Stellenbosch. Extent of the species distribution is not clear but recently also found on the flats between Macassar and Strand in Cape Town. **Endemism** Fynbos Biome.

3 Southern Caco *Cacosternum australis*

Dorsal coloration pale to dark brown with scattered dark markings. Upper lip is white with a darker line from the snout through the eye to the top of the forelimbs. The underparts are well marked with dark spots. **Length** 20mm. **Call** A rapid series of accelerating clicks often compared to a marble dropping in a glass bottle. Very similar to Klipheuwel and Flat cacos. **Habitat** A variety of shallow wetlands. Range appears to be centred on and around the Overberg but the species distribution is not clearly understood. **Endemism** Fynbos Biome.

4 Cape Caco *Cacosternum capense* **NT**

The largest caco, easily recognised by its size and multiple distinct dorsal glands. The most prominent are a pair of large glands low down on the back above the vent. Dorsal colour varies from light grey to dark brown, often with orange, brown or occasionally green markings. The underparts are white with large irregular olive blotches. **Length** 39mm. **Call** A harsh *creek* at night in late autumn and winter. **Habitat** Seasonal shallow wetlands in the western lowlands from Faure to about Graafwater. Able to persist despite some agricultural disturbances. **Endemism** Fynbos Biome. **Conservation status** Near Threatened.

1 Bronze Caco *Cacosternum nanum*

Dorsal colour varies from grey to brown or orange with a bronze hue. Scattered black markings present on back and limbs. Pale vertebral line occasionally present. Black line runs from snout through eye. Underparts heavily marked with black spots. Tympanum sometimes visible. **Length** 23mm. **Call** Regularly spaced *creek* note with bouts of rapid clicks. **Habitat** Inhabits various wetland types but favours smaller sites in the Fynbos Biome and a variety of other vegetation types. Found as far west as Swellendam. **Endemism** Southern Africa.

2 Flat Caco *Cacosternum platys* NT

Dorsal coloration varied; grey, green, brown or a combination of these colours. Variety of dark marks usually present; occasional pale vertebral stripe. White line runs from behind and below eye to top of forelimbs. Dark line runs from snout through eye to base of forelimbs. Underparts well marked with dark spots. **Length** 22mm. **Call** Rapid series of accelerating clicks often compared to a marble dropping in a glass bottle. Very similar to Klipheuwel and Southern cacos. **Habitat** Shallow temporary wetlands on sand. Occurs in the lowlands of the Cape Peninsula and Cape Flats. **Endemism** Fynbos Biome. **Conservation status** Near Threatened owing to very limited distribution and habitat loss. This species could possibly warrant a higher threat status as it is endemic to the City of Cape Town where much of its Cape Flats habitat is being lost to development.

Micro Frog *Microbatrachella*

The webbing on the hind feet distinguishes the monotypic Micro Frog from cacos (*Cacosternum*). Micro Frogs co-occur with Flat Caco on the Cape Peninsula and with Southern Caco in the Overberg. Tympanum not visible. While certainly small, the Micro Frog is not the smallest frog in the region, with many cacos being of a similar size and the moss frogs (*Arthroleptella*) being notably smaller.

3 Micro Frog *Microbatrachella capensis* CR

Dorsal coloration varied but usually brown, green, or yellowish green. Most individuals have some dark spots or flecks. Green metallic markings occasionally present. Many individuals also show a clear pale or yellowish green vertebral stripe. There is a dark line running from the eye to the base of the forelimbs. The ventral surface usually mottled with dark markings. Moderate webbing present between the toes. **Length** 18mm. **Call** A short insect-like *creek* uttered in quick succession. Calls during the day and night. **Habitat** Seasonal, shallow acidic wetlands usually with substantial aquatic sedges. **Endemism** Fynbos Biome. **Conservation status** Critically Endangered owing to habitat transformation and degradation across its limited range.

Montane marsh frogs *Poyntonia*

Monotypic. Morphologically distinct from all other Fynbos frogs. No tympanum visible. Moderate webbing between toes. Occurs in mountain seepage areas and appear to be well adapted to natural fire cycles.

4 Montane Marsh Frog *Poyntonia paludicola* NT

Dorsal coloration olive-grey to brown, usually with pale, yellow or orange vertebral line. Scattered orange to red markings occasionally present on the back. Appears rough due to granular skin and raised glandular areas. Upperparts can appear very dark. Distinctive pale line runs from each eye to corner of mouth. Other pale lines often run from eye to upper lip and from snout to upper lip. Underparts pale, usually well marked with dark spots. **Length** 30mm. **Call** A rapid series of up to ten short croaks. Calls during the day. Peak breeding season is during winter and spring. **Habitat** Very shallow mountain seeps, marshes and areas of surface flow usually with dark filamentous algae. Found in the highest-rainfall areas of the Fynbos Biome in the Hottentots Holland, Kogelberg and Kleinrivier mountains. **Endemism** Fynbos Biome. **Conservation status** Near Threatened.

Stream frogs *Strongylopus*

These medium-sized frogs are strong jumpers. The common name 'stream frog' is misleading, as they occur in a wide range of habitats. Sometimes mistaken for young river frogs (*Amietia*), but readily distinguishable by the very long feet and toes and by having minimal webbing at base of toes. Pupils horizontal. Tympanum present, but smaller than diameter of eye and not conspicuous. Five species occur in South Africa, three of which are found in the Fynbos.

1 Banded Stream Frog *Strongylopus bonaespei*

Dorsal coloration comprises a variety of light brown, dark brown, grey, cream and/or orange longitudinal stripes. Paler vertebral stripe usually present. Fine, longitudinal skin ridges present. Dark line runs from snout through nostril and expands behind eye to form a mask. This is bordered below by clear white line, which runs below eye to base of arm. Thighs strongly barred. Underparts pearly white with gold sheen. **Length** 40mm. **Call** Up to three harsh squawks followed by rapid cackle. **Habitat** Frequents marshes and seepage areas in mountain Fynbos. **Endemism** Fynbos Biome.

2 Striped Stream Frog *Strongylopus fasciatus*

Dorsal coloration pale yellow to light brown with numerous bold dark brown parallel stripes. Back smooth with low longitudinal skin ridges within dark stripes. Dark spots on inner thighs. Underparts white to pale yellow. **Length** 50mm. **Call** Burst of short sharp whistled notes, primarily at night. **Habitat** Fond of grassy areas near a variety of water bodies. Able to tolerate some disturbance and can be found in parks and gardens. Predominantly a summer-rainfall species, occurring as far west as Bonnievale.

3 Clicking Stream Frog *Strongylopus grayii*

The most frequently encountered frog in gardens of the region. Coloration extremely variable. Dorsal coloration brown, grey, yellow or reddish with variety of dark blotches or marks. Paler vertebral stripe usually present, which can be narrow or very broad. Numerous short longitudinal skin ridges present on back. Dark transverse bars on thighs. Underparts white. **Length** 50mm. **Call** Short, sharp clicking notes, the spacing of which is not constant. Calls during the day and night throughout wet season. **Habitat** Able to utilise a wide diversity of habitats. Can inhabit very degraded sites and persists in urban areas. **Endemism** Southern Africa.

Sand frogs *Tomopterna*

Medium-sized, stocky frogs that superficially resemble bull frogs (*Pyxicephalus*). Pupil horizontal. Limited webbing. Adapted to burrowing backwards, with distinctive, hardened metatarsal tubercle on heel of hind feet. Normally associated with sandy substrates. Breeding occurs in seasonal or perennial water bodies. Eight species occur in South Africa; one is found in the Fynbos Biome.

4 Cape Sand Frog *Tomopterna delalandii*

A thickset and short-legged frog. Underlying dorsal colour grey, with variably shaped white and grey to brown markings. Often with an olive or warm brown tone above. Narrow dorsal stripe often present. Dorsal skin bumpy; ventral side smooth and uniformly pale. Tympanum inconspicuous. **Length** 54mm. **Call** Very loud; quick succession of high-pitched and high-frequency knocking sounds. **Habitat** Favours lowland sandy substrates and valleys. **Endemism** South Africa.

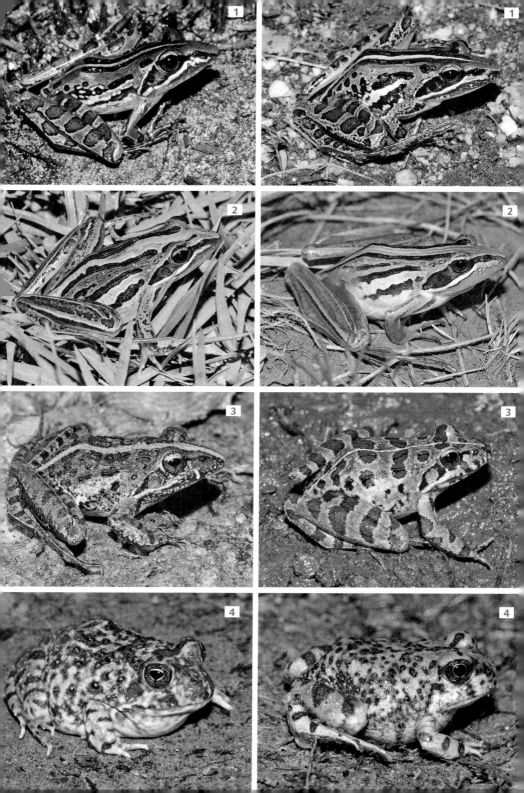

Reptiles

Two reptile orders occur in the Fynbos Biome, namely chelonians, i.e. tortoises and terrapins (order Testudines), and squamates, i.e. lizards and snakes (order Squamata). The reptile fauna of the Biome comprises 113 species in 20 families, representing just over a quarter of South Africa's reptile species and three-quarters of the families. This includes Common Dwarf Gecko (*Lygodactylus capensis*), which is not locally indigenous to the Biome but has been widely introduced to cities and towns in the region.

ENDEMISM

Of the 113 species of reptile included in this book, 24 (21%) are endemic to the Fynbos Biome. About half of these are obligatory rupicolous species. The diversity and endemism of the Biome's reptiles is mainly attributed to the region's large and distinctive mountain ranges. In general, snakes have much greater dispersal capabilities than lizards. Lizards, in contrast, tend to have smaller distribution ranges and exhibit higher endemism levels. This is illustrated by the fact that 23 of the 24 regional endemics are lizards. Four lizard genera are endemic to the Fynbos Biome. The Southern Adder is the only Fynbos endemic snake. Two other snakes, the Slender Thread Snake and Red Adder, are endemic to the greater Cape Floristic Region.

Reptile genera endemic to the Fynbos Biome	
Genus	Number of species
Southern rock lizard (*Australolacerta*)	1
Cliff lizards (*Hemicordylus*)	2
Blue-spotted lizard (*Ninurta*)	1
Swartberg leaf-toed gecko (*Ramigekko*)	1

Southern Adder

Swartberg Leaf-toed Gecko

CONSERVATION CONCERN

Eight species in the region are of conservation concern. This relatively low percentage (7%) can be attributed to the fact that the majority of the endemic and range-restricted species are confined to mountainous areas, where habitat transformation rates and threats are far less than on the highly impacted lowlands. Many of the reptiles found on the flats and lowlands have large geographic ranges. An obvious exception is the Critically Endangered Geometric Tortoise. This species is confined to lowland Renosterveld and alluvium Fynbos habitat types, which have been highly transformed for agriculture. Similarly, the Vulnerable Southern Adder is confined to limited lowland coastal areas.

LIFE HISTORY

Reptiles are cryptically patterned, silent and secretive. Many are also nocturnal. As such, most species are not easily observed.

All reptiles are ectothermic, relying on environmental heat sources to regulate their body temperature. This includes basking in sunlight (heliothermy) and flattening their body to increase contact with warm surfaces (thignothermy). Reptiles are very efficient at maintaining their body temperature, using minimal energy. They have very economical metabolic rates when compared to mammals and birds. This has significant advantages and reptiles are able to survive unfavourable conditions without the need to migrate as many birds and mammals do. In addition, reptiles live for much longer when compared to endothermic animals of a similar size.

While most reptiles lay eggs, many squamates are viviparous. There is usually no parental care. Most reptiles are solitary, although several species do live in colonies and many gecko species lay their eggs at communal sites.

Fynbos Biome reptiles are adapted to the fire-driven ecology. While many individuals succumb to fires, some always survive by sheltering in rocky refugia within unburnt patches or in burrows, enabling them to re-colonise the burnt areas as conditions improve after the fire. The eggs of most reptiles also survive fire events.

Reptile species of conservation concern		
Critically Endangered (CR)		
1	Geometric Tortoise	*Psammobates geometricus*
Endangered (EN)		
2	Speckled Dwarf Tortoise	*Chersobius signatus*
3	Southern Adder	*Bitis armata*
4	Dwarf Cliff Lizard	*Hemicordylus nebulosus*
Near Threatened (NT)		
5	Cape Dwarf Chameleon	*Bradypodion pumilum*
6	Armadillo Lizard	*Ouroborus cataphractus*
7	Kasner's Dwarf Burrowing Skink	*Scelotes kasneri*
8	Bloubergstrand Dwarf Burrowing Skink	*Scelotes montispectus*
Data Deficient (DD)		
9	Lambert's Bay Sandveld Lizard	*Nucras aurantiaca*

The iconic and highly venomous Cape Cobra

The Endangered Speckled Dwarf Tortoise

A NOTE ON REPTILE TAXONOMY

Snakes and lizards belong to the reptile order Squamata. Technically speaking, all members of this order are lizards, with snakes merely being specialised lizards. Snakes are carnivorous, while the other lizards are predominantly insectivorous.

IDENTIFYING REPTILES

Photography allows one to get detailed information without having to catch the animal. Some key aspects to look for when identifying reptiles include:

MORPHOLOGICAL FEATURES
- Shape and size
- The ratio of tail length compared to head–body length
- Scale type and arrangement
- Coloration and patterning of the dorsal and ventral surfaces. Note that coloration can be extremely variable in some species.

GEOGRAPHICAL DISTRIBUTION
Where an animal is found can be very useful in identifying it as many species occur in specific geographical ranges.

HABITAT
Many species are very specific regarding their preferred habitat. This can be of assistance when confirming the identification.

BEHAVIOUR
Some behavioural information, such as whether the animal is solitary or if they occur in colonies, can be of assistance with identification. While little is known about many of our reptiles' behaviour, one can obtain a great deal of enjoyment by watching an undisturbed animal going about its business.

NOTE: Modern molecular techniques have led to significant changes in reptile taxonomy in recent years. Ongoing research results in regular changes and advancements in reptile taxonomy.

Lateral head scales of a snake

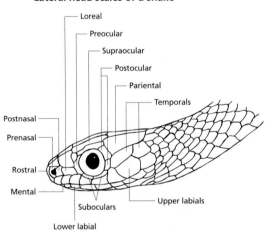

Ventral scales of a snake tail

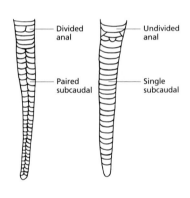

Head scales of a typical lizard

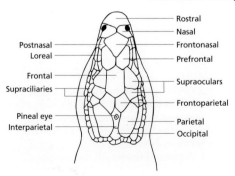

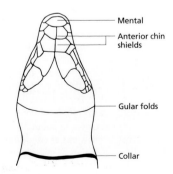

Chameleon identification features

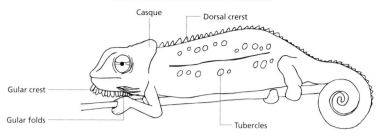

Casque

Dorsal crerst

Gular crest

Gular folds

Tubercles

Lizard belly / ventral side

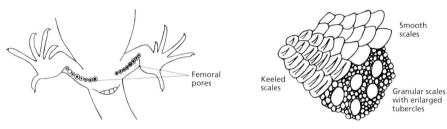

Femoral pores

Scale types

Smooth scales

Keeled scales

Granular scales with enlarged tubercles

Reptile measurements

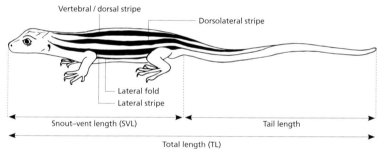

Vertebral / dorsal stripe

Dorsolateral stripe

Lateral fold

Lateral stripe

Snout–vent length (SVL)

Tail length

Total length (TL)

Tortoise shell scutes above

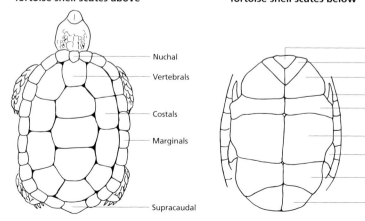

Nuchal

Vertebrals

Costals

Marginals

Supracaudal

Tortoise shell scutes below

Intergular

Gular

Humeral

Axillary

Pectoral

Abdominal

Inguinal

Femoral

Anal

55

Side-necked terrapins Family Pelomedusidae

Aquatic, with flattened shells and oar-like feet; webbing on hind feet. Retracts head and neck sideways under carapace. Primarily carnivorous, but will also eat some aquatic plants.

Marsh terrapins *Pelomedusa*

These terrapins have an unhinged plastron; the shell's front opening cannot close. Two species occur in South Africa, one of which is found in the Fynbos Biome.

1 South African Helmeted Terrapin *Pelomedusa galeata*
Relatively large. Shell dark, flat and thin. Carapace ranges from olive- to dark brown with paler edge; can have leathery appearance; may be densely mottled with blackish markings, especially in juveniles. Plastron uniformly blackish to chestnut-brown, often with variable pale centre. Head brown above, with black patterning; lighter below. Two small tentacles (barbels) visible underneath chin. Front limbs have prominent claws that aid in dismembering food items. Produces distinct odour from musk glands on carapace. **Length** 32cm. **Status and Habitat** Common. Adaptable; occurs in a wide variety of water bodies. Able to survive periods of drought; can move large distances. Widely distributed in South Africa and found throughout the Fynbos Biome. **Endemism** Southern Africa.

Tortoises Family Testudinidae

Terrestrial and herbivorous. Five species occur in the Fynbos, all endemic to South Africa.

Angulate tortoises *Chersina*

A unique feature is the undivided gular scute on the plastron. Closely associated with the CFR where they are common and can reach quite high densities. Monotypic, near-endemic to South Africa.

2 Angulate Tortoise *Chersina angulata*
The commonest tortoise in the Fynbos Biome. Medium-sized; carapace strongly curved. No central depression in vertabrals and costals. Shell light yellow, orange to reddish brown, with dark central markings and black edges to scutes. Marginal scutes can show almost triangular dark markings. Plastron varies from pale to bright reddish orange, with dark central markings. Beak not strongly hooked or serrated. Front limbs have five claws. **Length** 30cm. **Status and Habitat** Common in a variety of habitat types. Favours lower altitudes and particularly common in Strandveld. Largely absent from high-altitude mountain Fynbos habitats. **Endemism** Southern Africa.

Padlopers *Homopus*

Small, compact tortoises with the unique feature of having four claws on all limbs. Their small size and flattened shape enable them to take refuge in crevices, burrows and under rocks. This genus comprises two species, both found only in South Africa, with one occurring in the Fynbos Biome.

3 Parrot-beaked Tortoise *Homopus areolatus*
Carapace varies from reddish brown to orange. Dorsal scutes have central depressions, distinct rings and variable colourful bands of brown, green and reddish orange. Plastron yellowish, can have brown markings. Beak prominently hooked, with faintly serrated edge. Males show red flush to nasal scales when breeding. **Length** 16cm. **Status and Habitat** Fairly common in Renosterveld and Fynbos habitat throughout Fynbos Biome. Occasionally shelters under rocks. **Endemism** South Africa.

Jousting male Angulate Tortoises

Dwarf tortoises   *Chersobius*

These tortoises have five claws on their front feet and four claws on their hind feet. They are small and flattened, enabling them to make use of narrow rock crevices for shelter in their rocky habitats. Two species occur in South Africa, one of which is found in the Fynbos Biome.

1 **Speckled Dwarf Tortoise**   *Chersobius signatus*   EN

The smallest tortoise in the world. Extremely variable. Carapace coloration and patterning vary according to habitat substrate: light yellow, orange to brown or reddish, with variable dark flecks and black markings on scute edges. Dorsal scutes flat with central depressions. Plastron colour variable. No pronounced hook on beak, which has a serrated edge. Front limbs have five claws. **Length** 9.6cm. **Status and Habitat** Uncommon and seldom seen. Favours rocky outcrops along the West Coast of South Africa. Occurs inland as far as the Tankwa Karoo and Calvinia. Favours Succulent Karoo habitats but also utilises arid Fynbos. **Conservation Status** Endangered owing to habitat transformation, degradation and fragmentation, the impacts of climate change and illegal collecting for the pet trade. **Endemism** South Africa.

Tent and geometric tortoises   *Psammobates*

This genus comprises small, attractive tortoises. The raised scutes create a tent-like appearance, hence the common name. Three species, all endemic to southern Africa and found in South Africa.

2 **Geometric Tortoise**   *Psammobates geometricus*   CR

Small, handsome and one of the most threatened tortoises in the world. Carapace highly arched; scutes slightly raised. Strikingly patterned with bright yellow markings on black background forming distinctive geometric patterns. Each scute has yellow centre, with yellow lines radiating out towards edges. Plastron yellow, with black rays on edge and variable dusky marks, especially in centre. Beak hooked. Forelimbs have five claws. **Length** 16.5cm. **Status and Habitat** Lowland vegetation types on heavier soils, specifically alluvial Fynbos and Renosterveld habitats. Range greatly reduced, rare, with only scattered and isolated populations persisting. **Conservation Status** Critically Endangered owing to habitat transformation and degradation, climate change impacts and illegal collecting for the pet trade. **Endemism** Fynbos Biome.

Leopard tortoises   *Stigmochelys*

A monotypic genus that is widespread in southern and eastern Africa. Exceptionally large individuals can weigh up to 40kg.

3 **Leopard Tortoise**   *Stigmochelys pardalis*

The largest tortoise in South Africa. Coloration variable. Hatchlings differ markedly from adults: carapace flattened, with serrated edge; scutes bright yellow, black-edged, with one or two (occasionally three) irregular black blotches in centre. With age, carapace colour darkens and black blotches morph into irregular, smaller shapes. The adult's shell is markedly domed, with steep sides. Old individuals can be uniform brown or grey-brown. **Length** 65cm. **Status and Habitat** Common in various habitats. Occurs naturally in the eastern part of the Fynbos Biome but widely introduced and now widespread.

Geckos
Family Gekkonidae

These lizards are typically nocturnal, with large eyes that lack movable eyelids. Tails are easily shed (caudal autotomy). The regenerated tail can look very different. Geckos usually have highly specialised adhesive toepads (scansors), the exception being the burrowing terrestrial species. Most species feed on arthropods; a few drink nectar or eat flowers. Many live on buildings and feed on insects attracted to lights at night. All are oviparous, laying hard, calcareous shelled eggs. Females store calcium needed for the eggshells in endolymphatic sacs, which can be clearly visible on the neck. With limited dispersal capabilities, many species have very small geographic ranges. There are 86 species in South Africa, 18 of which occur in the Fynbos Biome.

Flat geckos *Afroedura*

Medium-sized geckos with distinctive scansors and small, smooth, granular scales dorsally. Head and body flattened; original tail marginally longer than body. The 32 currently described species are found in the southern part of Africa, with 23 occurring in South Africa. Three species are endemic to the Fynbos Biome, but two from the Kouga and Baavianskloof mountains are undescribed.

1 Hawequa Flat Gecko *Afroedura hawequensis*

A spectacular large and robust gecko with a velvety appearance. Distinctive scansor pairs (one large pair on fanned toe tip separated from smaller second and third pair) present on four toes. Dorsal coloration grey-beige to pinkish brown, with five or six blotchy, dark purple-brown bands, edged with yellow. These dark blotches and bands run across the body and flanks and continue onto the tail, limbs and head. Head has finer irregular, dark patterning, usually with grey patches above eyes. Large, metallic warm-brown eyes with dark vertical pupils. Ventrum whitish. Tail very broad, tear-drop shaped. **Length** SVL: 83mm. **Status and Habitat** Nocturnal, communal, rupicolous and uncommonly encountered. Restricted to a small range in Limietberg and Du Toitskloof mountains; on exposed sandstone rock faces and large boulders in mountain Fynbos. **Endemism** Fynbos Biome.

African leaf-toed geckos *Afrogecko*

Slender and covered with small, granular scales. Separated from pygmy geckos (*Goggia*) by having entire rostral scale (lacking a central crease), and no pre-anal pores in males. Single pair of leaf-shaped or rounded scansors visible under tip of each toe. Body scales homogenous. Originally endemic to the Fynbos Biome, but translocations have expanded this range to many urban environments, making them the most frequently encountered gecko in the Biome.

2 Marbled Leaf-toed Gecko *Afrogecko porphyreus*

A medium-sized, flattened gecko with a long, pointed snout and no enlarged chin shields. Beige to light brown or grey above with dark irregular, almost scalloped, dark brown to sooty patterning. Mostly mottled overall, but can be nearly uniformly pale; some with striking, pale vertebral stripe. Pale stripe running from snout through top part of eye to behind eye usually present. Ventrum pale, with mottling along edges. Thick, cylindrical tail normally longer than body. **Length** SVL: 51mm. **Status and Habitat** Communal, nocturnal and very common. Naturally rupicolous, sheltering in rock cracks, but also utilises bark and other shelters. Abundant on buildings. **Endemism** Natural distribution was confined to the Fynbos Biome.

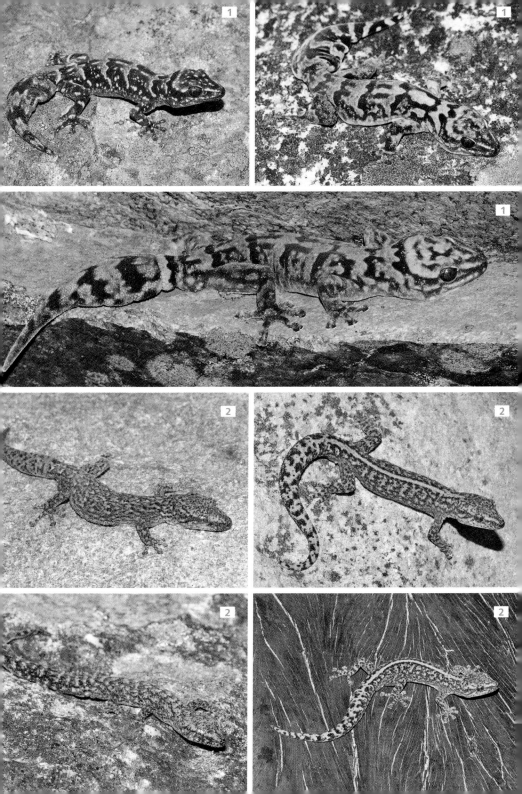

Giant geckos   *Chondrodactylus*

Beautiful, charismatic geckos that are robust and rough in appearance. Scansors undivided. Four species occur in South Africa, one of which is found in the Fynbos Biome.

1 **Bibron's Gecko**   *Chondrodactylus bibronii*

Very large. Back covered with very large, keeled tubercles separated by small, granular scales. Dorsal coloration tan to greyish light brown, with four or five very irregular and often diffuse bands across back. Approximately 8–10 bands continue onto tail. Bands warm brown to blackish with a few scattered white tubercles. Ventrum white. Original tail has whorls of strongly keeled, spiny scales. **Length** SVL: 100mm. **Status and Habitat** Nocturnal, gregarious and common (especially in the Karoo). Rupicolous but readily uses human structures in rural areas. Scattered records from across Cape Town are from accidental introductions.

Pygmy geckos   *Goggia*

Very small, except for one medium-sized species. All have a single pair of enlarged scansors under each toe tip, homogenous body scales (no enlarged tubercles), and a partly divided rostral scale. Pre-anal pores present in males. Nocturnal. A uniquely southern African genus comprising only ten species, five of which are confined to the CFR.

2 **Essex's Pygmy Gecko**   *Goggia essexi*

Very similar to the larger Hewitt's Pygmy Gecko, but not known to co-occur. Head and body flattened. Dorsal coloration light tan to grey-brown, with rows of pale spots across back. Anterior edges of these spots have dark margins, forming a scalloped effect. These dark margins are variable and can merge to form irregular and undulating crossbars or a reticulated pattern across the back. Ventrum grey. Original tail warm buff with variable irregular banding formed by the scalloped markings. Juveniles darker overall with brighter orange tail. **Length** SVL: 28mm. **Status and Habitat** Rupicolous. An Eastern Cape species from the Groot Winterhoekberge, that marginally enters the far eastern portions of the Fynbos Biome. **Endemism** CFR (in South Africa).

3 **Hewitt's Pygmy Gecko**   *Goggia hewitti*

A small gecko with a flattened body. Forms a species pair with the very similar but smaller Essex's Pygmy Gecko, but they do not co-occur. Dorsal coloration light tan to greyish brown with prominent scalloped markings across back. Anterior dark edges of these scallops merge to form irregular and undulating crossbars or a reticulated pattern. Ventrum cream with fine flecking. Original tail warmer in colour than the body, with variable irregular banding formed by scalloped markings. Juvenile darker brown with small pale buff spots. **Length** SVL: 38mm. **Status and Habitat** Rupicolous. Found in sandstone mountains of the southern Cape Fold Mountains from the Klein Swartberg to the Baviaanskloof Mountains. Inhabits mountain Fynbos and neighbouring Succulent Karoo and thicket habitats. **Endemism** CFR (in South Africa).

4 **Cederberg Pygmy Gecko**   *Goggia hexapora*

Small and flattened. Dorsal coloration tan or pale grey to dark brownish grey, with several rows of pale spots across back. These have broad, dark anterior margins, which merge to form a clear reticulated pattern. Ventrum pale grey with fine dark flecking, particularly on edges and under throat. Original tail a warmer tone than body, well marked with scalloped pattern. Juvenile darker with fine pale spots. **Length** SVL: 36mm. **Status and Habitat** Common in rocky areas in mountain Fynbos vegetation, extending into the Succulent Karoo. Rupicolous. Found in the northern and western Cape Fold Mountains from the Bokkeveld Mountains in the north to Limietberg Mountains near Wellington in the south. Also occurs on the Piketberg. **Endemism** CFR (in South Africa).

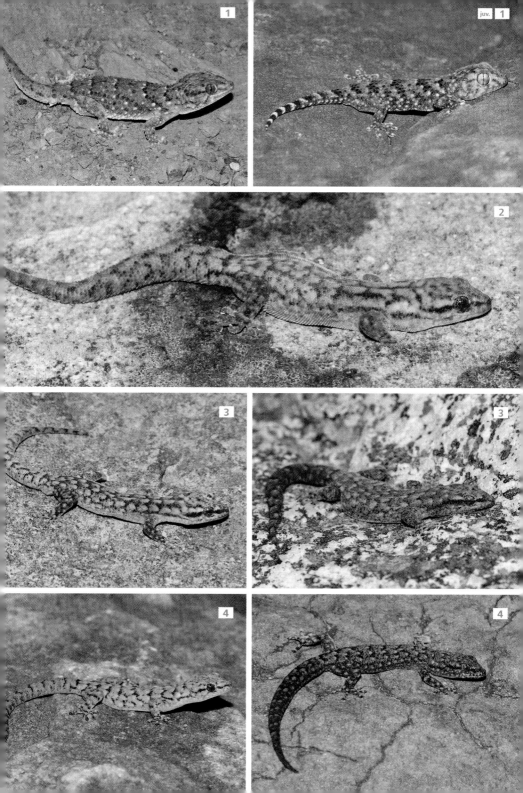

1 **Striped Pygmy Gecko** *Goggia incognita*

Diminutive, body not flattened as with the rupicolous *Goggia* species. Dorsal coloration grey to dark grey-brown. Darker markings in the form of chevrons arranged in diffuse, transverse rows. These chevrons may be pale centred. Some individuals also have four dark longitudinal stripes. Ventrum pale grey. Original tail marked with longitudinal dark lines or chevrons. Juvenile has brighter orange tail. **Length** SVL: 29mm. **Status and Habitat** Terrestrial, sheltering in vegetation debris or under stones and other objects. Found in western parts of the Fynbos Biome from south of the Knersvlakte, in the north, to Bokbaai in the south. Common in Strandveld on the West Coast. Also found in the western Cape Fold Mountains. Scattered records from the Karoo and Little Karoo. **Endemism** South Africa.

2 **Small-scaled Pygmy Gecko** *Goggia microlepidota*

Distinguished from other *Goggia* species by much larger size. Head and body flattened. Blotchy appearance overall. Dorsal coloration grey to dark grey, occasionally brownish grey. Blackish markings on back, flanks and top of head can be bold or subdued. Markings form roughly transverse but ragged bars. Ventrum pale grey. Juvenile darker overall with numerous paler flecks. **Length** SVL: 68mm. **Status and Habitat** Seldom encountered. Rupicolous. Inhabits large rock cracks in sandstone outcrops. Found in mountain Fynbos of Cederberg, Koue Bokkeveld and Groot Winterhoek mountains. The furthest southern locality is Keeromsberg near Worcester. **Endemism** Fynbos Biome.

Dwarf day geckos *Lygodactylus*

Small and agile, with a smooth appearance and rounded pupils. One digit on each hand and foot is vestigial, giving the appearance of only four digits. Paired scansors underneath each bulbous toe tip. A large genus with 11 species in South Africa, but only one introduced species in the Fynbos Biome.

3 **Common Dwarf Gecko** *Lygodactylus capensis* ❶

Body scales uniformly small and granular. Dorsal coloration shades of greyish brown to brown; generally appearing mottled, with scattered small white spots. Some with well-defined pale dorsolateral bands, which start on snout. These bands are bordered by black stripes. Lower stripe bold, running through eye. Both stripes usually become diffuse at about midbody on flanks. Some individuals also show variable pale vertebral stripe. Ventrum cream with dark flecking on throat, becoming yellow in breeding males. Elongated, conical tail equal to body in length. Juveniles more uniform darker brown with reddish tail. **Length** SVL: 43mm. **Status and Habitat** Diurnal and common in suitable habitat. Populations introduced to the Fynbos Biome primarily persists in suburban areas, making use of buildings and gardens. Well established in and around Cape Town, George and Gqeberha.

Thick-toed geckos *Pachydactylus*

Small, nocturnal, terrestrial or rupicolous lizards. Well represented in the arid western regions of southern Africa. There are 29 species in South Africa, nine of which occur in the Fynbos Biome.

4 **Austen's Gecko** *Pachydactylus austeni*

An attractive gecko confined to West Coast coastal sands. Large-headed with very big eyes and short snout. Dorsal scales small and uniform, no enlarged tubercles present. Toes only marginally dilated at tips. Coloration very variable. Dorsal coloration yellow, yellow-brown to brown; individual scales usually with darker brown centres, giving a fine speckled appearance. Randomly scattered white spots across back. Head usually purplish grey in centre; eye-rings often bright yellow or occasionally white. Lower flanks and belly white. **Length** SVL: 47mm. **Status and Habitat** Terrestrial. Fairly common, found in the narrow coastal strip from Koeberg north of Cape Town to the Holgat River in the Richtersveld. Frequents open sandy areas especially in vegetated coastal dunes, but can occur to almost 100km inland in suitable sandy areas. **Endemism** CFR (in South Africa).

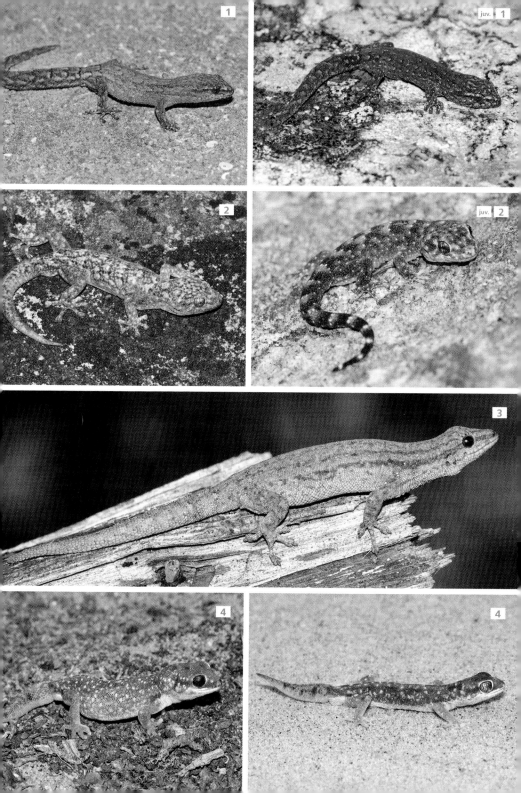

1 Southern Rough Gecko *Pachydactylus formosus*

An attractive, boldly marked gecko. Dorsal scales granular, keeled and intermixed with larger tubercles. Toes dilated at tips with five transverse scansors under middle toes. Basal dorsal coloration yellowish to reddish brown with five white to pale yellowish transverse bands, which are dark-edged. First pale band encircles back of head. Golden eye-ring or partial eye-ring usually present. Pale vertebral strip occasionally present. Original tail clearly banded, regenerated tail mottled or blotched. Juveniles more vividly patterned. Ventrum greyish white with fine speckling, especially on throat and chin. **Length** SVL: 60mm. **Status and Habitat** Common in mountainous regions of the western parts of the Fynbos Biome. Rupicolous. **Endemism** CFR (in South Africa).

2 Ocellated Gecko *Pachydactylus geitje*

Small, cylindrical, with uniformly, granular body scales. Toes short, only marginally flared at tips with four or five scansors under middle toes. Dorsal coloration grey to grey-brown or dark brown, often with orange hue. Variable white to pale orange spots with dark edging present. Dark edges can be extensive and may form blotches. Black line often runs from snout through eye to neck, and may extend onto flanks. Tail cylindrical, thick at base. Regenerated tail can be very fat. Juvenile has reduced pale spotting and the tail is brighter orange. Ventrum off-white, variably infused with grey. Grey spots on throat. **Length** SVL: 45mm. **Status and Habitat** Widespread and common. Terrestrial. Occurs in a diverse range of habitats. **Endemism** South Africa.

3 Thin-skinned Gecko *Pachydactylus kladaroderma*

A large, heavyset gecko with an astonishing defence mechanism. If grabbed by a predator, it will twist vigorously and large sections of its skin will tear off, allowing the gecko a chance to escape. Dorsal scales granular, intermixed with numerous enlarged tubercles. Pale brown to grey-brown with variable darker markings usually forming five irregular crossbands. Paler vertebral strip often present. Ventrum pale grey to cream. Tail shorter than head and body and faintly banded. **Length** SVL: 86mm. **Status and Habitat** Rupicolous. Prefers large and deep rock cracks and while primarily nocturnal, can be seen basking during the day. A Great and Little Karoo species, they occur peripherally in mountain Fynbos close to the Succulent Karoo edge and in the Groot Swartberg. **Endemism** South Africa.

4 Western Cape Gecko *Pachydactylus labialis*

Small, elongate and cylindrical. Toes relatively short, slightly broader at tips with five scansors under middle toes. Dorsal scales small and granular with evenly spaced large conical tubercles, roughly arranged in numerous longitudinal rows. Dorsal coloration tan or light to dark brown. Well marked with a variety of darker brown to sooty black markings. May also have various pale markings forming rough transverse bands or spotting, especially on flanks. Broad pale vertebral line may be present. Ventrum pale grey, often with dark mottling on throat and edges of belly. Juveniles more uniform dark brown. **Length** SVL: 86mm. **Status and Habitat** Terrestrial. Prefers sandy soil. Shelters under rocks or debris. Primarily a Namaqualand and Succulent Karoo species, but recorded in the sandveld north of Lambert's Bay. **Endemism** CFR (in South Africa).

5 Spotted Gecko *Pachydactylus maculatus*

A small, plump gecko with a rounded head and very short snout. Small, granular dorsal scales intermixed with enlarged tubercles, two or three times larger than granular scales. Toes short with three or four scansors under each tip. Grey to greyish brown above with four longitudinal rows of large, elongated or rounded dark brown to blackish spots. Spots never white-edged as with Golden Spotted Gecko. Spots may merge to form transverse bands. Ventrum white, usually heavily flecked with brown markings. Tail round and tapering abruptly to a point. Readily shed. **Length** SVL: 58mm. **Status and Habitat** Terrestrial. Primarily found in summer-rainfall areas of South Africa. Common from about Cape St Francis eastwards. Occurs in mountain Fynbos in the Baviaanskloof with scattered records as far west as the mountains near De Doorns. **Endemism** Southern Africa.

1 Common Banded Gecko *Pachydactylus mariquensis*

A small, terrestrial gecko with a rounded head, short snout and cylindrical body. Limbs long and thin. Toes relatively short, with three or four scansors. Dorsal scales small and granular, with no enlarged tubercles. Grey to light brown above. Most individuals have five or six dark brown, black-edged, irregular bands across back. Bands may be highly fragmented, resulting in a mosaic of dark and pale blotches. Dark spot on snout. Ventrum white to off-white. **Length** SVL: 57mm. **Status and Habitat** Terrestrial. Widespread in South Africa, but few records from the Fynbos Biome. Recorded in Renosterveld just north of Cape Town, but appears to be rather rare. Potentially under-recorded from Renosterveld habitats. **Endemism** South Africa.

2 Golden Spotted Gecko *Pachydactylus oculatus*

Closely related to Spotted Gecko. However, snout slightly longer, more flattened and pointed. Enlarged tubercles on back more varied in size and more conical than in Spotted Gecko. Most adults have a regenerated tail. Toes relatively short, with three or four scansors under each tip. Pale brown to beige above with four longitudinal rows of brown to reddish-brown spots. Spots always clearly white-edged in adults. Juveniles more brightly coloured and dorsal spots are black-edged. Ventrum white. **Length** SVL: 53mm. **Status and Habitat** Terrestrial. Peripheral in the Fynbos Biome. Primarily a karroid and grassland species that occurs in mountain Fynbos along the interior edge of Cape Fold Mountains. Occurs in Groot Swartberg Mountains. **Endemism** South Africa.

3 Weber's Gecko *Pachydactylus weberi*

Small and flattened with granular dorsal scales. Scales larger and more prominent on sides of back and flanks. Toes dilated at the tips, with 5–7 transverse scansors under middle toes. Middle row of scales above scansors enlarged. Grey to greyish brown above with irregular dark brown to reddish-brown markings forming roughly transverse bands across back. Ventrum grey with pinkish hue. Original tail banded with alternating dark and pale bands. Regenerated tail brownish grey, usually with irregular blotches or mottling. Juvenile brighter and more boldly patterned, with three prominent pale transverse bands on back of head and body. **Length** SVL: 49mm. **Status and Habitat** Rupicolous. Less common than Southern Rough Gecko, with which it often co-occurs. Found in mountain Fynbos from about Ceres northwards. Also inhabits smaller isolated rocky habitat to sea level on the West Coast. **Endemism** Southern Africa.

Swartberg leaf-toed geckos *Ramigekko*

A monotypic genus, split from *Afrogecko* (African leaf-toed geckos) in 2014. They have a single pair of leaf-shaped or rounded scansors under the fanned tip of each toe, and retractile claws. Distinguished by larger size and larger, smooth tubercles on back, surrounded by smaller granular scales. African leaf-toed geckos (*Afrogecko*), flat geckos (*Afroedura*) and pygmy geckos (*Goggia*) all have uniform covering of similarly sized granular scales.

4 Swartberg Leaf-toed Gecko *Ramigekko swartbergensis*

A beautiful, large and highly flattened gecko. Larger tubercle scales surrounded by smaller granular scales on back. Dorsal coloration warm brown, with shades of grey and beige mottling. Irregular whitish to cream patches on back form a diffuse series of bars that are interspersed with fine, sooty brown, jagged lines. Original tail marginally shorter than head–body length and shows seven or eight paler bands. Ventrum evenly pale in adults but blotchy in juveniles. **Length** SVL: 77mm. **Status and Habitat** Rupicolous. Range-restricted endemic limited to the higher-altitude northern slopes of the Klein and Groot Swartberg mountains, including the Oukloofberge. Associated with large sandstone outcrops in mountain Fynbos. Uncommon and rarely encountered. **Endemism** Fynbos Biome.

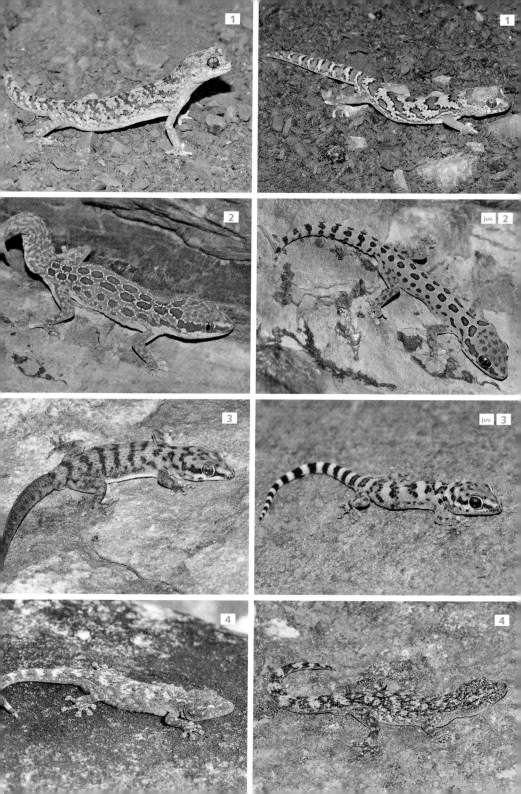

Lacertids/Old World lizards   Family Lacertidae

Small to medium-sized, typical, diurnal lizards with a long tail. Most lacertids are built for speed. Many species are adapted specifically to sandy substrates, but some are rupicolous. There are 27 species in South Africa, ten of which occur in the Fynbos Biome.

Southern rock lizards *Australolacerta*

Monotypic. They superficially resemble mountain lizards (*Tropidosaura*) but are distinguished by dorsolateral lines of reddish spots and a well-defined collar.

1 Southern Rock Lizard *Australolacerta australis*

A truly beautiful lizard. Medium-sized with small, smooth granular dorsal scales. Original tail twice head–body length. Distinct collar. Dorsal coloration sooty black, densely marked with creamy beige irregularly shaped spots. Spots are pale grey-green or blueish green, particularly on hindquarters. Dorsolateral lines of reddish spots run towards hind legs. Pale markings on top of head form short lines. Tail dull sage, black-flecked, with blueish tone towards tip. Juvenile has a bright greenish-blue tail. Ventral coloration pale with dark-edged scales. **Length** SVL: 70mm. **Status and Habitat** Diurnal, solitary and uncommonly encountered. Rupicolous, inhabiting rocky mountain Fynbos, preferring large sandstone outcrops. Restricted to Cape Fold Mountains from Clanwilliam in the north to Waboomsberge in the western Langeberg.

Desert and savanna lizards *Meroles*

Alert and adapted to moving quickly over loose, sandy substrates. Streamlined shape, small, granular scales on back and obvious collar. Easily confused with sand lizards (*Pedioplanis*) but can be distinguished by the presence of fringing on toes and in that the subocular scale does not reach the lip. Five species in South Africa, one in the Fynbos Biome.

2 Knox's Desert Lizard *Meroles knoxii*

Small to medium-sized with fine, granular dorsal scales. Coloration variable, corresponding to substrate. Pale grey to warm brown above. Heavily patterned with brown, black and dark grey blotches forming distinct longitudinal bands that contain white spots. Ventrum uniformly whitish. Top of legs spotted. 13–22 femoral pores on each thigh. Supranasal scales in contact. Breeding males develop yellow coloration on head, throat, vent and base of tail. Individuals from coastal areas generally paler. Juveniles more brightly marked. **Length** SVL: 68mm. **Status and Habitat** Diurnal, darting between shrubs, particularly on sandy substrates. Primarily a species of the West Coast lowlands but extending as far inland as the Tankwa Karoo. **Endemism** Southern Africa.

Sandveld lizards *Nucras*

Beautiful lizards with a cylindrical shape and a very long, often colourful, tail. All have small, granular dorsal scales, a distinct collar and toes that lack fringing. Tail has rectangular scales that are strongly keeled above and arranged in whorls. Diurnal, but generally secretive and rarely encountered. Nine species occur in South Africa, with four species in the Fynbos Biome.

3 Lambert's Bay Sandveld Lizard *Nucras aurantiaca* DD

Enigmatic, described in 2019. Body extremely elongated. Dorsal coloration plain orange-beige with grey shading on head and forebody. Very faint, short, grey barring along spine. Tail extremely long, orange to bright orange. Pale orange flanks merge gradually with orange upperparts and white ventral side. In *N. tesellata* var. *elegans* there appears to be no merging of coloration on the back and flanks, creating a two-tone effect. Range of variations in coloration not known. **Length** SVL: 75mm. **Status and Habitat** Little known. Well-vegetated shrubland with a sandy substrate near Lambert's Bay. **Conservation Status:** Data Deficient; proposed threat status of Endangered owing to threats from agriculture and development. **Endemism** Fynbos Biome.

1 Delalande's Sandveld Lizard *Nucras lalandii*

Large, robust, generally spotty in appearance with no defined dorsal stripes. Warm brown to greyish brown above with longitudinal lines of white-centred black spots. Black blotches can merge into bands, sometimes containing white spots. Black spotting continues down brownish tail. Lips, cheeks and flanks usually boldly marked with irregular white and dark markings that can form vertical white bars, especially on side of neck. Ventrum whitish with striking black spotting. Juveniles darker above with more prominent white spots. **Length** SVL: 110mm. **Status and Habitat** Cryptic and rarely encountered. Occurs in well-vegetated moist Fynbos. Rare in Fynbos Biome and restricted to the narrow southern coastal strip as far west as Cape Town (no recent records). **Endemism** Southern Africa.

2 Karoo Sandveld Lizard *Nucras livida*

The smallest of the Fynbos sandveld lizards. Dark sooty black above with six thin pale stripes down back. Irregular white to yellowish spotting on flanks and upper surface of legs. Spotting can form varying degrees of white and black barring on side of neck and flanks. Adults have reddish-brown coloration to the lower back. Tail reddish brown with faint dark flecking. Ventrum uniformly whitish. Juvenile has blue colour to hind legs and tail. **Length** SVL: 85mm. **Status and Habitat** Secretive and rarely encountered. Predominantly associated with well-vegetated sandy areas of the Succulent Karoo, but may enter arid Renosterveld or Fynbos habitats along the arid edges. One old record from north of Cape Town but no other confirmed records from the West Coast. **Endemism** South Africa.

3 Western Sandveld Lizard *Nucras tessellata*

Anterior part of body usually sooty black with 2–4 thin, whitish to orange dorsal stripes or stippled lines. Striking black-and-white barring on flanks fades at about midbody as the brilliant red colour of hindquarters and tail starts. This red colour can be a subdued pale red-brown. In juveniles, black-and-white barring continues further down body. Ventrum uniform white. The unmarked form var. *elegans* resembles Lambert's Bay Sandveld Lizard, but has more scale rows across the mid-back (45–47 as opposed to 39–41). Some from the West Coast resemble Karoo Sandveld Lizard but they have a maximum of five stripes (not six) on the nape. **Length** SVL: 92mm. **Status and Habitat** Secretive but the most frequently encountered sandveld lizards in Fynbos. Encountered in arid mountain Fynbos of the Cape Fold Mountains, as well as Strandveld of the West Coast north of Velddrif. **Endemism** Southern Africa.

Sand lizards *Pedioplanis*

Relatively small lacertids with a cylindrical body, distinct collar and long tail. Diurnal, alert and adapted to running extremely quickly over sandy substrates. Separated from desert lizards (*Meroles*), in that subocular scale borders lip and there is no fringing on toes. An African genus with five species in South Africa and two in the Fynbos Biome.

4 Burchell's Sand Lizard *Pedioplanis burchelli*

Small, granular scales on back. Distinct collar and faint gular fold present. Coloration highly variable. Juvenile has sooty black upperparts with five pale buff to orange longitudinal stripes. Central stripe may be forked towards head or double. Tail orange or blueish grey. Legs sooty black with distinct buff spots. This coloration can persist in some adults, but most are more cryptically patterned. Stripes fade to varying degrees, resulting in broken lines of white spotting and irregular black lines or linear blotches on a grey, brown to warm beige background. **Length** SVL: 57mm. **Status and Habitat** Relatively common in the southern and eastern parts of South Africa. Preference for flat, rocky areas with sparse vegetation. In the Fynbos Biome, primarily found in mountain Fynbos from the Cederberg southwards. **Endemism** Southern Africa.

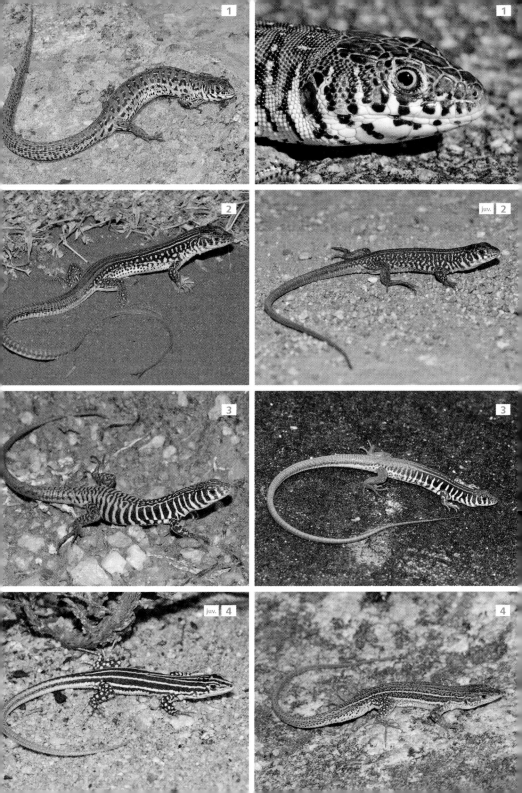

1 **Common Sand Lizard** *Pedioplanis lineoocellata pulchella*

Extremely variable. Distinguished from Burchell's Sand Lizard by row of distinct 'eyes' or spots along flanks. These characteristic spots are blueish to greenish white, bordered by black. Dorsal coloration usually shades of warm brown. Head usually greyish brown. 2–4 rows of black blotches on back and upper flanks that sometimes merge to form continual strips, especially towards head. Stripes or rows of spots often bordered by thin white stripes or small white spots. Some individuals are rather uniform, but normally retain characteristic flank spots to some degree. Ventrum white. Males can have blue-grey shading on throat. Juvenile has four black longitudinal stripes and bright orange-red tail. Distinct collar present, lacking gular fold. **Length** SVL: 58mm. **Status and Habitat** Common in the Cederberg. Absent from the western coastal plain, Overberg and wet mountain Fynbos. Preference for flat, rocky areas. **Endemism** Southern Africa.

Mountain lizards   *Tropidosaura*

These smallish, slender lizards are attractively patterned. Males develop bright colours on flanks when breeding. They lack a collar, but a gular fold is present, although sometimes indistinct. Body scales large, strongly keeled and mucronate. A small genus comprising four diurnal species found only in South Africa, two of which occur in the Fynbos.

2 **Cape Mountain Lizard** *Tropidosaura gularis*

Similar to the smaller Common Mountain Lizard, but the pale dorsolateral stripes are usually broken up into rows of spots and a distinct gular fold is present. Granular scales on nape and side of neck smooth. Scales on back in 23–29 rows at midbody. 7–12 femoral pores on each thigh. Dark brown to black above with lighter brown, greenish or yellow-orange broken bands down back. Pale lateral stripe usually broken up to form series of pale spots along each flank. Broken band of yellow-orange scales also present low down on each flank, becoming bright orange in breeding males. Tail brown or dark blueish green, occasionally bright turquoise. Ventrum off-white with variable black spotting. **Length** SVL: 62mm. **Status and Habitat** Solitary, shy and uncommon. Restricted to rocky mountain Fynbos habitat, often in moist situations. **Endemism** Fynbos Biome.

3 **Common Mountain Lizard** *Tropidosaura montana montana*

Has more defined pale dorsolateral stripes than larger Cape Mountain Lizard. Gular fold very faint. Scales on side of neck and nape small and keeled. Scales on back in 20–23 rows at midbody. 5–8 femoral pores on each thigh. Light to olive-brown above, with dark brown to sooty vertebral stripe. Pale dorsolateral stripes bordered on both sides by darker stripes. Variable (sometimes indistinct) pale lateral stripe present on flanks. These are also bordered by dark longitudinal stripes. Pale yellow band or row of spots present on lower flanks. When breeding, this intensifies to bright orange. Tail brown with dark markings. Ventrum greyish white with variable dark spots. **Length** SVL: 58mm. **Status and Habitat** Solitary, shy and uncommon. Prefers lush, moist, rocky mountain slopes. **Endemism** South Africa. The subspecies *T. m. montana* restricted to the Fynbos Biome.

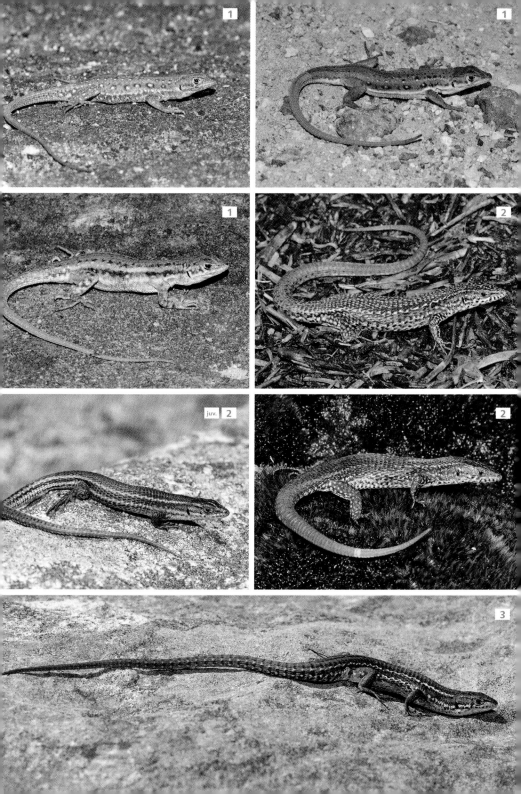

Cordylids or spinytail lizards   Family Cordylidae

Recognised by their scales, which are arranged in regular girdles on the body and form whorls or rings along the tail. The tail scales are spiny or markedly keeled. These lizards also have a short tongue. An African endemic family, with South Africa containing some 50 species. There are 13 species in the Fynbos Biome, where almost half of this number are endemic.

Grass lizards   *Chamaesaura*

These extremely elongated lizards are specialised for moving through grass-like vegetation and are referred to as grass swimmers. Limbs residual. The very long tail is easily shed in self-defence. While the tail is re-growing, movement is significantly impaired. Three species of this African genus occur in South Africa, one of which is found in the Fynbos biome.

1 Cape Grass Lizard *Chamaesaura anguina anguina*
Extremely elongated with heavily keeled scales and a large head. All limbs present but significantly reduced and with one or two clawed digits on each. Tail extremely long (±3–4 times the length of the body). Coloration variable. Some individuals uniform brown above, but most distinctly striped. Back variable shades of brown from nose to tail tip, usually with pale central stripe. Two pale tan dorsolateral stripes run through eyes and down length of body and tail. These stripes occasionally bordered below by warm buff band. Flanks greyish brown to pale brown. Ventrum off-white to pale yellow. **Length** SVL: 140mm. **Status and Habitat** Diurnal and solitary. Cryptic but can be common. Found in grassy and restio-dominated areas, predominantly in Fynbos. **Endemism** South Africa.

Girdled lizards   *Cordylus*

These lizards have a distinctly triangular head. Most are significantly flattened, enabling them to shelter in narrow rock cracks. All have well-developed limbs. Scales along tail arranged in concentric rings, spiny. Tail regeneration slow and inefficient. Diurnal. There are nine species in South Africa and six in the Fynbos Biome.

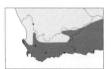

2 Cape Girdled Lizard *Cordylus cordylus*
Attractive and robust with large, rough dorsal scales. 16–22 scales in a row across the middle of the back. These scales have prominent keels, forming longitudinal ridges. Flanks scales also keeled. Scales on side of neck and tail spiny. Subocular scale does not reach lip as it does in Black Girdled Lizard. Dorsal coloration variable but generally dull to brighter shades of brown, yellowish or orange, with irregular dark sooty markings that can create a checkered appearance. Top of head darker than back and largely unmarked. Irregular pale dorsal stripe or series of blotches may be present. Ventrum beige-yellow to orange-brown; ventral scales smooth. 4–10 femoral pores on each thigh of male. **Length** SVL: 98mm. **Status and Habitat** Colonial, widespread and common. Rupicolous, occurring from sea level to high mountain peaks. **Endemism** Southern Africa.

3 Rooiberg Girdled Lizard *Cordylus imkeae*
An attractive Fynbos Biome endemic with a very restricted range. The smallest of the Fynbos girdled lizards. Dorsal scales strongly keeled, the keel being obliquely orientated on each scale. 24–26 scales in a row across the middle of the back. Dorsal coloration yellowish brown with numerous irregular dark markings that can create a blotchy appearance. Dark markings can form broken bands across back. Scales on side of neck and tail spiny. Ventrum whitish with smooth ventral scales. Both sexes have 4–6 femoral pores on each thigh. **Length** SVL: 67.8mm. **Status and Habitat** Rupicolous. Uncommon with a highly restricted range which it doesn't share with any other *Cordylus* species. Endemic to arid Kamiesberg Granite Fynbos on the Rooiberg Mountain in the Northern Cape. **Endemism** Fynbos Biome.

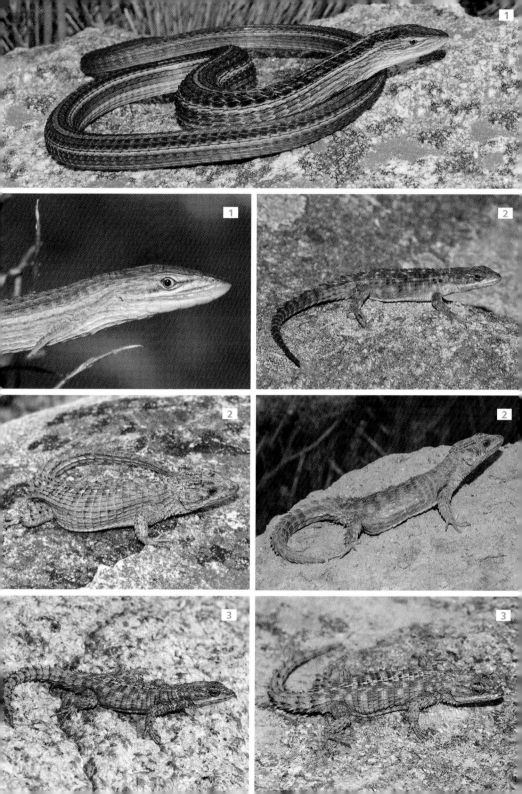

1 Large-scaled Girdled Lizard *Cordylus macropholis*

A small, stocky lizard with very large, strongly keeled dorsal scales and a rough overall appearance. Terrestrial, with a rounded head and cylindrical body, unlike the flattened body shape of the rupicolous girdled lizards. 14–18 scales in a row across the middle of the back. Scales on flanks and tail spiny. Upperparts grey, brownish grey to dark chocolate-brown with irregular light brown, beige to greyish markings. Fine dark flecking evident on paler scales. Lips and throat paler than rest of head, with some dark spotting. Ventrum pale grey; ventral scales keeled. 10–12 femoral pores on each thigh. **Length** SVL: 70mm. **Status and Habitat** Secretive and not regularly encountered. Terrestrial. Found in small colonies. Restricted to three subpopulations along the West Coast from Port Nolloth to Yzerfontein. Within the Fynbos Biome, in Strandveld vegetation close to the coast. **Endemism** CFR (in South Africa).

2 McLachlan's Girdled Lizard *Cordylus mclachlani*

A small girdled lizard with a restricted range. Scales on back in 21–25 rows at midbody. These scales have prominent keels that are obliquely orientated on each scale. Scales on neck, flanks and tail larger and spiny. Dorsal coloration orange-brown to brown. Variable but usually extensive irregular blackish markings on back, flanks and tail. Often with small pale yellow spots on back. Head predominantly dark. Ventrum whitish with smooth scales. 7–12 femoral pores on each thigh. Range does not overlap with the similar Rooiberg Girdled Lizard, which has fewer femoral pores (4–6). **Length** SVL: 73mm. **Status and Habitat** Diurnal and rupicolous. Inhabits low rocky outcrops in arid Fynbos and Succulent Karoo. Extends from the Bokkeveld Mountains down the Cederberg to the Koue Bokkeveld Mountains in the south. **Endemism** CFR (in South Africa).

3 Black Girdled Lizard *Cordylus niger*

Medium-sized with a rough overall appearance. Distinctive in that it is usually uniformly black. Dorsal scales keeled. 16–22 scales in a row across the middle of the back. Subocular scale reaches the lip, unlike the Cape Girdled Lizard. Tail spiny. Dorsal coloration sooty black, usually lacking any distinctive patterning or markings. Some individuals may show some dull diffuse markings, especially on flanks. Ventrum uniform sooty grey. 5–10 femoral pores on each thigh. **Length** SVL: 92mm. **Status and Habitat** Common in suitable habitat. A range-restricted species with populations on the Cape Peninsula, Jutten Island, at Langebaan and Saldanha where they inhabit rocky outcrops in Fynbos and Strandveld. They can make use of very small outcrops and artificial structures. **Endemism** Fynbos Biome.

4 Oelofsen's Girdled Lizard *Cordylus oelofseni*

A small girdled lizard that occurs in three distinct populations, possibly representing separate species. Tail has prominent rings of spiny scales. Dorsal scales keeled, the keels forming parallel ridges. 18–22 scales in a row across the middle of the back. Scales on flanks more prominently keeled. Dorsal coloration generally uniform, dull sooty brown to matt-black. Some individuals show a pale yellowish-white vertebral stripe or some pale yellowish to orange-brown spotting on body and tail. Sides of neck and lips can be paler than rest of upperparts. Ventral scales smooth and greyish. Both sexes have 6–9 femoral pores on each thigh. **Length** SVL: 69mm. **Status and Habitat** A common but localised rupicolous mountain Fynbos endemic. Colonies occur in large and small rocky outcrops from near Citrusdal in the north to the Hottentots Holland Mountains in the south. They also occur on the Piketberg. **Endemism** Fynbos Biome.

Cliff lizards *Hemicordylus*

This special genus is endemic to the Fynbos Biome and contains only two species. They are slender, melanistic and lack spiny body scales. These lizards have well-developed limbs and are adept at navigating vertical rocks at high speed. Both species are diurnal, rupicolous and live in small colonies.

1 **Cape Cliff Lizard** *Hemicordylus capensis*

Slender, flattened and lacking spiny scales on its head and body. Tail long, thin and spiny. Keeled scales on back in approximately 10–12 rows at midbody, with central line of very small scales along spine. Flanks have only granular scales. The much rarer Dwarf Cliff Lizard has keeled scales on its flanks. Dorsal coloration dark slaty, charcoal or black with yellow flecking or spotting in some. Yellow flecks or spots can merge to form fine vermiculations or rough crossbars. Jaws with whitish or orange spotting. Markings on neck, throat and eyebrow can be orange. Ventrum slate-grey with paler central belly. 15–20 femoral pores on each thigh. **Length** SVL: 78mm. **Status and Habitat** Restricted to higher altitudes of the Cape Fold Mountains, where fairly common. Favours vertical cliffs. Very alert and quick to retreat. **Endemism** Fynbos Biome.

2 **Dwarf Cliff Lizard** *Hemicordylus nebulosus* **VU**

This rare, slender lizard is similar to Cape Cliff Lizard. They differ in that the flanks have large, keeled scales interspersed with granular scales, and the larger scales on the back are not divided by a median line of very small scales. The large dorsal scales are keeled. Dorsal coloration slaty-brown to black with variable fine yellow spotting, especially along spine and around neck. Ventral surface black. Tail long and slender with whorls of spiny scales. 9–11 femoral pores on each thigh. **Length** SVL: 76mm. **Status and Habitat** Rare with a highly restricted distribution. Occurs at high altitude in moist, rocky habitats in Kogelberg Sandstone Fynbos. Only one population is known to occur in the Hottentot Hollands Mountains. **Conservation Status:** Vulnerable. Particularly vulnerable to the potential impacts of future climate change. **Endemism** Fynbos Biome.

Karusa lizards *Karusasaurus*

Differs from all other Fynbos cordylids by the high number of scale rows across the back. Only the very different Cape Crag Lizard has more scale rows. The only Fynbos cordylid with smooth dorsal scales and keeled scales on flanks. A southern African endemic genus containing two widespread species. One species occurs in South Africa and the Fynbos Biome.

3 **Southern Karusa Lizard** *Karusasaurus polyzonus*

Large, with a triangular head and flattened body. Back scales small, numerous and relatively smooth; flank scales keeled. 28–40 scales in a row across the middle of the back. Spiny scales on neck, upper limbs and tail. Coloration highly variable. Generally light to dark brown, charcoal, olive-brown or orange-brown above. Some predominantly uniform, others with regularly arranged dark or light blotches along length of body. Dark patch on side of neck clearly visible in paler individuals. Ventrum pale yellow to off-white. Throat occasionally infused with grey vermiculations. Melanistic populations on the West Coast near Langebaan and Saldanha. Juveniles brown, boldly marked with dark and pale blotches. **Length** SVL: 113mm. **Status and Habitat** Diurnal, gregarious and common. Very alert and quick to retreat. Widespread in semi-arid rocky habitat but absent from the Overberg and coastal areas of the southern Cape. **Endemism** Southern Africa.

Blue-spotted lizard   *Ninurta*

A monotypic genus endemic to the Fynbos Biome. The single colonial species is diurnal and rupicolous. No spines on neck or tail.

1 Blue-spotted Lizard   *Ninurta coeruleopunctatus*

An attractive medium-sized lizard with a triangular head and robust body. Body scales small and strongly keeled but not spiny. Some granular scales present on neck and flanks only. 20–22 scales in a row across middle of back. Predominantly slaty-grey above, with varying degrees of irregular paler olive- to yellowish-brown markings. These often form roughly linear patterns or lines down body. Diagnostic small metallic powder-blue spots scattered along cheeks, neck and flanks. Ventrum greyish with yellow to orange throat. This bright yellow-orange coloration can extend onto the chest and belly as well as onto the snout, cheeks, eyebrows and flanks. **Length** SVL: 82mm. **Status and Habitat** Common in suitable habitat within its limited range. Occurs in the Cape Fold Mountains from the Langeberg to Oubosstrand area where they prefer moist rocky habitat. **Endemism** Fynbos Biome.

Armadillo lizards   *Ouroborus*

A monotypic genus endemic to CFR. They have a characteristic defence mechanism: they roll into a ball by biting onto the tail, protecting their soft underbelly. While still common and widespread, illegal collecting has decimated both the colonies and habitat at some easily accessible and well-known sites. Their low reproduction rate (usually one offspring/year/female) means that colony resilience is low, and recovery is slow. Diurnal and gregarious.

2 Armadillo Lizard   *Ouroborus cataphractus*   `NT`

A charismatic, endearing and attractive lizard. Robust and flattened with heavy plated and spiny appearance. Large scales on triangular head, ending in sharp backward-pointing spines. Large, keeled scales arranged in 15–17 overlapping concentric bands down body. Similar bands of scales extend down legs onto toes and down tail. Scales on flanks, upper legs and tail also have spines. Yellow to brown above, with shades of orange. Some with darker patches. Area around the eyes, nostrils, lips and throat have dark, blackish markings. Ventrum shades of yellow with darker patches. **Length** SVL: 105mm. **Status and Habitat** Common in suitable habitat. Primarily associated with the Succulent Karoo but occurs in the western and northern parts of the Fynbos Biome in arid, rocky habitats. **Conservation Status** Near Threatened. **Endemism** CFR (in South Africa).

Crag lizards   *Pseudocordylus*

This southern African endemic genus contains some of the largest cordylids. Similar to gridled lizards (*Cordylus*) in appearance but differ in that they have granular scales on the back and neck, and the tail is less spiny. They are exclusively found in rocky environments, mostly at high altitude. Five species occur in South Africa, with only one found in the Fynbos Biome.

3 Cape Crag Lizard   *Pseudocordylus microlepidotus microlepidotus*

An impressive, large lizard with a very broad, triangular head. Numerous small, granular scales cover back, with 36–46 scales in a row across the mid-back. No spines on back, flanks, neck or head. Scales on tail form pattern of concentric rings ending in spiny points. Dark charcoal-brown to black from head down length of back and tail. Lower flanks yellow to orange. This coloration extends up flanks and forms faint to pronounced light yellow stripes (seven or eight) across back. In some, the yellow is more of a mottled intrusion onto the black. Lips and snout yellow or black. Ventrum pale blueish white to yellow. Males and juveniles more brightly coloured. The throat in males have a variable sooty black patch which can extend over entire throat area. **Length** SVL: ±140mm. **Status and Habitat** Diurnal, generally solitary and shy. Common in suitable habitat along the Cape Fold Mountains. Dependent on rocky habitat with a preference for smaller rocky outcrops. **Endemism** South Africa. The subspecies *P. m. microlepidotus* is a Fynbos endemic.

Plated lizards and relatives — Family Gerrhosauridae

Closely related to cordylids (family Cordylidae). Named for the rectangular body scales, which create a plated appearance. The family contains lizards with a wide range of sizes, shapes and features. Limbs and digits vary from being well developed to highly reduced or absent.

Dwarf plated lizards *Cordylosaurus*

This monotypic African genus is superficially similar to plated snake lizards (*Tetradactylus*). *Cordylosaurus* is however brightly coloured in contrast to the cryptic coloration of the plated snake lizards. The single diurnal species is restricted to the arid western portion of southern Africa.

1 Dwarf Plated Lizard *Cordylosaurus subtessellatus*
A very attractive and distinct little lizard. Limbs well developed. Tail very long, being up to double head–body length. Dorsal scales variably keeled. Coloration bold with marked striped appearance. Black to sooty brown above. Two bold cream to pale orange dorsolateral stripes run from the snout (where they meet) down the body onto the tail. From base of tail, the pale stripes become striking turquoise to royal blue. The bright tail is readily shed when harassed. Legs variable shades of red. Lateral fold present. Ventrum white with blueish or greenish tinge. **Length** SVL: 55mm. **Status and Habitat** Primarily found in more karroid habitats and uncommonly encountered in the Fynbos Biome. Enters the Biome on the arid peripheral border with the Succulent Karoo. Associated with rocky outcrops. Extremely fast and evasive.

Plated lizards *Gerrhosaurus*

Medium-sized to large robust lizards, with well-developed but relatively small limbs. Defined lateral fold present on flanks; dorsal scales keeled. In some species, both sexes have femoral pores, but these are more pronounced in males. Diurnal, solitary, relatively slow-moving and shy. Bask in sunlight with their limbs raised, resting on their belly, and slide down slopes in this position. The long tail is used for fat storage and is easily shed. Four species occur in South Africa, with two in the Fynbos Biome.

2 Yellow-throated Plated Lizard *Gerrhosaurus flavigularis*
Large, slender lizard with no distinct neck and a relatively small head. Back and upper flanks reddish brown to brown with two pale yellow longitudinal stripes running down the body, from just above the eye to halfway down the tail. Between these stripes, the back can be uniform or variably flecked with black and occasionally white spots. Flanks uniform or with black or pale spots or vertical barring. Juveniles boldly marked. White dorsolateral stripes often broken, forming stippled line. There are roughly paired white spots and variable dark flecking on back. Sides of head and flanks show bold black-and-white vertical barring which extends onto tail. Ventrum white to yellowish white. Breeding males can develop bright red, yellow or blue coloration on lower sections of face, throat and chest. **Length** SVL: 142mm. **Status and Habitat** Fairly common but shy. In the Fynbos Biome, confined to the coastal regions.

3 Karoo Plated Lizard *Gerrhosaurus typicus*
The only plated lizard found along the West Coast and in the Karoo. Cylindrical, with no distinct neck and a smallish, rounded head with a short snout. Dorsal coloration light to dark brown. Two white to cream, dark-edged dorsolateral stripes present. These start from behind each eye and run onto the tail. Dark flanks show bold white flecking, extending onto long tail. Ventrum uniformly whitish, including lower lips and throat. Breeding males can develop orange-reddish coloration at base of tail and underside of limbs. **Length** SVL: 114mm. **Status and Habitat** Shy and rarely encountered. Utilises dry, sandy and rocky habitats. Few records from the Fynbos Biome, but associated with the Strandveld of the West Coast as far south as Koeberg. Also recorded from Renosterveld; probably more common and widely distributed than records indicate. **Endemism** South Africa.

Plated snake lizards/seps *Tetradactylus*

These beautiful lizards are specialist grass swimmers. Extremely elongated and can be mistaken for a snake when glimpsed briefly. Closely associated with grassy and restio-rich habitats. Diurnal and solitary. The genus contains eight species, all confined to the southern half of Africa. Six species occur in South Africa (one of which is extinct), with three in the Fynbos Biome.

1 FitzSimons' Long-tailed Seps *Tetradactylus fitzsimonsi*

Distinguished from the other two Fynbos Biome species of *Tetradactylus* by the lack of forelimbs and the highly reduced hind limbs, which have only a single toe (inset). Dorsal scales have pronounced keels. An obvious lateral fold is visible. Dorsal coloration light bronze-brown to olive-brown. A fine dark mark on each scale creates the appearance of indistinct longitudinal stripes. Flanks paler. Some dark spots on head and distinct dark barring from behind eye onto neck. This barring extends above lateral fold. Ventrum uniformly pale. Tail very long, more than three times the head–body length. **Length** SVL: 71mm. **Status and Habitat** Rarely encountered. Recent records between George and the area around Mazeppa Bay (Eastern Cape). Habitat preference appears to be coastal grassy or restioid areas. **Endemism** South Africa.

2 Short-legged Seps *Tetradactylus seps*

Very dark overall with well-developed front and hind legs, both of which have five toes (inset). Small, elongated and cylindrical with no distinct neck and a long tail. Tail normally double the head–body length, but many individuals have shorter regenerating tail. Dorsal scales striated or, on occasion, very slightly keeled. Distinct lateral fold present. Dorsal coloration generally different shades of metallic bronze to dark brown. A series of white spots on top lip usually very conspicuous. White spotting can also occur on the neck. These rarely extending onto flanks and tail. Ventrum white to pale grey. **Length** SVL: 68mm. **Status and Habitat** Common in suitable habitat but difficult to see and not often encountered. Associated with moist grassy and restio-rich habitats. They often make use of logs and leaf litter for shelter. **Endemism** South Africa.

3 Cape Long-tailed Seps *Tetradactylus tetradactylus*

This seps has diminutive front and hind limbs, each with four toes (inset). Dorsal scales keeled and striated. Distinct lateral fold is present. Tail very long (three times the length of the body). Dorsal coloration light bronze-brown to olive-brown with darker marks in each scale, creating striped appearance of varying intensity. Dark brown dorsolateral bands present, often bordered by pale buff stripe below. Flanks paler. Top of head has variable dark spots. Short, dark bars run from top of lip to forelimbs. These bars are below the lateral fold. Ventrum pale. **Length** SVL: 74mm. **Status and Habitat** Associated with drier grassy and restio-rich habitats. Does not occur in Strandveld. Common, but extremely fast and usually only glimpsed briefly as it 'swims' away in grassy habitat with serpentine movements. Navigates gaps between grass and restio tufts with impressive spring-like jumps. **Endemism** South Africa.

Skinks
Family Scincidae

These lizards have notably smaller limbs compared to other families. Skinks inhabit a wide range of habitats, but the highest diversity is associated with sandy substrates that cater for fossorial species. Of the Fynbos Biome skink species, only typical skinks (*Trachylepis*) and dwarf burrowing skinks (*Scelotes*) are able to shed and regenerate their tail.

Legless skinks *Acontias*

Fossorial and completely limbless, often mistaken for snakes. Elongated and cylindrical with no discernible neck. An overall smooth, glossy appearance with a short, blunt-tipped tail. Small, dark eyes with transparent or opaque lower eyelids, but no upper eyelids. Snout bluntly pointed, with large rostral shield. Twenty-one species occur in South Africa, with four species found in the Fynbos Biome. This genus is currently under scrutiny and several taxonomic changes are expected.

1 Gray's Dwarf Legless Skink *Acontias grayi*

Previously considered a subspecies of Striped Dwarf Legless Skink and may well be lumped again. Dorsal coloration orange with a dark mark in the front half of each scale, which creates a spotted appearance. These spots can form parallel lines in some individuals. The size of the dark marks can increase around the head and eyes, creating dusky areas of variable intensity and extent. **Length** SVL: 148mm. **Status and Habitat** Fossorial and restricted to the sandy coastal region on the West Coast between the Berg River and the Olifants River where they are fairly common. **Endemism** Fynbos Biome.

2 Striped Dwarf Legless Skink *Acontias lineatus*

Closely related to Coastal and Gray's Dwarf Legless Skinks, both of which expected to be lumped with this species. Dorsal coloration varies greatly from strongly striped to completely uniform. Most individuals are yellow above with up to 10 longitudinal stripes or rows of spots. Uniformly coloured purplish-black individuals are occasionally encountered. Ventral coloration ranges from purplish black to pinkish and is usually partially translucent. Variable amounts of dark coloration around eyes create masked effect in paler individuals. **Length** SVL: 148mm. **Status and Habitat** Fossorial and found in sandy substrates across a wide range of habitats within the Western and Northern Cape provinces. Within the Fynbos Biome, they are found north of Citrusdal. **Endemism** Southern Africa.

3 Coastal Dwarf Legless Skink *Acontias litoralis*

Likely to be lumped with Striped Dwarf Legless Skink. This small skink has uniform golden-orange or purplish-black dorsal coloration. Individuals with a purplish-black back have golden-orange flanks, creating a distinct two-tone appearance. Some orange individuals have dark spots on the scales just behind the head, resulting in short lines or rows of spots on the nape. Variable dark mask-like markings around eyes. Ventral coloration pinkish and somewhat translucent. **Length** SVL: 119mm. **Status and Habitat** Fossorial and common in suitable habitat. Limited to sparsely vegetated sandy substrates where it is generally found under leaf litter or at the base of shrubs. Found on the coastal strip between Velddrif and Port Nolloth. **Endemism** CFR (in South Africa).

4 Cape Legless Skink *Acontias meleagris*

The largest and most common of the region's legless skinks. Tail short and thick. Coloration variable. Dorsal surface smooth, glossy, usually a shade of yellow or olive but can be grey, brown or blackish brown. Occasionally uniform but the back is usually a darker tone with variable dark markings on each scale, resulting in a spotted or vaguely striped appearance. Ventrum paler, usually unmarked, but occasionally mottled. Juvenile has a more heavily striped appearance and darker head. **Length** SVL: 250mm. **Status and Habitat** Fossorial and very common. Occurs in a wide variety of habitats in Fynbos, Strandveld and Renosterveld throughout the Fynbos Biome. **Endemism** South Africa.

Blind legless skinks *Typhlosaurus*

These insectivorous lizards are completely limbless. A key feature distinguishing them from legless skinks (*Acontias*) is the loss of functional eyes. A specialised fossorial genus with five species, all in southern Africa. Four species occur in South Africa, with only one in the Fynbos.

1 **Southern Blind Legless Skink** *Typhlosaurus caecus*

Blind, vestigial eyes visible as dark spots underneath head scales. Adapted to a subterranean lifestyle, the body is elongated, cylindrical, smooth and limbless. No defined neck; head ends in pointed snout covered by large scale. Tail tip almost rounded. Scales smooth and polished. Dorsal coloration an attractive orange with pinkish collar behind head. Division between orange upperparts and pink flanks marked; edge irregular. Ventrum pinkish to flesh coloured and somewhat translucent. **Length** SVL: 213mm. **Status and Habitat** Fossorial. Common but restricted to the narrow coastal strip on sandy substrates of the West Coast between Cape Town and Strandfontein. **Endemism** Fynbos Biome.

Typical skinks *Trachylepis*

Relatively robust, small to medium-sized lizards with well-developed limbs. Cylindrical in shape, with no distinct neck and a smooth, shiny appearance despite most having keeled scales. Eyes have movable eyelids. Tail can be shed when threatened. They occupy a wide range of habitats and are all diurnal. There are 15 species in South Africa, with five in the Fynbos Biome. Cape Skinks are one of few reptiles that can persist in areas of urban sprawl.

2 **Cape Skink** *Trachylepis capensis*

Dorsal and lateral scales have three low keels; most pronounced on back. Dorsal coloration varies from sandy brown to warm darker brown or olive-grey; often with metalic sheen. Broken, horizontal dark bars cross back and flanks, extending onto tail. Individual paler scales can produce a fine spotted appearance. Three whitish to buff longitudinal stripes present; one along spine, two at top of flanks. Vertebral stripe can be broad with stippled dark line in centre. Uniformly pale grey, brown or sooty brown forms can occur, sometimes with paler stripes present, but no other markings. Ventrum pale whitish, usually infused with brownish grey. Can be separated from Western Three-striped Skink by slightly keeled scales on flanks and numerous small ear lobe scales. **Length** SVL: 135mm. **Status and Habitat** Very common in a diversity of habitat types, including suburban gardens.

3 **Red-sided Skink** *Trachylepis homalocephala*

An attractive skink; breeding males develop varying degrees of pale orange to bright reddish-orange coloration on flanks, legs, lower jaw and throat. Dorsal scales each have three low keels. Upperparts olive-brown to greyish brown. Darker longitudinal stripes on back; these may be broken, absent, or replaced by rows of squarish spots. Variable pale flecking can also be present. Broad, black dorsolateral bands run from snout onto base of tail. These are bordered below by distinct white to cream stripes. Ventrum whitish, variably infused with orange in males. Subocular scale does not taper to where it reaches the lip as it does in Variegated Skink. **Length** SVL: 79mm. **Status and Habitat** Common in moist habitats. Found throughout the Fynbos Biome, associated with coastal shrub, moist Fynbos, wetlands and riverine fringes. **Endemism** Southern Africa.

1 Western Three-striped Skink *Trachylepis occidentalis*

Similar to Cape Skink but generally more slender and often more brightly coloured. Lacks the broken, dark bars across the back and flanks evident in many Cape Skinks. Dorsal scales keeled; lateral scales smooth. Three enlarged ear lobe scales evident. Warm light brown, dark brown or bright rufous-brown above. Three pale whitish, longitudinal stripes run from behind head to base of tail. These are edged with darker scales, which form stippled or solid dark lines. Flanks can be slightly darker, with broken dark spots. Pale flank stripes present. Ventral coloration uniformly pale. **Length** SVL: 95mm. **Status and Habitat** Uncommon. Found in arid environments, only entering the fringes of the Fynbos Biome where they are found in sandy areas with an open shrub component. Not found in gardens.

2 Western Rock Skink *Trachylepis sulcata sulcata*

A rupicolous skink with a flattened head and body. Dorsal scales strongly keeled with 3–5 keels on each scale. Significant sexual dimorphism. Female pale to olive-brown with six dark brown longitudinal stripes running from behind head parallel along back to tail. Ventrum off-white to pale grey with variable black spotting on throat. Juveniles similar to females. Male uniform black or bronze-brown in colour. Can be variably two-toned; black with bronze-brown coloration on hindquarters or bronze-brown above with black flanks. Ventrum in males uniformly black or densely black spotted. **Length** SVL: 81mm. **Status and Habitat** Common, gregarious and found in rocky outcrops and mountainous areas in arid habitats. **Endemism** Southern Africa.

3 Variegated Skink *Trachylepis variegata*

A small skink. Each dorsal scale has three keels. Coloration variable. Light greyish brown to dark brown above. Back can be plain but usually has variable black spots or marks arranged in longitudinal rows. White to cream dorsolateral and lateral stripes present. Pale vertebral stripe may also occasionally be present. Uniform, unmarked specimens can occur. Ventrum uniformly white. Breeding males develop reddish-brown flush on vent, hind legs and base of tail. Similar to Red-sided Skink but in Variegated Skink the subocular scale narrows markedly to where it reaches the lip. Subocular scale almost rectangular in Red-sided Skink. **Length** SVL: 53mm. **Status and Habitat** Associated with a variety of arid, rocky or sandy habitats. In the Fynbos Biome, associated with the drier habitats particularly on the Succulent Karoo fringes. Most frequently encountered in the Strandveld and mountain Fynbos in the western parts of the Biome.

Dwarf burrowing skinks *Scelotes*

A small genus of highly specialised, fossorial African skinks. Body elongated, cylindrical and smoothly polished, with no distinct neck. Small, dark eyes visible in all Fynbos species. Tail readily shed in self-defence. Regenerated tail has a different appearance to the original. They have varying degrees of reduced limbs and toes, the number of which aids in the identification of species, along with distribution and coloration. They live in subsurface layers of loamy and sandy soils or in leaf litter. The leaf litter species have more well-developed limbs, while those moving through sand have more significant limb reduction. There are 18 species in South Africa, with six in the Fynbos Biome.

4 Silvery Dwarf Burrowing Skink *Scelotes bipes*

This small skink has no forelimbs. The reduced hind limbs (inset) each have two toes. Variable amounts of black around eyes can form a mask-like appearance. Dorsal coloration silvery-grey; back often with buff tones. Numerous rows of dark spots on back and flanks, which can merge to form continuous stripes. These lines of spots or stripes continue onto original tail. Original tail shorter than head–body length. Regenerated tail pale with more diffuse spotting. Ventrum faintly spotted and silvery-white with pinkish hues. **Length** SVL: 79mm. **Status and Habitat** Fossorial and common. Distribution is patchy along sandy soils of coastal areas. Occurs roughly from Mossel Bay in the east to Velddrif in the west. **Endemism** Fynbos Biome.

1 Cape Dwarf Burrowing Skink *Scelotes caffer*

The smallest of the Fynbos burrowing skinks and the only one with forelimbs and relatively well-developed hind limbs. Each limb has three toes. Dorsal coloration is light to dark coppery brown. Each scale has dark central spot. Some have faint, pale dorsolateral stripes that run from above each eye down length of body. Snout shorter and more rounded than in the other Fynbos dwarf burrowing skink species. Tail longer than body and greyish to bright blue. They readily lose their tail if handled. **Length** SVL: 55mm. **Status and Habitat** Found under rocks and burrowing amongst leaf litter in sandy areas. The patchy distribution stretches across the CFR. Common on the West Coast north of Velddrif. Also numerous scattered records from mountain Fynbos. **Endemism** CFR (in South Africa).

2 Gronovi's Dwarf Burrowing Skink *Scelotes gronovii*

A small burrowing skink with minute hind limbs that have only one toe (inset). Dorsal coloration silvery to buff with several rows of stippled, longitudinal stripes down back and flanks. These markings are variable and can be a series of diffuse spots or continuous bold stripes. Two bold dark stripes on each flank merge to form mask-like stripe through eye to snout. Paler ventral side a warm light greyish colour with variable flecking. **Length** SVL: 70mm. **Status and Habitat** Fossorial and primarily found under objects on sparsely vegetated Strandveld sand dunes, often very close to the high-water mark. Common within restricted range from Bokbaai in the south to Doringbaai in the north, extending inland to about Graafwater. Also found on Robben and Dassen islands. **Endemism** Fynbos Biome.

3 Kasner's Dwarf Burrowing Skink *Scelotes kasneri* NT

Large, similar to Bloubergstrand Dwarf Burrowing Skink. Lacks forelimbs; reduced hind limbs each have two clawed toes (inset). Dorsal coloration warm buffy beige to caramel. Dark mark on each scale. These are very subdued on back, but well defined on flanks, usually forming three distinctive dorsolateral stripes which can merge to form a defined black band. Ventrum pale greyish to yellowish white, can be spotted beneath tail. In adults, the original tail is usually pale with a blueish hue. However, some have bright orange-red tail. Juvenile has blue tail. **Length** SVL: 129mm. **Status and Habitat** Fossorial. Fairly common under objects and at the base of plants in coastal sands from around Lambert's Bay in the north to at least Velddrif in the south and inland to about Clanwilliam. **Conservation Status** Near Threatened owing to habitat transformation within its restricted range. **Endemism** Fynbos Biome.

4 Bloubergstrand Dwarf Burrowing Skink *Scelotes montispectus* NT

The largest *Scelotes* species. Similar to Kasner's Dwarf Burrowing Skink but differs in that it lacks distinct lateral stripes extending from the mask down the length of the body. Lacks forelimbs; hind limbs each with two toes. Warm sandy-buff above, pale greyish white below. Short dark stripe runs through eye but does not extend down the body. Dark flecking on each dorsal scale can create impression of faint longitudinal stripes down the back. The original tail is a beautiful pinkish to orange. Juvenile has bright orange-red tail and the black mask can extend in a broken line onto the flank. **Length** SVL: ±134mm. **Status and Habitat** Fossorial. Fairly common in coastal dunes, Strandveld and Sand Fynbos from Bloubergstrand to Velddrif, inland to Mamre. **Conservation Status** Near Threatened owing to coastal habitat transformation and degradation. **Endemism** CFR (in South Africa).

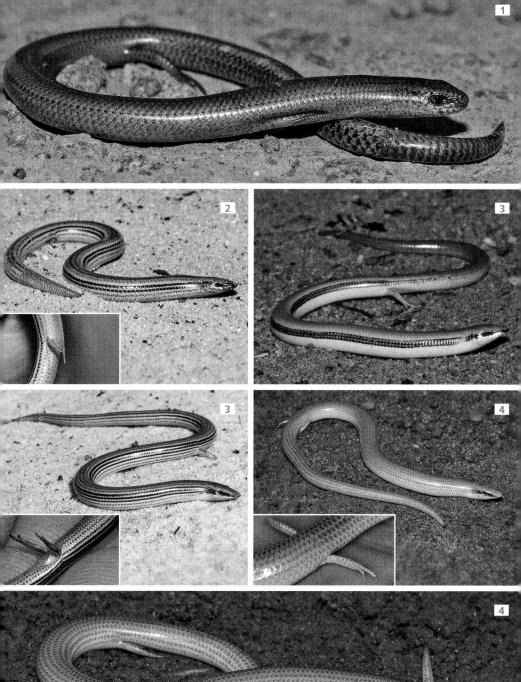

1 Striped Dwarf Burrowing Skink *Scelotes sexlineatus*
Similar to Silvery Dwarf Burrowing Skink, but larger, with a more defined striped appearance, and the original tail is longer than head–body length. Only reduced hind limbs present, each with two clawed toes. Dorsal coloration warm buff to sandy-silver; flanks usually paler than back. Dark spots on each scale form longitudinal rows of spots or merge to form continual stripes along back and flanks. These stripes are most pronounced on flanks. Dark stripe from tip of pointed snout through eye. Ventrum greyish white with pinkish hues. Original tail pale with pinkish-blue hue. Juvenile has bright purplish-blue tail. **Length** SVL: 98mm. **Status and Habitat** Seldom encountered. Fossorial, inhabiting sandy soils along the West Coast from near Lambert's Bay to around Alexander Bay. Occurs as far inland as about Clanwilliam. **Endemism** CFR (in South Africa).

Chameleons   Family Chamaeleonidae

Well known and highly distinctive. Most famous for their ability to change colour, which is not done as a means of camouflage, but rather for thermoregulation, when showing aggression or for intraspecific communication. They have very good eyesight, their eyes being in highly mobile turrets, enabling them to look independently in all directions. Arboreal and adapted to climbing, with fused toes that form opposite clasping digits. Diurnal ambush predators; their long tongue shoots out to a distance that can exceed their body length.

Dwarf chameleons   *Bradypodion*

A feature unique to the genus is the ridge of enlarged gular scales on the throat. The size and shape of these are important for identification. There is little overlap in their natural distribution ranges. However, chameleons are prone to being translocated. There are 20 species in South Africa, with seven found in the Fynbos Biome. Two Western Cape species occur in Southern Afrotemperate Forest: Knysna Dwarf Chameleon (*B. damaranum*) and Grootvadersbosch Dwarf Chameleon (*B. venustum*).

2 Swartberg Dwarf Chameleon *Bradypodion atromontanum*
Similar to Little Karoo Dwarf Chameleon, but ranges mutually exclusive. Casque reduced and barely elevated. Gular crest comprises small conical cones or irregularly shaped lobes. At least one enlarged, pale blue gular groove present. Weak dorsal crest present, small conical tubercles extending to tail. Row of enlarged tubercles present on flanks. Background coloration greenish, greyish or orange-brown. When not displaying, it is mostly rather dull. Dark band runs from behind eye to top of shoulder. Flanks usually mottled, distinctive pale lines may be present. When displaying, coloration much brighter greenish overall with yellow and blueish-white markings on the head. Eye turrets orange or brick-red. Tail significantly shorter than head–body length. **Length** TL ±12cm. **Status and Habitat** The only chameleon found in the mountain Fynbos of the Klein and Groot Swartberg mountains, where it is common. **Endemism** Fynbos Biome.

3 Beardless Dwarf Chameleon *Bradypodion barbatulum* [NE]
Only described in 2022. Very similar to Baviaans Dwarf Chameleon. While they occur on neighbouring mountain ranges, not known to co-occur. Small, relatively dull chameleon. Tail shorter than head–body length. Casque slightly elevated. Gular crest comprises very small tubercles. Not actually 'beardless', but gular crest much reduced. Gular grooves shallow and pale. Low dorsal crest of small, pointed tubercles runs from nape to base of tail. Enlarged tubercles form vague rows on flanks. Background coloration pale greenish or yellowish brown to grey. Variable darker brown or grey blotches on flanks and back. Blotches on flanks sometimes orange. **Length** TL 11cm. **Status and Habitat** Common in mountain Fynbos in Langkloof and Kouga mountains, as well as on northern slopes of Tsitsikamma Mountains. **Endemism** Fynbos Biome. **Conservation Status** Not evaluated. Unlikely to be threatened.

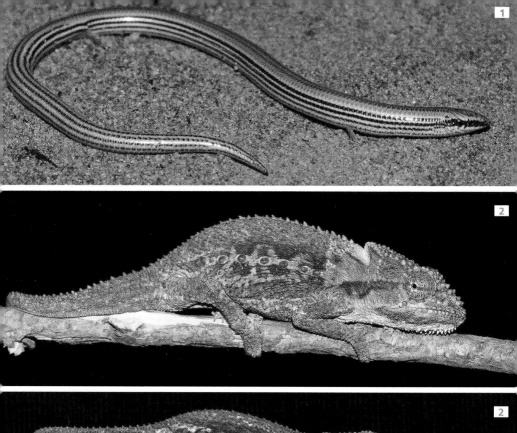

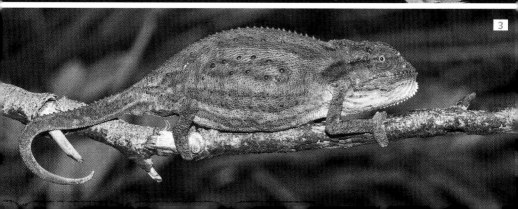

1 **Baviaans Dwarf Chameleon** *Bradypodion baviaanense* NE

The only chameleon to occur in the Baviaanskloof Mountains. Only described in 2022. Very similar to the Beardless Dwarf Chameleon, but their ranges are not known to overlap. Casque slightly elevated. Tail shorter than head–body length. Gular grooves pale. Low gular crest comprises small conical lobes. Low dorsal crest comprising small conical tubercles to base of tail. Enlarged tubercles on flanks, some forming indistinct rows. Coloration similar to Beardless Dwarf Chameleon, being grey to greenish brown with variable darker brown or grey blotches on flanks and back. **Length** TL 11cm. **Status and Habitat** Only known to occur in mountain Fynbos on Baviaanskloof Mountains in the eastern part of the Fynbos Biome. **Conservation Status:** Not Evaluated. Unlikely to be threatened. **Endemism** Fynbos Biome.

2 **Little Karoo Dwarf Chameleon** *Bradypodion gutturale*

Casque prominent and slightly elevated. Many enlarged tubercles on head. Gular crest very variable but in many individuals (especially from the more karroid areas) comprises very large overlapping lobes that are much longer than broad. Individuals from Koue Bokkeveld and Groot Winterhoek areas have much reduced, conical gular lobes. Off-white to yellowish gular grooves present. Dorsal crest variable, but most have large to very large conical tubercles that extend along much of tail. Body scales vary greatly in size. The very large tubercles may be arranged in a row or scattered on flanks. Enlarged tubercles cream, green, black, orange or various shades of brown. Tail shorter than head–body length. Background coloration variable; usually greyish to olive-brown. Area behind crest (nuchal fold) often yellowish brown. **Length** TL ≥15cm. **Status and Habitat** Common in Fynbos and Renosterveld of the Overberg and in mountain Fynbos from the southern Cederberg to the Outeniqua Mountains. **Endemism** CFR (in South Africa).

3 **Western Dwarf Chameleon** *Bradypodion occidentale*

A greyish chameleon with a prominent gular crest comprising up to 22 large, overlapping, flap-like lobes (inset). Two or three deep gular grooves present. When harassed, the throat is extended and these grooves open to show deep purplish-black, yellow or orange skin. Dorsal crest variable but usually prominent with conical tubercles from nape to almost the end of tail. Body scales vary greatly in size. Minimum one but up to four rows of enlarged flattened tubercles on flanks. Background coloration pale to dark grey. Variable pale blaze usually evident on flanks. There may also be darker markings and mottling on flanks. Tail shorter than snout–vent length. **Length** TL 16cm. **Status and Habitat** Found in coastal belt from just north of Cape Town to Lüderitz in southern Namibia. Primarily inhabits Strandveld vegetation but also found in Renosterveld and Succulent Karoo. **Endemism** CFR and southern Africa.

4 **Cape Dwarf Chameleon** *Bradypodion pumilum* NT

Occurs in two distinct forms: larger, brighter green, lowland form, and smaller, duller, mountain Fynbos form. Lowland form: Casque narrow and fairly prominent. Gular crest comprises up to 20 large non-overlapping scaled lobes; longer than they are wide. Gular grooves orange. Dorsal crest of small conical tubercles extends more than halfway down tail. Usually at least one row of enlarged tubercles present on sides of body. Background coloration bright green, usually with orange blaze on flanks; latter often bordered by bright turquoise-blue. Mountain Fynbos form: Smaller with shorter tail and less pronounced casque. Gular lobes wider than they are long. Gular folds yellow. Tubercles on flanks smaller than in lowland form. Coloration generally brown to green. Often well patterned, but lacks brightly coloured flanks of lowland form. **Length** TL 18cm. **Status and Habitat** Common within its small range. Occurs in Strandveld as well as lowland and mountain Fynbos. Lowland form has adapted to suburban gardens. Often translocated to gardens outside of natural range. **Conservation Status:** Near Threatened. **Endemism** Fynbos Biome.

Lowland form   Fynbos form

1 Elandsberg Dwarf Chameleon *Bradypodion taeniabronchum*

A small chameleon with reduced and slightly elevated casque. Gular crest comprises numerous pointed tubercles. Gular region pale with two or three diagnostic dark maroon grooves. Uppermost groove shorter than rest. Row of small conical tubercles runs down ridge of back, becoming smaller on tail. Row of enlarged tubercles present on upper flanks. These are relatively small and usually not very prominent. Background coloration usually dull yellowish to greenish brown. Pale stripes often present on flanks. White line running from below eye to top of front leg may be present. **Length** TL ±11cm. **Status and Habitat** Locally common in mountain Fynbos vegetation in the Elandsberg. Also occurs in the Kareedouw and Suuranys mountains west of Humansdorp. **Endemism** Fynbos Biome.

Agamas   Family Agamidae

Medium-sized to large lizards with a flattened body. They are closely related to chameleons. The fragmented scalation of the head is characteristic. The limbs are well developed and relatively long. They do not exhibit caudal autotomy and the tail cannot be regenerated if lost. Represented by only one genus in Fynbos Biome.

Agamas *Agama*

Robust but agile lizards. Large triangular head, distinct neck and a rough texture with varying degrees of small spines across back. They develop attractive coloration when breeding, particularly in males. Diurnal. Five species occur in South Africa, two in the Fynbos Biome.

2 Southern Rock Agama *Agama atra*

A large agama. Variable short dorsal crest formed by spiny scales on nape. This can extend down spine onto tail. Spiny protrusions can also be present on neck and flanks. Ventrum pale with smooth scales and honeycomb or striped patterning on throat extending onto chest. Much variation in coloration. Non-breeders and juveniles predominantly mottled shades of grey, olive or brown. Pale dorsal stripe or series of connected blotches often present. There can be variable, but usually diffuse, broad darker bars across the back. When present, bars become more pronounced on tail. In breeding males, head and anterior part of body shades of blue. Body usually dark sooty brown to black with prominent and contrasting pale vertebral stripe. Breeding females also develop blueish head and flanks; back becomes variably yellow-orange with rusty blotches. Males have bright purple-blue throat and chest. **Length** SVL: 135mm. **Status and Habitat** Colonial. Very common and widespread. Closely associated with rocky habitats. **Endemism** Southern Africa.

3 Southern Spiny Agama *Agama hispida*

Easily distinguished from Southern Rock Agama by habitat preference and spinier back. Dorsal crest subtle and does not reach tail. Scales small with prominent keels. Multiple spiny protrusions across back, neck and upper legs. Spines on back form indistinct longitudinal rows. Dorsal coloration variable shades of beige, brown, olive and grey. Overall mottled appearance with four or five dark irregular bands or blotches on back. Banding continues onto tail and legs. Intensity of patterning variable, very bold in some. Breeding males are a variety of striking shades of bright yellowish green. Ventral scales keeled. Ventrum in females and juveniles whitish with shades of pale green or with reticulated pattern of sooty grey. Breeding male's ventrum blueish green, sometimes with darker throat. **Length** SVL: 110mm. **Status and Habitat** Associated with flat, arid and often sparsely vegetated areas. Found as far south as Strand on the Cape Flats but rather scarce in the southern part of range. Solitary. Terrestrial, but readily climbs onto shrubs and fence posts. **Endemism** Southern Africa.

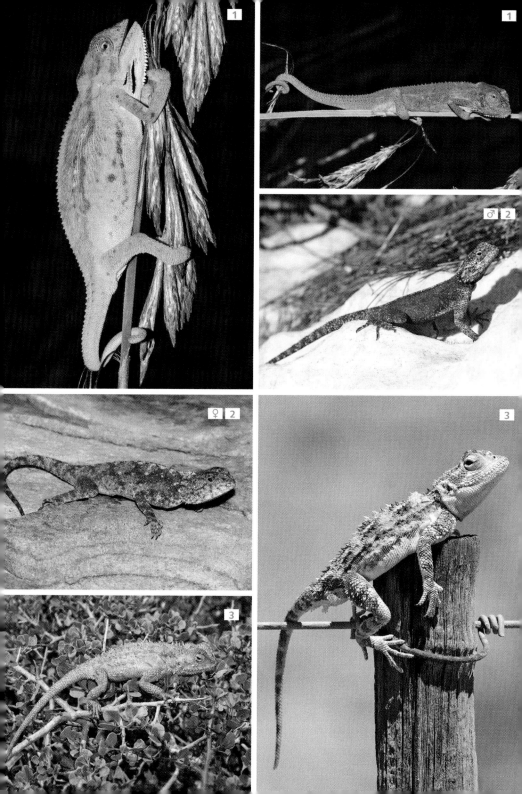

Blind snakes   Family Typhlopidae

Fossorial. Their body is the same thickness along much of its length, with a very short tail. Scales highly polished. They prey on invertebrates, most feeding on ants, termites and their larvae. Flowerpot Snake (*Indotyphlops braminus*) is introduced and established in and around Cape Town.

Beaked blind snakes   *Rhinotyphlops*

These snakes have a beaked snout, broad rostral scale and vestigial eyes. Two species in South Africa.

1 Delalande's Beaked Blind Snake *Rhinotyphlops lalandei*
Only naturally occurring blind snake in the Fynbos. Prominent sharp-edged beak. Eyes reduced to black spots, visible beneath head shields. Basal coloration pink to pinkish grey. Each dorsal scale has variable dark grey or brownish central mark. Markings absent from lower flanks and pinkish belly, resulting in two-tone effect with clear but irregular divide. Tail very short, spine-tipped. Much larger than thread snakes (*Leptotyphlops*) and alien Flowerpot Snake. **Length** TL ≤35cm. **Venom** None. **Status and Habitat** Various habitats, including Fynbos, Strandveld and Renosterveld. Widespread, common, fossorial. **Endemism** Southern Africa.

Thread snakes   Family Leptotyphlopidae

Highly distinctive, specialised snakes. Extremely small and thin, with a small, blunt head and tail. Fossorial, living on the eggs, larvae and workers of social insects. They use chemical camouflage (pheromones) to blend into the colonies of their prey. Two species occur in the Fynbos Biome.

Typical thread snakes   *Leptotyphlops*

Eight morphologically similar species found in South Africa. One species occurs in the Fynbos Biome.

2 Black Thread Snake *Leptotyphlops nigricans*
Tiny, with a very short tail. Body cylindrical, with smooth, glossy scales, black to purplish black in colour. Overlapping area of scales can appear silvery-grey. Silver-grey patterning more prominent in drier environments. Shorter and not as elongate as Slender Thread Snake. Resembles the alien Flowerpot Snake, which is not recorded in natural habitats. It is purplish to pale brown with smaller body scales (20 scale rows at midbody compared to 14 in the thread snakes). **Length** TL ±20cm. **Venom** None. **Status and Habitat** Fossorial, found in variety of habitats. Does not appear to occur north of Langebaan on the West Coast. **Endemism** South Africa.

Namib thread snakes   *Namibiana*

A small genus, historically part of *Leptotyphlops* but separated owing to differences in scalation and more elongated body. Two species occur in South Africa.

3 Slender Thread Snake *Namibiana gracilior*
Very slender, even for a thread snake. Scales smooth and glossy, black to sooty black in colour, usually with pale silvery edges. The drier the conditions, the more prominent these silvery edges with only the centre of the scales appearing black. In such specimens, the head is often darker than the body. Longer and more elongated than Black Thread Snake. **Length** TL <20cm; up to 24cm. **Venom** None. **Status and Habitat** Rarely encountered. Mostly a Succulent Karoo species. However, occurs in arid mountain Fynbos. Old records from the Riviersonderend area. **Endemism** CFR (in South Africa).

Adders
Family Viperidae

Most snakes in this family are thickset, with cryptic coloration. All are rear-fanged, with cytotoxic venom that aids with digestion. They have vertical pupils.

African adders *Bitis*

Ambush predators with large, hinged fangs. Large, triangular head covered with small, fragmented scales. Distinct neck separates head from stocky body. Body scales keeled. Tail short, especially in females. Eleven species occur in South Africa, five in the Fynbos Biome.

1 Puff Adder *Bitis arietans* ☠

Known for swift strike and threat display of puffing and hissing while repeatedly inflating the body. Large and very thick. Dorsal coloration variable: various shades of brown, beige or yellow with darker brown or black markings. Series of dark chevron-shaped markings usually present. Fynbos specimens usually vivid yellow and black. No enlarged scales or horns above eyes. Distinct narrow pale bar usually present behind eyes. **Length** TL ≥1m; exceptionally 1.4m. **Venom** Powerful cytotoxic venom. Bites medical emergency. **Status and Habitat** Most widely distributed viper in Africa. Common throughout the Biome in wide range of habitats.

2 Southern Adder *Bitis armata* ☠ **VU**

A small, enigmatic snake with a cluster of short erect scales above each eye. Two off-white bars radiate from each eye to the upper lip. Dorsum grey with series of dark irregular blotches, which are often paler brown, grey or tan in centre. Ventrum pearly grey-white. Told from baby Puff Adders by short cluster of horns above eyes and absence of pale bar behind eyes. Can co-occur with Berg Adder, which lacks raised scales above eyes. **Length** TL ±30cm; exceptionally >40cm. **Venom** Little known. No human envenomation documented. Likely similar to most other small adders. **Status and Habitat** Cryptic. Rare in limestone and coastal Fynbos. Discontinuous distribution in coastal strip from Langebaan to Infanta. Recently recorded near Theewaterskloof Dam in mountain Fynbos. Predominantly crepuscular. **Conservation Status** Vulnerable owing to small global range, habitat degradation and transformation of coastal lowlands. **Endemism** Fynbos Biome.

3 Berg Adder *Bitis atropos* ☠

Fynbos Biome Berg Adders may constitute a separate species in future. Lacks raised ridges or tufts of scales above eyes. Beautifully but variably patterned: usually grey, olive-grey or brown with series of regular semi-circular to triangular dark marks along back; these marks usually pale-edged. Distinctive pale dorsolateral stripes usually present. Head triangular, more elongated than in other local adders. Prominent pale line runs from back of eye to gape. Ventrum off-white to dusky-grey. **Length** TL ±40cm; occasionally >50cm. **Venom** Unlike most adders, venom has strong neurotoxic properties. Bites considered a medical emergency. **Status and Habitat** Mountain Fynbos, often in moist habitats, from sea level to mountain peaks. Primarily found in the southern and eastern mountain ranges of Fynbos Biome. Rare in, if not absent from, the Cederberg, where Red Adder is more frequently encountered. Diurnal, not often encountered. **Endemism** Southern Africa.

4 Many-horned Adder *Bitis cornuta* ☠

Diagnostic elaborate tuft of horns above each eye. Dorsum usually grey, but can be brown or reddish brown. Two rows of dark markings on back and single rows on flanks. Rows on back may merge to form large blotches, often pale-edged. Bold pale line runs from behind eye to lower jaw. Additional pale line usually runs from nostril to lower jaw. Ventrum off-white, with variable grey speckling. **Length** TL ±35cm; occasionally >50cm. **Venom** Little known. Cytotoxic, causing pain, swelling and some necrosis. Bites rare but require medical assistance. **Status and Habitat** Dry rocky habitats and gravel plains on West Coast from near Graafwater northwards, inland to about Calvinia. Marginally enters arid Fynbos and Strandveld. **Endemism** Southern Africa.

1 **Red Adder** *Bitis rubida* 🖤

Taxonomic uncertainties remain with this species and its close relatives. Various colour forms occur. Red phase easily identified by brick-red coloration, usually with diffuse patterning. Brown to grey-brown phase usually boldly patterned with black and grey markings. Scales above eye raised to form ridge or occasionally short tuft of erect scales. Co-occurs with prominently horned Many-horned Adder in north of its range. Boldly marked grey form similar to Berg Adder, which lacks raised scales above eyes. **Length** TL ±30cm; some >40cm. **Venom** Little known. No human envenomations documented. Likely similar to that of most other small adders. **Status and Habitat** Fairly common in rocky mountain Fynbos, Renosterveld and Succulent Karoo habitats on inland side of Cape Fold Mountains from northern Cederberg to Groot Swartberg. Mainly crepuscular. **Endemism** CFR (in South Africa).

Night adders *Causus*

Night adders differ from most other adders by their more slender body and large head scales. Head only slightly wider than body. Pupil round. Two species occur in South Africa.

2 **Rhombic Night Adder** *Causus rhombeatus* 🖤

Stout and thickset, but not as thick as adders in the genus *Bitis*. Scales soft, weakly keeled, appearing smooth. Dorsal colour variable: shades of brown, greyish brown, olive, bright buff or even pinkish brown. Series of irregular, dark brown blotches on back, usually white-edged. Large dark brown or black V-shaped mark on head, pointing towards snout. Belly coloration variable: ivory-white, pinkish or sooty black. Superficially similar to Rhombic Egg-eater, which has vertical pupils, a thinner body and is much rougher in texture. **Length** TL <1m; usually much less. **Venom** Produces large quantities of diluted venom, causing pain and swelling. No human fatalities documented. Medical assistance must be sought. **Status and Habitat** Mainly active at and after dusk, but regularly encountered during the day. Moist habitats in Fynbos, forest and thickets as far west as Swellendam. Often found close to water.

Shovel-snouts   Family Prosymnidae

A unique, monotypic African family.

Shovel-snouts *Prosymna*

Predominantly fossorial, with broad, sharp-edged rostral scales that aid in moving through topsoil and leaf litter. Highly specialised, feeding almost exclusively on reptile eggs. They have an elaborate defence display where they coil up in a tight spring and rapidly uncoil and recoil if threatened. Six species occur in South Africa.

3 **Sundevall's Shovel-snout** *Prosymna sundevallii*

Distinctive, secretive and not often observed. Head not distinct from body. Rostral scale large, flattened, sharp-edged and slightly upward-pointing. Basal colour yellow to orange or greyish brown, variably flecked with white. Large, dark brown mark on nape and broad dark bar across snout in front of eyes. Two (occasionally four) rows of brown spots down back. Ventrum pearly white. Tail ends in short, sharp spike. **Length** TL ±25cm; some >30cm. **Venom** None. Harmless. **Status and Habitat** Thinly distributed in mountain Fynbos. Some records from Renosterveld habitats. Appears to be absent from Strandveld. **Endemism** Southern Africa.

Sand snakes *Psammophis*

Elongated, fast-moving, diurnal, rear-fanged snakes that hunt small vertebrate prey, especially lizards. Nine species occur in South Africa, with three in the Fynbos Biome.

1 Cross-marked Grass Snake *Psammophis crucifer*

Small and attractive; most specimens very boldly marked. Grey, olive or brownish above, with prominent dark brown band down centre of back. One or two broad transverse bars usually present on nape. These form the 'cross' or 'crucifix' as per common names. Dark brown bands on either side of body. Ventrum yellow to orange or occasionally cream, edged with thin dark lines or a row of spots. Some specimens lack bold markings and are uniformly olive-brown to olive-grey above. **Length** TL <60cm. **Venom** Mild venom of no threat to humans. **Status and Habitat** Common and widespread in region, from sea level to mountain summits. Found in Fynbos, Strandveld and Renosterveld. **Endemism** Southern Africa.

2 Cape Sand Snake *Psammophis leightoni*

Attractive, very slender and extremely fast. Grey-brown to dark brown above, with narrow black and pale spotted vertebral line. Peach to buff-brown lines run down flanks. Upperparts always with black flecking or spots. Head more pointed than in Karoo Sand Snake. Three white to pale peach vertical bars present on sides of head between eye and neck. Ventrum off-white with variable dark flecking or mottling. Some have rows of black triangular sooty blotches on the edge of each ventral scale. **Venom** Mild venom of no threat to humans. **Length** TL ±80cm. **Status and Habitat** In the Biome, restricted to the Strandveld and Sand Fynbos of the West Coast from Cape Town to the mouth of the Olifants River. Less common than Karoo Sand Snake, with which it co-occurs.

3 Karoo Sand Snake *Psammophis notostictus*

Coloration very variable. Dorsum light grey to dark brown, uniform in colour or boldly patterned. Some with dark and pale spotted vertebral line. Sides of body often paler than back. Well-defined pale or dull orange stripes may run down flanks. Head patterning very variable, some having intricately marked head. Ventrum yellow to dull orange-brown with white edging. Intricately marked individuals can look similar to Cape Sand Snake, but Karoo Sand Snake does not have the three paler vertical bars on side of the head. **Length** TL ±80cm. **Venom** Mild venom of no threat to humans. **Status and Habitat** Common in the West Coast lowlands and drier Fynbos. Seemingly absent from much of the Overberg and rare in the southern Cape.

Grass snakes *Psammophylax*

Historically called Skaapstekers (Afrikaans for 'sheep stabbers'), now commonly referred to as grass snakes. These diurnal, active foragers prey on small vertebrates. An African genus of six species. Two species occur in South Africa.

4 Spotted Grass Snake *Psammophylax rhombeatus*

In the Fynbos, dorsal coloration usually light grey-brown to olive-brown. Four rows of brown spots, edged with black, run down back and flanks. Middle two rows usually merge to form large irregular spots, which link up towards tail, forming continuous stripes. Top of head uniform grey-brown to olive-brown. Large dark mark runs from each eye to nape of neck. Variable rufous flecking often present along flanks and side of belly. Ventrum variable; pearly white to grey with range of black and rufous marks. **Length** TL ≤90cm. **Venom** Rear-fanged; mild venom of no threat to humans. **Status and Habitat** One of the most common and widespread snakes in the Fynbos Biome. Found in diverse habitats. **Endemism** Southern Africa.

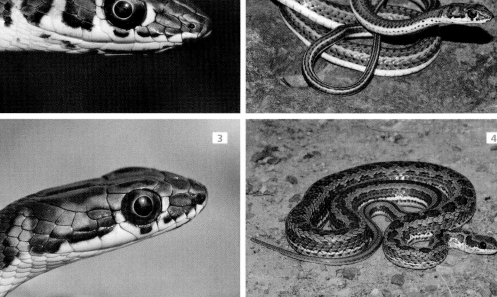

Burrowing asps
Family Atractaspididae
Interesting fossorial snakes with small eyes and smooth scales.

Harlequin snakes *Homoroselaps*
Small, colourful snakes that feed on other fossorial reptiles. Two species are endemic to South Africa.

1 Spotted Harlequin Snake *Homoroselaps lacteus*
A small, beautiful snake with variable coloration. Basal colour yellow, with bright orange dorsal stripe. Variable black spotting along flanks, often joining on back to form irregular bands. Specimens from eastern coastal parts of region have largely black flanks with variable yellow spotting. Variable ventrum with black central stripe or dusky mottling. **Length** TL <40cm; some >60cm. **Venom** Not well studied. Bites rare, can cause significant symptoms (swelling, bruising and headache). **Status and Habitat** Common throughout Biome. Semi-fossorial. Often found under rocks and debris. Feeds on especially legless skinks (*Acontias*). **Endemism** Southern Africa.

Mole snake and allies
Family Pseudaspididae
A small, interesting family of four species, two from Africa.

Mole snakes *Pseudaspis*
Monotypic, viviparous, with smooth polished scales. These useful, diurnal snakes grow very large in the Fynbos Biome, an adaptation that enables them to prey on large Cape Dune Mole-rats.

2 Mole Snake *Pseudaspis cana*
Largest snake in the Biome. Adults identified by large size and small, pointed head. Most uniform black, occasionally olive-brown or yellowish brown. Hatchlings and juveniles very different and often misidentified: usually yellowish brown to olive-brown with variable darker brown spots. Spots form four rows; each spot usually partially edged in white. Spots can merge to form zigzag stripe down middle of back. Spotted Grass Snake separated by large dark mark running from eye to nape; absent in juvenile mole snakes. Adult ventrum normally black to dusky; occasionally off-white in very pale specimens. Juvenile belly yellowish, variably infused with grey. **Length** TL <2m. **Venom** None. Powerful constrictor; can inflict painful bite. **Status and Habitat** Widespread. Especially common on Cape Flats and sandy lowlands of West Coast. Scarce in mountain Fynbos, especially the southern Cape.

House snakes and allies
Family Lamprophiidae
Some of the region's most common, well-known snakes. No venom; constricts vertebrate prey.

House snakes *Boaedon*
Harmless constrictors. Two species occur in South Africa.

3 Brown House Snake *Boaedon capensis*
Widespread, often associates with houses; invaluable in rodent control. Dorsal coloration yellowish brown to dark brown, occasionally reddish brown. Distinctive pale stripes on head, most prominent of which runs from snout above eye to back of head. Second stripe runs from eye to gape of mouth. Stripes often continue along forepart of body, can become diffuse, forming spotted or mottled effect on flanks, especially in juveniles. Ventrum pearly white to yellowish cream. **Length** TL <1m; exceptionally >1m. **Venom** None. **Status and Habitat** Nocturnal. Common throughout most of Biome. Seldom in moist mountain Fynbos and Strandveld.

Dwarf house snakes *Lamprophis*
Harmless, nocturnal constrictors. Four species occur in South Africa.

1 Aurora Snake *Lamprophis aurora*
Beautiful and docile. Dorsum usually yellowish to greenish olive. Diagnostic bright orange to yellow vertebral stripe down centre of back. Juvenile has dark spotting on head scales and dark-edged body scales, creating speckled effect. Ventrum white to yellowish. **Venom** None. **Length** ±TL 60cm; exceptionally ±90cm. **Status and Habitat** Uncommon in Fynbos Biome. Most frequently encountered on Cape Flats, but scattered records throughout southern portions of Biome. Usually associated with moist habitats. **Endemism** Southern Africa.

2 Yellow-bellied Snake *Lamprophis fuscus*
Small, secretive and rarely observed. Plain olive-brown to greenish yellow above. Upper lip and lower flanks cream to yellow and brighter than rest of upperparts. Ventrum yellow to cream. Can be confused with Brown Water Snake, which is generally darker brown above with distinct two-tone appearance. Olive Ground Snake is larger and more robust with over 21 scale rows compared to 19, and lacks brighter cream to yellow lower flanks present in Yellow-bellied Snake. **Length** TL <70cm. **Venom** None. **Status and Habitat** Rare in the Fynbos Biome, with few scattered records along south coast. Most records from moist mountain Fynbos. **Endemism** Southern Africa.

3 Spotted Rock Snake *Lamprophis guttatus*
Attractive, with distinctly flattened and broad head. Basal colour brown, olive-brown or beige. Markings very variable. Rows of distinctive dark spots or blotches run from behind neck down body, usually becoming smaller and more diffuse towards the tail. Blotches often have paler centres. Head can be plain or intricately marked, with small, paler-centred blotches. Ventrum pearly white to pale buff, occasionally with rows of dark spots. **Length** TL <60cm. **Venom** None. **Status and Habitat** Uncommon, occurs in mountain Fynbos. Rupicolous, always associated with rocky habitats. **Endemism** Southern Africa.

Water and ground snakes *Lycodonomorphus*
Small to medium-sized, mainly brown snakes. These harmless constrictors are closely related to house snakes (*Boaedon*). Closely associated with aquatic habitats. Four species occur in South Africa.

4 Olive Ground Snake *Lycodonomorphus inornatus*
Uniform olive, olive-grey or brown. Often has metallic sheen, especially when freshly shed. Occasionally yellowish brown or very dark grey or brown. In the Fynbos Biome, head of juvenile usually greyer and darker than rest of body. Lips typically paler, but seldom contrast as strikingly with rest of head as in Brown Water Snake. Ventrum usually same colour as upperparts, but often slightly paler. Underparts also never contrast with upperparts as distinctly as in Brown Water Snake. **Length** TL ±75cm; exceptionally ±1.3m. **Venom** None. **Status and Habitat** Common throughout southern and eastern parts of Fynbos Biome. Nocturnal. Utilises a variety of habitats, usually favouring moister environs. Occurs as far north as Velddrif. **Endemism** Southern Africa.

5 Brown Water Snake *Lycodonomorphus rufulus*
Slender, predominantly aquatic. Scales smooth and polished. Back and flanks uniform dark chocolate-brown to light brown. Ventrum and upper lips usually pearly white to cream, but may be yellowish or pink. Marked contrast between back and belly. Olive Ground Snake larger, more thickset and with less contrast between back and belly. **Length** TL ±60cm; rarely >80cm. **Venom** None. **Status and Habitat** Common. Closely associated with wetland and rivers. Largely absent from the dry Strandveld of the West Coast. Predominantly nocturnal but regularly active during the day. **Endemism** Southern Africa.

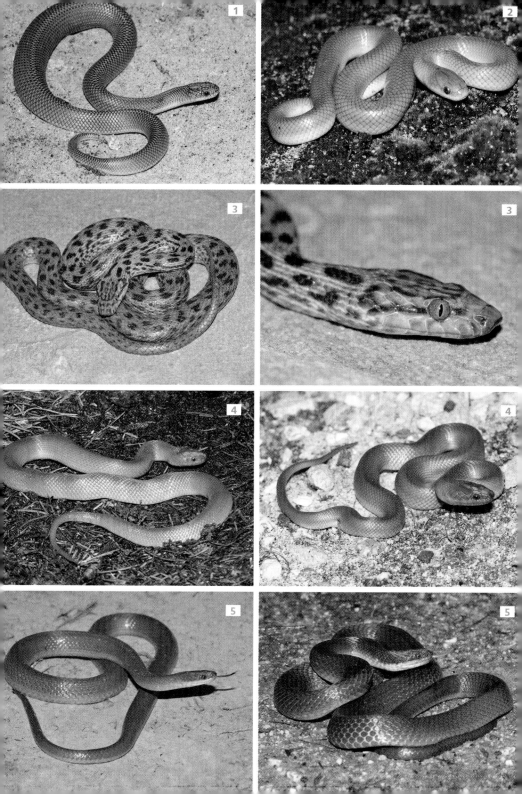

Wolf snakes   *Lycophidion*

Docile, nocturnal constrictors with relatively large, recurved teeth, hence the common name. Head only marginally wider than neck and significantly flattened. Eyes small with elliptical pupils. Three species occur in South Africa, one entering the Fynbos Biome.

1 **Cape Wolf Snake** *Lycophidion capense*

Small, secretive and seldom encountered in the Fynbos. Back and flanks brown, black or purplish black. Dorsal scales each have variable white or pale grey tip, creating speckled appearance. Scales on flanks usually have larger pale spots. Some can lack spotting, particularly in larger individuals. Head markedly compressed, usually with fine white or pale grey speckling or a reticulated pattern. Ventrum pearly white, occasionally infused with darker markings. **Length** TL ±40cm; occasionally >50cm. **Venom** None. **Status and Habitat** Very scarce in the Fynbos Biome, but undoubtedly under-reported owing to secretive behaviour. Occasionally recorded from moist or mesic fynbos as far west as Pringle Bay.

Madagascar brook snakes   Family Pseudoxyrhophiidae

Predominantly from Madagascar; only five species occur on the African mainland. Two species are found in the Fynbos Biome.

Many-spotted Snake   *Amplorhinus*

Secretive, diurnal snakes that favour wetland areas, where they prey on frogs and lizards. Currently monotypic, but scattered southern African populations are under taxonomic review.

2 **Many-spotted Snake** *Amplorhinus multimaculatus*

Rarely encountered. Dorsal colour brown to olive-brown. Two broad yellowish-brown to pale olive dorsolateral stripes run down length of body, bordered by rows of black spots that fade away towards tail. Variable white flecking present on upperparts. Centres of upper labials and preocular often white. Ventrum off-white with blueish hue. Uniform bright green form of this species not known to occur in the Fynbos Biome. **Length** TL ±50cm. **Venom** Mildly venomous and bites readily. Bites can cause very mild and localised swelling, inflammation and pain. **Status and Habitat** Undoubtedly under-recorded. Found near streams and wetlands in mountain and lowland Fynbos from Cape Town eastwards. Recorded as far north as Limietberg Mountains. **Endemism** Southern Africa.

Slug-eaters   *Duberria*

Small, nocturnal, viviparous snakes. They lack venom and are specialist feeders on slug and snail prey. Two species occur in South Africa, one of which is found in the Fynbos Biome.

3 **Common Slug-eater** *Duberria lutrix*

One of few snakes that can persist in suburban areas, where it fulfils a great service to gardeners. Blunt-headed with relatively large eyes and a short tail. Dorsal colour reddish brown, tan, light brown or olive-brown. Thin black stripe, or series of fine black marks, may be present down centre of back. Flanks same colour as back, or shades of grey. Flank scales occasionally with paler centres, creating reticulated effect. Ventrum white to pale yellow. Each ventral scale usually has dark grey or black spots on outer edges, creating dark edging to pale belly. **Length** TL ±30cm; exceptionally >40cm. **Venom** None. **Status and Habitat** Very common. Nocturnal, but can be encountered during day. Absent from dry West Coast lowlands, but occurs in moist mountain Fynbos as far north as Clanwilliam. **Endemism** Southern Africa.

Colubrids
Family Colubridae

Rear-fanged and oviparous. Historically a 'wastebasket taxon' for species of uncertain affinities.

White-lipped snakes *Crotaphopeltis*

These snakes have an impressive threat display: the head is flattened while they hiss and strike repeatedly. Only one widespread species occurs in South Africa and the Fynbos Biome.

1 Red-lipped Snake *Crotaphopeltis hotamboeia*

Small to medium-sized, with smooth, polished scales. Dorsal coloration varies: olive-green, brown, greyish or yellowish brown. Back with variable white flecking that can form diffuse bands. Distinctive large, black patches on side of head start behind eyes and usually join on nape. Often with blue or purple sheen. Upper lip red, orange-red, yellow or cream. Ventrum pearly white to cream. **Length** TL 50–75cm; very large specimens ±1m. **Venom** Mild, of no consequence to humans. Minor, localised symptoms such as swelling at the bite site possible. **Status and Habitat** Nocturnal. Common and widespread in the Fynbos. Preference for eating frogs and toads, so usually associated with moist habitats.

Egg-eaters *Dasypeltis*

Toothless and lack venom. Highly specialised to prey on bird eggs and can swallow eggs far larger than their head. Vertebrae in the neck protrude into the throat and are used to saw through the eggshell. The contents of the egg is ingested and the shell regurgitated. Egg-eaters have elaborate defensive displays, which involve rubbing the rough scales together to produce a hissing sound while flaring their jaws and striking with an open mouth. Three species occur in South Africa.

2 Rhombic Egg-eater *Dasypeltis scabra*

Head rounded, not distinct from body. Body scales elongated, with pronounced keels. Dorsal colour varies from grey to various shades of brown. Series of large angular spots down middle of back; spots can have paler centres or edges; spaces between spots may be much paler than rest of body. Irregular bar-like spots on flanks alternate with spots along back. Distinct V-shaped marking often present on nape of neck. Some individuals have very faint markings. Ventrum pearly white. Inside of mouth black. **Length** TL ±75cm; occasionally >1m. **Venom** None. **Status and Habitat** Nocturnal. Common throughout the Fynbos Biome in diverse array of habitats.

Boomslang *Dispholidus*

Long, arboreal snakes with very large eyes. Equipped with small fangs in the rear of the mouth and potent hemotoxic venom. Diurnal. One species occurs in South Africa.

3 Boomslang *Dispholidus typus typus* ☠

Any snake in a bush or tree is often mistakenly called a Boomslang. However, Boomslang can be identified by the short snout, very large eyes and heavily keeled body scales. Males from the Fynbos Biome are strikingly patterned, black above and yellow or cream below. Females dull brown to olive-brown above and pale brown below. Juveniles very attractive: grey to brown above with paler flanks and fine dense speckling; variable buff-yellow wash on neck; upper and lower jaws white; large eyes emerald-green. When threatened, they inflate their neck, exposing the black skin between the scales (inset). **Length** TL ±1.5m; exceptionally >2m. **Venom** Small quantities of extremely potent hemotoxic venom. Bites can prove fatal and medical assistance is critical. This snake avoids conflict as far as possible and most bites are provoked. **Status and Habitat** Arboreal, inhabiting thickets and shrublands. Fairly common but wary and often escapes detection. **Endemism** This subspecies is endemic to South Africa.

Red-lipped Snakes flare their jaws as a threat display.

Green snakes *Philothamnus*

Slender, green, diurnal and arboreal. Five species in South Africa, two species entering the south-eastern part of the Fynbos Biome.

1 **South-eastern Green Snake** *Philothamnus hoplogaster*

Bright green to olive-green above. May have dark maroon or black spots on upperparts of anterior portion of body. On occasion, turquoise base and edging to dorsal scales may be evident. Ventrum yellowish or white with blue or green hue. Very similar to Western Natal Green Snake, but has smooth ventral scales and two temporal scales in single row on each side of head. **Length** TL ±60cm; extremely large specimens ±1m. **Venom** None. **Status and Habitat** Inhabits reedbeds, thickets and Fynbos near water. Localised in the Fynbos Biome, being scarce in the southern Cape as far west as Mossel Bay.

2 **Western Natal Green Snake** *Philothamnus occidentalis*

The more common and widespread of the two green snake species in the Fynbos Biome. Bright emerald to olive-green above. Tail and head often have turquoise hue. Base of some scales turquoise, resulting in scattered turquoise speckles on back and flanks. Ventrum yellowish or white with greenish tinge. A rare dusky grey form with a blueish-grey belly has been recorded in the southern Cape. Very similar to South-eastern Green Snake, but has keeled ventral scales and temporal scales are usually in two rows on either side of head. **Length** TL 90cm; but can be >1m. **Venom** None. **Status and Habitat** Common in forest edge, thickets and moist Fynbos east of Swellendam. Usually near water. **Endemism** Southern Africa.

Elapids   Family Elapidae

This large family is characterised by having permanently erect, short, hollow fangs in the front of their mouth and by the lack of loreal scales. They are alert, with good eyesight. Many species have a distinctive threat display where they rear up and flatten their neck to form a distinctive hood. All are venomous, many with potent neurotoxic venom.

Shield cobras *Aspidelaps*

Easily recognised by the presence of the enlarged shield-like rostral scale on the snout. Largely fossorial, spending a great deal of time underground. One of two species occurs in the Fynbos Biome.

3 **Coral Shield Cobra** *Aspidelaps lubricus lubricus* ☠

A short, stocky and beautiful coral-red to orange snake with numerous black bands along its body and tail. Black bands may totally encircle body and tail, especially in juveniles. Black bands always narrower than orange bands. Distinctive enlarged rostral scale forms a shield, which is used when burrowing. Black band runs from upper lip through eyes. Ventrum creamy yellow, except where black bands encircle body. Very quick to get into a defensive position and spread a narrow hood, hissing and striking repeatedly. **Length** Southern subspecies (*A. l. lubricus*) TL ≤50cm. **Venom** Little known. Bites are rare. Venom appears to be dangerously neurotoxic and bites must be treated as a medical emergency. **Status and Habitat** Nocturnal, most often active during and after rain. Found in a variety of habitats but with a preference for more arid rocky areas. Appears to be absent from West Coast Strandveld and the southern coastal plain.

Rinkhals   *Hemachatus*

A monotypic genus restricted to southern Africa. Closely related to the true cobras, but differs in that they are viviparous, have keeled body scales and lack solid teeth on the maxilla. Well known for their ability to 'spit' venom and for feigning death (thanatosis).

1 **Rinkhals**   *Hemachatus haemachatus* 💀

Thickset and very variable in coloration. Most Fynbos Biome specimens are black with irregular yellow banding. Banding can be very dull, especially in large individuals. Elsewhere in range, dorsal coloration olive-brown or black with fine black barring. Ventrum black with two or three white bands across neck. Bands very obvious when the snake is in a defensive position, with the front part of the body raised off the ground and a broad hood spread. Spits venom but only from a hooded position. Body and tail scales strongly keeled. **Length** TL ±1m; exceptionally 1.5m. **Venom** Dangerous neurotoxic venom. A bite or venom in the eyes needs urgent medical attention. **Status and Habitat** Rare and localised in the Fynbos Biome. Historically occurred on the Cape Flats but most recent records are from the Agulhas Plain and Grabouw areas. Also recorded from moist mountain Fynbos in the southern Cape. Predominantly diurnal. **Endemism** Southern Africa.

Typical cobras   *Naja*

True cobras. All have the ability to raise the front part of their body off the ground and spread a hood in a defensive pose. They can inflict potentially lethal bites and several species have evolved the ability to 'spit' venom. All lay eggs and have smooth scales. There are five species in South Africa, two of which occur in the Fynbos Biome.

2 **Cape Cobra**   *Naja nivea* 💀

The most frequently encountered cobra in the Fynbos Biome. Very variable in coloration: brown, reddish brown, yellow, tan or brownish black, with or without black speckling. Many Fynbos Biome individuals are dark reddish brown with black or pale speckling. Some are particularly attractive, being bright yellow with variable black speckling. Juveniles are olive-yellow to yellow with a broad dark throat band. Quick to assume a defensive position and spreads an impressive hood if threatened. **Length** TL ±1.3m; exceptionally >1.6m. **Venom** Potent neurotoxic venom. Urgent medical attention is needed, as death can occur very quickly owing to respiratory failure. **Status and Habitat** Widespread and common throughout the Biome. Predominantly diurnal. **Endemism** Southern Africa.

3 **Black Spitting Cobra**   *Naja nigricincta woodi* 💀

Large, black snake with smooth, polished scales. Rears up and spreads an impressive hood if threatened. Juveniles grey with black head, throat and belly. Adults easily confused with rare dark form of Cape Cobra, which is more brownish black and does not spit. Also potentially confused with Mole Snake, which is more thickset, with a head that is not distinct from the body, and does not spread a hood. **Venom** Primarily cytotoxic, but some neurological symptoms also occur. Spits readily from any position. Bites and venom entering eyes must receive urgent medical attention. **Length** TL ±1.25m; up to 2m. **Status and Habitat** A species of the arid western parts of South Africa and southern Namibia. In the Fynbos it occurs in rocky, dry environments as far south as the Piketberg. It is generally scarce and appears to occur at low densities. Predominantly diurnal. **Endemism** This subspecies is a southern African endemic.

Rinkhals feigning death

Birds

To date, 865 bird species have been recorded in South Africa. This book features 162 species in 58 families, representing the birds of the Fynbos Biome specifically. Selecting these species was challenging, as non-Fynbos Biome habitats are interspersed throughout the region. Species associated with major wetlands and marine environments were excluded, along with forest-dwelling species occurring in Afrotemperate Forest patches, and species found primarily in the bordering Succulent Karoo. Being extremely mobile, birds can rapidly colonise suitable new areas as habitats change. Human-induced changes have enabled a multitude of species to colonise the region over the past few decades. Many are closely associated with altered habitats, such as intense agriculture, alien thickets and suburbia. These species are not featured in this book. Vagrants and rare visitors are excluded too. See page 266 for a full list of excluded species.

Protea Canary is one of the eight Fynbos Biome endemic birds.

ENDEMISM

No fewer than 96 bird species are endemic to southern Africa (almost 10% of this region's bird fauna). The centres of endemism are the arid Karoo, the highland grasslands and the Fynbos. Two bird families are endemic to southern Africa: sugarbirds (Promeropidae) and rockjumpers (Chaetopidae). Both are represented in the Fynbos Biome.

Bird species endemic to the Fynbos Biome	
Fynbos Buttonquail	Turnix hottentottus
Cape Rockjumper	Chaetops frenatus
Agulhas Long-billed Lark	Certhilauda brevirostris
Victorin's Warbler	Cryptillas victorini
Cape Sugarbird	Promerops cafer
Orange-breasted Sunbird	Anthobaphes violacea
Protea Canary	Crithagra leucoptera
Cape Siskin	Crithagra totta

CONSERVATION CONCERN

Habitat loss and degradation negatively affect almost all bird species in the Fynbos Biome. Infrastructure, such as wind turbines, overhead powerlines and fences, pose a danger to many species. Several raptor species are also threatened by direct persecution.

Of the 162 species included in this book, 16 are of conservation concern. Four are Fynbos Biome endemics and eight are raptors.

Numerous other species, once widespread in the Fynbos Biome historically, are now locally extinct. These include iconic species such as the Southern Bald Ibis (*Geronticus calvus*), Bearded Vulture (*Gypaetus barbatus*) and Wattled Crane (*Bugeranus carunculatus*). Species currently at risk of suffering the same fate include the Cape Vulture, which has only one breeding colony left in the region, and the African Grass Owl, which persists at a few isolated sites in the Overberg.

The Fynbos Biome is highly vulnerable to the long-term effects of climate change. As such, other species confined to these habitats may well become threatened in the future.

LIFE HISTORY

The Fynbos Biome supports several generalist species that occur in a diverse array of habitats, as well as specialist species that require specific habitat features.

The birds associated with Fynbos are well adapted to fire as the driving force of the Biome. Species dependent on specific food plants or habitat structure will leave recently burnt areas until such time as the habitat has recovered to provide their specific requirements. Nectar-feeding birds, for instance, return to an area as soon as the plants that they depend on are flowering again. The Fynbos Buttonquail will only recolonise an area once the vegetation structure is dense enough. In contrast, some species are very quick to take advantage of recently burnt area. For example, Nicholson's and Plain-backed Pipit will move into a recently burnt area in a matter of days. They favour the post-fire open habitat, which provides excellent forging opportunities.

Of the 162 species of bird covered in this book, 140 (86%) are considered to be resident. Many of these species will undertake local movements and some are strongly nomadic.

The Endangered African Marsh Harrier is dependent on extensive wetland habitats.

Bird species of conservation concern		
Endangered (EN)		
1	Cape Vulture	*Gyps coprotheres*
2	Martial Eagle	*Polemaetus bellicosus*
3	Black Harrier	*Circus maurus*
4	African Marsh Harrier	*Circus ranivorus*
5	Fynbos Buttonquail	*Turnix hottentottus*
Vulnerable (VU)		
6	Verreaux's Eagle	*Aquila verreauxii*
7	Secretarybird	*Sagittarius serpentarius*
8	Denham's Bustard	*Neotis denhami*
9	Southern Black Korhaan	*Afrotis afra*
10	Striped Flufftail	*Sarothrura affinis*
11	African Grass Owl	*Tyto capensis*
12	Lanner Falcon	*Falco biarmicus*
Near Threatened (NT)		
13	Blue Crane	*Grus paradisea*
14	Cape Rockjumper	*Chaetops frenatus*
15	Agulhas Long-billed Lark	*Certhilauda brevirostris*
16	Protea Canary	*Crithagra leucoptera*

The nectar-feeding Southern Double-collared Sunbird

Migratory Pearl-breasted Swallow

The Cape Grassbird is a very vocal species.

African Pipit

Nicholaon's Pipit

Given reasonable views, even the challenging pipits can be identified to species level.

There are also 22 summer migrants that spend the austral summers in the region. These include non-breeding visitors from the Palearctic region, such as Barn Swallow, Common Buzzard and Lesser Kestrel. Intra-African migrants also move into the area during our summers, including breeding visitors such as Common Reed Warbler, Pearl-breasted Swallow and Diederik Cuckoo.

Birds rely heavily on sound to communicate. Most species call for a variety of reasons, including to attract mates, defend territory and to keep in touch with their mates or with members of a flock. Species that live in dense habitats, where visual communication is less effective, tend to be very vocal. While some species call throughout the year, most species become far more vocal during the breeding season. The vast majority of the birds in the Fynbos Biome breed in spring and early summer.

BIRDING IN THE FYNBOS

Birding in the Fynbos Biome is generally straightforward. The region lacks complex groups of birds with numerous similar-looking species. Even the little brown jobs (LBJs) are relatively easy to work out, given practice. The trickiest groups in the region are perhaps the cisticolas and the pipits. Non-breeding bishops are also challenging, but fortunately the biome does not have very many species to contend with. In addition, juvenile birds can cause a bit of confusion, African Harrier-Hawk juveniles being especially problematic, as they are extremely variable and differ from the distinctive adults.

Most people carry cameras nowadays, and even poor photos can be sufficient to identify many species. If you are close enough to a calling bird, record the call on your cell phone and post photos and calls on the citizen science platform iNaturalist (**www.inaturalist.org**), where participants will propose identifications. An extremely valuable resource for the local birder is the mobile app BirdLasser (**www. birdlasser.com**) which allows one to log bird species. This creates a spatially referenced database of all the birds you have logged. It is an efficient way to contribute to the Southern African Bird Atlas Project 2 (**www.sabap2. birdmap.africa**). In addition, there are various bird clubs that offer member outings and support to the like-minded and keen birders out there. The largest bird club in the region is the Cape Bird Club (**www.capebirdclub.org.za**). There are also public-benefit organisations dedicated to the protection of South Africa's birds and their habitats, such as the well-known BirdLife South Africa (**www.birdlife.org.za**).

Identification features

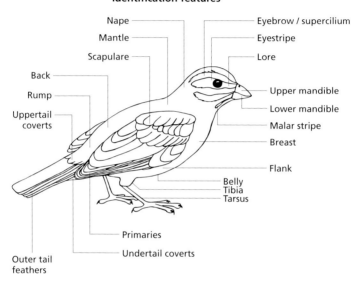

Nape · Mantle · Scapulare · Back · Rump · Uppertail coverts · Outer tail feathers · Primaries · Undertail coverts · Belly · Tibia · Tarsus · Flank · Breast · Malar stripe · Lower mandible · Upper mandible · Lore · Eyestripe · Eyebrow / supercilium

Bird wing from above

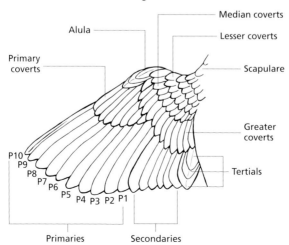

Alula · Primary coverts · P10 · P9 · P8 · P7 · P6 · P5 · P4 · P3 · P2 · P1 · Primaries · Secondaries · Tertials · Greater coverts · Scapulare · Lesser coverts · Median coverts

Ostriches Family Struthionidae

The largest and fastest running birds in the world. They feed on plant matter. Farmed for their meat, eggs and feathers. Only one species is found in South Africa and the Fynbos Biome.

1 Common Ostrich *Struthio camelus*
Unmistakable. Male body feathers black; vestigial wings with soft, plume-like, white feathers. Head small, with huge eyes and long eyelashes. Beak short with blunt tip. Head and neck very long, pale grey to beige, with short, downy feathers. Tail buff or white. Legs long, mostly naked; feet with two toes. Female dull greyish brown. Juvenile resembles female. Hatchlings have dark spots, stripes on neck and rufous crown. **Size** 120–200cm; 60–80kg. **Call** Loud booming, heard mainly at night. **Status and Habitat** Fairly common reintroduced resident. Historically occurred on coastal plains. Commonly farmed; self-sustaining populations reintroduced to larger protected areas.

Guineafowl Family Numididae

Large terrestrial birds that live in flocks. They roost in trees when not incubating eggs or raising chicks. They differ from pheasants, fowl and allies (family Phasianidae) by their largely featherless heads. Omnivorous. One introduced species occurs in the Fynbos Biome.

2 Helmeted Guineafowl *Numida meleagris* ❶
Unmistakable. Head and upper neck featherless and blue. Prominent pale brown casque on crown, surrounded by red skin. Cere red. Bill horn, with reddish base. Prominent blue moustachial wattles with red tips. Plumage black to greyish black, densely speckled with small white spots. Powerful legs and toes dull black. Female has smaller casque. Juvenile has dark greyish facial skin and much reduced wattles and casque. **Size** 55–60cm; 1.1–1.8kg. **Call** Rapid cackling, *kek, ek, ek, kaaaaaa*. Male and female perform plaintive duetting call during breeding season. **Status and Habitat** Common introduced resident from the Eastern Cape (race *mitrata*). Interbred with domesticated birds (race *galeata*) in many places. Introductions and expanding agricultural activities facilitated their colonisation of the Fynbos and Karoo biomes. Alien trees and telephone lines provide required roosting sites in previous treeless areas. Favours degraded open areas.

Pheasants, fowl and allies Family Phasianidae

Medium-sized to large stocky, terrestrial birds with short, powerful legs. Five species occur in the CFR. Red-necked Spurfowl (*Pternistis afer*) inhabits forest edges and thickets and has been excluded.

3 Grey-winged Francolin *Scleroptila afra*
Intricately marked. Basal colour greyish brown, densely striped, barred and spotted with white, buff, black and chestnut. Throat grey and finely speckled. In flight, primaries dull rufous. Belly off-white with fine black barring. Bill dark grey. Legs dull yellow. Male has short spurs on back of leg. Juvenile has white throat when very young. Much rarer and more localised Red-winged Francolin is distinguishable by its rufous nape, white throat and bright rufous flight feathers. **Size** 30–33cm; 370–520g. **Call** Variable loud and piercing *pi, pi, pi, pip, pi-weeu*. **Status and Habitat** Common resident in Strandveld, Renosterveld and Fynbos habitats, from sea level to high altitudes. **Endemism** Southern Africa.

Chick

1 Red-winged Francolin *Scleroptila levaillantii*

As intricately patterned as Grey-winged Francolin, but bright rufous on sides of neck and nape is unspotted. Throat white and unmarked. Broad black-and-white-spotted collar present. In flight, rufous in wing brighter and more extensive than in Grey-winged Francolin. Belly buff. Bill dark grey with yellow base. Legs dull yellow, male with short blunt leg spurs. Juvenile duller overall. **Size** 33–38cm; 360–550g. **Call** Similar to Grey-winged Francolin. High-pitched *tuip, tuip, tuip, tuip, tuip-chee-tchoo*. The *tuip-chee-tchoo* often repeated several times. **Status and Habitat** Rare in moist mountain Fynbos from Swellendam eastwards. More common in eastern part of region, where it also occurs in lower-lying areas. **Endemism** Southern Africa.

2 Cape Spurfowl *Pternistis capensis*

A large, dark chocolate-brown spurfowl. Feathers intricately patterned with off-white edges and fine chevrons. Throat off-white with dark flecking. Lower breast and belly feathers have broad white to pale buff central stripes. Cere and base of upper mandible yellowish horn. Lower mandible orange. Legs orange, with large, upturned spurs in males. Juvenile duller overall. The Red-necked Spurfowl, which inhabits forest edges and thickets (from Grootvadersbosch to the east), is easily distinguished by its bare orange-red throat and facial skin. **Size** 40–43cm; 650–1,000g. **Call** Various versions of a harsh, ringing *ka, ka, ka-reek, ka-reek, ka-reek*. **Status and Habitat** Common resident in dense Fynbos, Strandveld and Renosterveld shrublands. Will utilise almost any habitat as long as there is sufficient cover. Artificial water sources facilitated colonisation of more arid areas. **Endemism** Southern Africa.

3 Common Quail *Coturnix coturnix*

Secretive, seldom seen in the open. Upperparts richly patterned with shades of brown, buff, off-white and black. Long, whitish eye stripe present. Chest rufous; flanks streaked with rufous, pale buff and black. Belly pale buff. Bill black. Legs pinkish to yellow or brown. Male has pale buff to rufous throat with variable blackish central marking, often in the shape of an inverted T. Female lacks bright rufous coloration, with streaked breast and plainer throat. Juvenile less streaked overall. Distinguished from scarcer Fynbos Buttonquail by larger size and habit of gliding for short periods when flushed. **Size** 16–20cm; 80–115g. **Call** Well-known, fast *whit, wit-wit* usually rendered as 'wet my lips'. **Status and Habitat** Common spring- and summer-breeding visitor throughout the Fynbos Biome. Favours grasslands and crops (especially wheat and lucerne) but also utilises natural vegetation.

Ducks, geese and swans · Family Anatidae

Medium-sized to large waterbirds. Bill usually broad and flattened; many species have lamellae which are used to filter food from the water column. Mostly vegetarian. Eleven species occur in the CFR in wetland habitats, but are not considered Fynbos birds. Four are regularly encountered in small wetlands or disturbed natural vegetation in the Fynbos Biome.

4 Egyptian Goose *Alopochen aegyptiaca*

Noisy and pugnacious. Face and throat pale grey. Nape and back of head pale brown. Dull orange eye surrounded by large, dark brown eye patch. Upperparts dark brown and chestnut. Rump, tail and flight feathers black. Underparts pale greyish brown with fine dark vermiculations, especially on flanks. Distinctive dark brown spot on lower breast. Bill pink with black tip. Legs and feet pink. Juvenile lacks brown eye and chest patches. Easily told from South African Shelduck by brown chest, eye patches and being browner overall. **Size** 60–75cm; 1.5–3.5kg. **Call** Male and female call together; male hisses while female produces loud harsh honking noise. **Status and Habitat** Abundant, adaptable and opportunistic resident. Locally indigenous, but increased greatly in numbers owing to artificial wetlands, agricultural and lawned areas.

1 South African Shelduck *Tadorna cana*

A richly coloured duck. Breast and vent buff. Remainder of under- and upperparts parts bright russet. Rump, tail and flight feathers black. Secondaries have metallic green sheen. Forewing white in flight. Eyes and bill black. Legs and feet black. Male has all-grey head. Female has variable white face. Juvenile has brownish head. **Size** 60–65cm; 900–1,800g. **Call** Rather plaintive honking by both sexes. **Status and Habitat** Common, widespread resident and nomad. Nests in holes in the ground, most frequently in disused Aardvark burrows. Nest sites can be some distance from water. Feeds in water, on exposed mud flats and in agricultural areas. Utilises wide range of water bodies, but prefers shallow wetlands with exposed shoreline.

2 African Black Duck *Anas sparsa*

Dark chocolate-brown overall. Back with numerous large white marks, forming rough bars. Metallic blue speculum bordered by black and white bars, visible in flight and sometimes at rest. Underwing coverts white. Eyes dark brown. Bill black and blueish grey. Feet bright orange to dull yellow. Juvenile browner with pale underparts; markings on upperparts buff, not white. **Size** 48–58cm; 780–1,200g. **Call** Typical duck quacking by female, usually in flight. Male utters soft wheezy *peeep*. **Status and Habitat** Fairly common resident, but occurs at low densities. A distinct preference for perennial rivers, including relatively small rivers in mountainous areas. Occasionally utilises other wetland types, such as dams or sewage works.

3 Yellow-billed Duck *Anas undulata*

The only all-brown duck with a bright yellow bill. Bill has large black centre spot and smaller black spot on tip. Head dark brown and finely streaked, eye brown. Upperparts dark brown, feathers with fine buff edging. Metallic green speculum bordered by black and white bars, visible in flight. Underparts with dark brown central feather spots. Spots very large on flanks, resulting in a scaled appearance. Belly appears finely spotted. Feet dark olive-grey. Bright orange feet are a sign of hybridisation with alien Mallard Duck (*A. platyrhynchos*). Juvenile similar but more uniform brown. **Size** 52–58cm; 700–1,150g. **Call** Female quacks, male mostly silent but does utter a soft whistle. **Status and Habitat** Common resident. Highly mobile and utilises great variety of wetland types. Readily utilises relatively small wetlands in natural areas.

Bustards — Family Otididae

This family contains the heaviest flying birds in the world. They are adapted for walking and feed on a wide range of vegetation and invertebrates. They breed on the ground where they are very vulnerable to disturbance. Two species occur in the Fynbos Biome.

4 Denham's Bustard *Neotis denhami* VU

Large and stately. Nape and upper mantle rich chestnut. Back appears uniform brown. Large, mottled, black-and-white panel evident on folded wing. Head with distinctive black stripes. Throat and front of neck blueish grey. Female smaller, has more mottled back and less white in upper wing in flight. Juvenile has freckled crown and paler chestnut nape. Ludwig's Bustard (*N. ludwigii*), a rare visitor, has a dark brown face, crown and front of neck. Lacks large areas of white in folded wing. **Size** 90–120cm; 4–14kg. **Call** Mostly silent. Displaying male utters soft popping sound, seldom heard. In display, male inflates and erects long neck and breast feathers to form a large white balloon that is visible from a great distance. The chestnut mantle feathers are also erected. **Status and Habitat** Uncommon resident, largely confined to the lowlands of the south coast. Favours agricultural areas, especially old lands. **Conservation Status** Vulnerable owing to habitat loss and degradation, collisions with powerlines, and hunting.

Male displaying

1 Southern Black Korhaan *Afrotis afra* VU

Attractive, small bustard. Male has black neck and head. Top of crown brown, heavily scaled with white. Large white circular cheek patches present. Upperparts heavily barred buff and blackish brown. Folded wing has broad white edge. White collar extends onto breast. Underparts black. Bill bright pink with grey tip. Legs yellow in both sexes. Female lacks black on head and neck. Neck densely barred with fine dark brown and buff bars. Bill dark grey with some pink on lower mandible. Juvenile similar to female. **Size** 48–52cm; 600–900g. **Call** Raucous series of *kreea* or similar notes. Calls from ground or in flight. **Status and Habitat** Fairly common but declining. Occurs in lowland Strandveld, Fynbos and Renosterveld. Largely avoids transformed areas. **Conservation Status** Vulnerable. Recent significant population decrease probably due to loss of lowland habitat. **Endemism** South Africa.

Flufftails   Family Sarothruridae

Small, terrestrial birds. Secretive and difficult to observe. Three species occur in the CFR. The Buff-spotted Flufftail (*Sarothrura elegans*) is confined to Afrotemperate Forest and dense thicket.

2 Red-chested Flufftail *Sarothrura rufa*

Male has bright chestnut head, neck and breast. Rest of plumage black, with narrow white stripes and spots. Tail black with small white spots. Female dark brown above, with fine buff to brown speckling. Underparts off-white to dull buff, with dense scaling and spotting, particularly on flanks and sides of breast. Tail black with fine white spots. Juvenile like female, but darker, with less markings. **Size** 15–17cm; 30–46g. **Call** Very vocal, with a diverse array of calls. Most common is a series of *duu* notes increasing in volume and intensity. Gives an alarm like *wha-wha-wha-wha*. **Status and Habitat** Fairly common but cryptic. Inhabits wetlands with reeds, frequenting edges.

3 Striped Flufftail *Sarothrura affinis* VU

Male has bright chestnut head, nape and tail. Rest of plumage black, heavily streaked with white below and pale buff above. Female upperparts dark brown with narrow, buff barring. Underparts buff, breast and flanks heavily spotted with dark brown. Flanks barred. Tail dull chestnut with dark brown barring. Juvenile like female but has less barring and spotting. **Size** 14–15cm; 25–30g. **Call** Low, hooting *whoooo*. More frequently heard territorial call is harsh rattled *ki-ki-ki-ki-ki* followed by series of *ker* notes. **Status and Habitat** Uncommon localised resident in mountain Fynbos. Associated with marshes and seepage areas in the Fynbos. Does not occur in reedbeds. **Conservation Status** Vulnerable. Threatened primarily by habitat loss and inappropriate fire regimes, particularly in the grassland parts of its range.

Cranes   Family Gruidae

Large, very tall birds with a long neck and legs. Unlike herons (Ardeidae), cranes fly with their neck outstretched. Opportunistic omnivores. One species occurs in the Fynbos Biome.

4 Blue Crane *Grus paradisea* NT

South Africa's beautiful and elegant national bird. Soft blue-grey overall. Top of large, bulbous head white. Elongated tertial and inner secondary feathers extend past tail. Eyes dark brown. Bill pale pink. Legs grey to dark grey. Juvenile has smaller head and lacks elongated tertials. **Size** 100–120cm; 4–5.5kg. **Call** Far-carrying, guttural *kaaraaak*. **Status and Habitat** Common resident. Found predominantly on low-lying coastal plains, particularly abundant in the Overberg. Distinct preference for open agricultural areas. Absent from mountain Fynbos. Utilises wetlands for roosting at night. **Endemism** Southern Africa. **Conservation Status** Near Threatened owing to habitat loss and changes in agricultural practices. Collisions with powerlines considered biggest threat.

Buttonquails
Family Turnicidae

Unlike quails, buttonquails do not have a crop or a hind toe. These odd waders are polyandrous, females being larger and more brightly coloured than males. Females have a specialised vocal organ that enables them to produce a call. One species occurs in the Fynbos.

1 Fynbos Buttonquail *Turnix hottentottus* EN

Enigmatic and elusive, the most challenging of the Fynbos endemic birds to see. Intricately marked. Upperparts rufous with extensive black barring and spotting. Feathers white-edged. Male has buff throat; breast heavily spotted and barred with black. Female more brightly coloured; eyebrows, face and upper breast rich orange. Belly off-white. Legs flesh-coloured to pink. Smaller than Common Quail, with richer coloration, and does not glide for short periods when flushed. **Size** 14–15cm; 40–60g. **Call** A soft hooting, similar to Striped Flufftail. **Status and Habitat** Uncommon resident with local movements. In mountain Fynbos, they prefer younger restio-dominated veld. Also occurs in Strandveld and Sand Fynbos habitats. **Endemism** Fynbos Biome. **Conservation Status** Endangered. Threats include alien plant invasion, inappropriate fire regimes and development of lowland habitats. Climate change may pose significant threat.

Thick-knees
Family Burhinidae

Large, cryptically coloured waders with a preference for open areas. They have long legs, a heavy bill and large yellow eyes. Primarily nocturnal insectivores, but vertebrate prey is also occasionally taken. Two species occur in South Africa and the Fynbos Biome. The Water Thick-knee (*Burhinus vermiculatus*) is primarily associated with wetlands, and excluded.

2 Spotted Thick-knee *Burhinus capensis*

A large, distinctive wader that is predominantly nocturnal. Buff-coloured with dense, large, dark brown spots on upperparts. Head streaked; short diffuse eyebrow present. Throat white. Underparts pale buff, streaked brown on breast, flanks and upper belly. Eyes large and yellow. Bill black with extensive yellow base. Feet and long legs yellow. Juvenile more streaked above. Water Thick-knee is finely streaked (not spotted) on upperparts and has distinctive two-tone bar on folded wing. **Size** 43cm; 380–600g. **Call** Loud piping *phi, phi, phi, phiw, phiw, phiw phi, phi.* Heard mainly at night. **Status and Habitat** Common resident throughout much of the Fynbos Biome, but largely absent from mountainous areas. Favours open habitats, especially heavily grazed areas, and extensive lawns. Readily utilises suitable open spaces in urban areas.

Plovers
Family Charadriidae

Small to medium-sized waders that frequent open wet or dry habitats. Most species have a short, straight bill. They have short toes. While 17 species have been recorded in the CFR, several are rare visitors or vagrants and the majority are associated with wetland habitats.

3 Crowned Lapwing *Vanellus coronatus*

A smart-looking lapwing of terrestrial habitats. Top of head and lores black; distinctive white band encircles top of head. Rest of upperparts, neck and breast tan-brown. Black band separates brown breast from white belly. Tail white with broad black band towards tip. Eyes yellow. Bill bright coral-red with an extensive black tip. Long legs coral-red. Juvenile scaled above and on the breast. **Size** 29–31cm; 150–220g. **Call** A loud *kreeek*. **Status and Habitat** Common resident. Distinct preference for open areas and frequents ploughed, mown and heavily overgrazed habitats. Also utilises recently burnt natural areas. Seldom seen in mountainous areas.

Storks
Family Ciconiidae

Large birds that stand tall, with a long neck and legs. Carnivorous, feeding on a variety of prey. Unlike herons (Ardeidae), the head and neck are held outstretched in flight. Two species occur regularly in the Fynbos. The Black Stork (*Ciconia nigra)* has not been included as it is a rare visitor.

1 White Stork *Ciconia ciconia*

Elegant and distinctive. White overall, with black flight feathers. Tail white. Bill long, dagger-like and orange-red. Long, red legs often fouled with excrement, appearing whitish. Feet stick out well beyond tail in flight. Juvenile has buff-tinged plumage, dull red legs and a black bill with a red base. **Size** 100–120cm; 2.4–4kg. **Call** Silent, except at the nest where a mechanical bill-clicking display is given. **Status and Habitat** Common migratory summer visitor from the Palearctic. Vast majority are non-breeding visitors, but a handful of birds breed in the Western Cape. Most abundant in the Overberg and the coastal plain to the east. Scarce on the West Coast and in the Swartland. Primarily utilises agricultural areas. Will also utilise recently burnt areas and readily scavenges at landfill sites.

Ibises and spoonbills
Family Threskiornithidae

A small family comprising two distinctive forms, the ibises and the spoonbills. They nest colonially, frequently alongside a variety of other waterbirds in mixed heronries. They feed on invertebrates and small vertebrates. Four species are common in the CFR. Three are obligatory waterbirds and only the ubiquitous Hadada Ibis is terrestrial and included. The Southern Bald Ibis (*Geronticus calvus*) historically occurred in the Biome but was extirpated by the early 1900s.

2 Hadada Ibis *Bostrychia hagedash*

Head, neck and underparts grey. Back dark olive-brown with green to bronze metallic sheen on wing coverts. Bill black, long and decurved, with dark red line on top half of upper mandible. Legs dark grey with red markings on toes. Juvenile lacks metallic sheen; bill all black and shorter when recently fledged. **Size** 76–85cm; 1–1.5kg. **Call** Vocal. A loud repeated *hah* and familiar onomatopoeic *hah, hah, da, dah*. **Status and Habitat** Extremely common resident throughout much of Biome. Impressive westward range expansion since the 1980s. Prefers mesic grasslands, but adapted well to all lawn or open areas, including low or open Fynbos habitats. Dependent on trees for nesting, benefiting from widespread establishment of alien trees.

Herons
Family Ardeidae

Medium-sized to large birds that are mostly associated with wetlands or coastlines. They have a long neck and legs. All but one have a dagger-like bill for stabbing prey. A diverse family with a variety of food items. They their neck in while flying. Most species nest colonially, often alongside other heron species, ibises and spoonbills. Eleven species are regular in the CFR and six are rare visitors or vagrants. Most are obligatory waterbirds, with only two species more terrestrial.

3 Western Cattle Egret *Bubulcus ibis*

Smallest and most terrestrial egret. Non-breeding birds pure white, with yellow eyes and bill. Legs and feet dark olive-brown. Breeding birds develop long pale-rufous plumes on crown, nape, chest and mantle. Bill becomes orange to red and eye red. Legs and feet become reddish or dull yellow. Juvenile has grey to blackish bill, legs and feet. **Size** 48–54cm; 280–540g. **Call** Mostly silent, except at breeding colonies, where they utter a variety of croaking and grunting calls. **Status and Habitat** Very common resident throughout Biome. Distinct preference for grassland and agricultural areas, but readily utilises most disturbed habitats. Closely associated with cattle and large game.

1 Black-headed Heron *Ardea melanocephala*

A terrestrial heron. Adults have distinctive black crown, ear coverts and hindneck. Remaining upperparts dark grey. Upper throat white, lower throat with short, thick, black streaking. Underparts grey. Bill heavy with a grey upper mandible and a greenish yellow lower mandible. Legs and feet black. In flight, underwing coverts are white, contrasting with dark flight feathers. Juvenile has paler underparts and dark grey crown and hindneck. Throat washed with brown. Separated from more aquatic Grey Heron (*A. cinerea*) by dark ear coverts and two-tone underwing in flight (Grey Heron has uniform grey underwings). **Size** 86–94cm; 1.2–1.9kg. **Call** Harsh guttural *ku-aaark* or similar. A variety of croaking notes at nest. **Status and Habitat** Common resident. Favours dry open habitats; will occasionally forage in wetlands. Quick to respond to fires, where it forages in recently burnt areas.

Secretarybird   Family Sagittariidae

Monotypic. African endemic, totally different to other raptors. Highly specialised for hunting on the ground. They walk through open vegetation, stamping prey with their strong feet.

2 Secretarybird *Sagittarius serpentarius* VU

A wonder of African ornithology. A highly distinctive, very large, long-legged raptor with a long neck. Body pale grey, flight feathers black. Black leggings on tibia. Face unfeathered and bright orange. Tail long, with elongated central tail feathers. Long black feathers on nape can be erected. Bill pale blue-grey. Juvenile has browner plumage, yellow facial skin, and shorter tail. **Size** 1.25–1.5m; 2.8–5kg. **Call** Usually silent. Utters deep guttural croaking in vicinity of nest. **Status and Habitat** Uncommon resident encountered throughout the region in flat open habitats. Most common on the southern coastal plain. **Conservation Status** Vulnerable. Declining owing to a variety of threats including habitat transformation, bush encroachment and collision with powerlines.

Kites, hawks and eagles   Family Accipitridae

A family with a huge variety of sizes, colours and shapes. Occurs in almost all available habitats. Predatory, hunting on the wing or from a perch. Twelve species regularly utilise Fynbos habitats.

3 Black-winged Kite *Elanus caeruleus*

Beautiful, small and distinctive. Pumps its tail in display and hovers readily while hunting. Upperparts grey, becoming lighter on nape and crown. Black shoulder distinctive. Underparts bright white. White below in flight except for black undersides to primaries. Eye striking red, bordered above by short dark eyebrow. Bill black; cere and gape yellow. Feet bright yellow with black talons. Juvenile browner above with white-tipped feathers. Crown, nape and sides of breast variably streaked with tawny brown. Eyes dull orange-brown. **Size** 30–33cm; 210–290g. **Call** A variety of calls including a *whee–aargh*. **Status and Habitat** Very common resident throughout the Fynbos Biome. Most abundant in lowland areas. Rare or absent from dense mountain Fynbos.

4 African Harrier-Hawk *Polyboroides typus*

Adults easily identifiable. Blueish grey overall, with broad, black tips to flight feathers. Bare facial skin yellow, flushing pink when excited. Eyes and tip of bill black. Base of bill pale pinkish grey. Tail black with white tip and broad white bar in middle. Belly, vent, flanks, leggings and underwing coverts finely barred. Long-legged; tarsi unfeathered and yellow. Juvenile extremely variable. Can be various shades of brown to buff and can vary from dark brown to completely white below. Best identified by very broad wings, small head, shaggy nape feathers and long legs with unfeathered tarsi. **Size** 60–66cm; 620–950g. **Call** High-pitched, two-noted whistle *pee-weep*. **Status and Habitat** Common resident. Usually associated with urban areas and alien thickets but regularly forages in natural areas.

1 Cape Vulture *Gyps coprotheres* EN

Large, pale buff vulture, with pale underwing coverts that do not contrast strongly with darker secondaries. Secondaries dark-tipped, forming dark bar on trailing edge of wing. Head and long neck largely unfeathered and grey. Eyes dull yellow. Bill black. Juvenile darker than adult, with dark eyes. Vagrant White-backed Vulture is smaller, with dark eyes, and has strong contrast between pale underwing coverts and uniformly dark secondaries. **Size** 100–118cm; 7.4–10.8kg. **Call** Usually silent, but has a variety of screeches, hisses and cackles when at a carcass or colony. **Status and Habitat** Rare, localised resident. Only remaining Fynbos Biome colony is in De Hoop Nature Reserve. Only frequently encountered in the Overberg. **Endemism** Southern Africa. **Conservation Status** Endangered. Persisting main threat is direct persecution through poisoning. Other threats include collision with powerlines, wind turbines and other infrastructure, and presence of nonsteroidal anti-inflammatory drugs in domestic food sources.

2 Martial Eagle *Polemaetus bellicosus* EN

Large and powerful. Upperparts and head blackish brown. Short, shaggy crest on back of head and nape. Breast dark brown, remainder of underparts white, finely spotted with dark brown. In flight, underwing dark brown with barred flight feathers. Eyes yellow. Bill greyish black; cere grey. Juvenile very pale, with white, unmarked underparts and face. Upperparts grey-brown with buff-edged feathers. Underwing coverts white; flight feathers dark and heavily barred. **Size** 78–86cm; 2.4–5.2kg. **Call** Usually silent, but may produce plaintive series of *klooee* notes. **Status and Habitat** Rare resident. Utilises a diversity of habitats but avoids urban areas. **Conservation Status** Endangered. Main threat is direct persecution from small-stock farmers. Drowning in reservoirs, electrocution and a reduction of their natural prey base are contributing threats.

3 Booted Eagle *Hieraaetus pennatus*

A small, polymorphic eagle. Pale phase most prevalent. Upperparts brown with paler panels in wing. Underparts pale buff with variable brown streaking on throat, breast and flanks. Underwing coverts pale buff, contrasting with the dark flight feathers. Eyes orange-brown. Bill dark grey with a yellow cere. Less common dark morph has brown underparts with darker streaking. All have characteristic spots or landing lights on leading edge of the wing, where the wing meets the body. These are evident in flight. **Size** 44–55cm; 520–1,200g. **Call** Mostly silent. Breeding birds utter series of *ki, ki, ki* notes. **Status and Habitat** Common breeding visitor from early spring to summer. Most birds in the Fynbos Biome are probably from the local breeding population, but Palearctic breeding visitors may occur in summer. Nest sites usually on cliffs, but forages widely and can be seen in all habitats.

4 Verreaux's Eagle *Aquila verreauxii* VU

Striking, large and powerful. Predominantly black with large white rump and V-shaped mark on back. Shaggy black leggings and yellow toes. Broad wings have bulging secondaries that get shorter towards body, giving wings distinctive shape. Pale windows in primaries. Bill blueish grey with darker tip. Cere, gape, and eye-ring bright yellow. Juvenile scaled brown and buff with buff crown and tawny nape. **Size** 80–96cm; 3–5.6kg. **Call** Series of high-pitched *tchup* notes. Also produces a plaintive whistled scream, *peeeeeu*, although mostly silent. **Status and Habitat** Fairly common resident; occurs at low densities. A cliff nester, primarily associated with mountainous areas. **Conservation Status** Vulnerable. Threatened by persecution from small-stock farmers, disturbance at breeding sites, drowning in reservoirs and collision with powerlines and other infrastructure.

Pale morph

Dark morph

1 Pale Chanting Goshawk *Melierax canorus*

A beautiful raptor. Head and upperparts blue-grey. Breast blue-grey, rest of underparts finely barred grey and white. In flight, very pale secondaries and white rump evident. Eyes dark; lores dusky. Bill tip dark grey. Gape, cere and base of bill reddish orange. Tarsi unfeathered, toes and legs reddish orange. Juvenile brown with white eyebrow and rump. Breast brown, heavily streaked, rest of underparts heavily barred. Eyes pale yellow. Juveniles best distinguished from harriers and buzzards by long, orange legs. **Size** 48–62cm; 620–1,400g. **Call** A melodious *kleeu-kleeu-klu-klu-klu*. **Status and Habitat** Fairly common resident. Preference for arid areas and absent from mesic mountain Fynbos. Occurs regularly in Strandveld vegetation to the north of Velddrif. Uncommon in the Overberg and towards Mossel Bay. Regularly recorded around St Francis Bay.

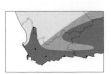

2 Rufous-breasted Sparrowhawk *Accipiter rufiventris*

A small, attractive raptor. Upperparts uniform slate-grey. Underparts plain rufous-orange with paler throat and white vent. Underside of flight feathers heavily barred brownish black. Underwing coverts pale rufous. Long tail has broad dark and pale bars. Eyes and cere yellow. Bill grey with dark tip. Legs and toes yellow. Female similar to male, but browner above and significantly larger. Juvenile browner above, has thin, pale buff eyebrow; underparts mottled. The larger, juvenile Black Sparrowhawk (*A. melanolucus*) is also rufous below, but heavily streaked with black. **Size** 30–38cm; 105–210g. **Call** A high-pitched *kew-kew-kew* or similar notes. **Status and Habitat** Uncommon resident. Primarily a forest species but readily breeds in small copses of trees (particularly alien Poplars) in Fynbos Biome. Hunts in surrounding natural vegetation.

3 African Marsh Harrier *Circus ranivorus* EN

Upperparts dark brown with rufous-edged feathers, variably flecked with white. Facial disk demarcated by white-spotted ruff. Underparts and underwing coverts rich brown, heavily streaked with pale buff. Long, narrow wings with heavily barred flight feathers. Tail long, narrow and barred. Eyes bright yellow. Bill grey; cere greyish yellow. Juvenile darker brown, lacks streaking below, has variable cream breast band. Distinctive pale shoulders and nape patch. Secondaries uniform brown; primaries and tail only faintly barred. Eyes dark brown. **Size** 44–50cm; 360–680g. **Call** Various notes, including nasal *nhee* and high-pitched *tseee*. **Status and Habitat** Uncommon resident, associated with extensive wetlands in the lowlands, but will feed over neighbouring terrestrial habitats. **Conservation Status** Endangered owing to wetland loss and degradation.

4 Black Harrier *Circus maurus* EN

A spectacular raptor. All sooty black when perched. In flight shows a bold white rump. Long tail has broad black and pale grey bars. Flight feathers white below with broad dark tips. Underwing coverts black. Eyes bright yellow. Bill black with a yellow cere. Legs and feet yellow. Juvenile blackish brown above with buff-edged feathers. Sides of neck brown, almost forming complete collar. Underparts pale buff with light black streaking on flanks. **Size** 42–50cm; 350–600g. **Call** Series of high-pitched, plaintive notes, *tee, tee, tee*. Also produces a rattling *treep*. **Status and Habitat** Uncommon resident with extensive local movements. Favours lowland Fynbos, Strandveld and Renosterveld, but does utilise mountain Fynbos. Will forage over agricultural areas. **Endemism** Southern Africa. **Conservation Status** Endangered. Threatened by habitat loss and disturbances. Proliferation of wind farms also likely to be a significant threat.

1 **Yellow-billed Kite** *Milvus aegyptius*

A graceful and well-known raptor. Upperparts brown with dark central feather shafts. Head brown, face variably grey and streaked. Breast brown with fine dark streaking. Underparts rufous-brown. Tail long with distinctive fork. Eyes dark brown. Bill and cere bright yellow. Juvenile has black-tipped bill and dark eye patch; more heavily streaked above. Often misidentified as vagrant Black Kites, but latter have pale eyes. **Size** 50–58cm; 570–760g. **Call** Tremulous whistle. Also produces a plaintive *tui, ti-ti ti*. **Status and Habitat** Common spring- and summer-breeding visitor from central Africa. Found throughout the region but avoids mountain Fynbos. Most nest in large alien trees.

2 **Common Buzzard** *Buteo buteo*

Coloration highly variable, with several morphs. Typically greyish brown above. Underparts of paler morphs white, with dense broad streaking on throat and breast. Streaking on lower breast usually more diffuse, forming pale breast band. Belly and flanks barred. Underwing coverts dark, contrasting with paler flight feathers. Broad, black trailing edge to wing. Eyes brown. Bill black with yellow cere. Juvenile has streaked underparts and finely barred tail without prominent subterminal bar present in adults. Eyes pale yellow. Forest Buzzard, which inhabits forest edges, best separated by having paler underparts with blotched, not barred, flanks. Hybrids known to occur. **Size** 46–52cm; 540–920g. **Call** A seldom heard high-pitched *pee-ooo*. **Status and Habitat** Very common summer visitor, most abundant in agricultural lowlands. Most are non-breeding visitors from Palearctic. Some dark morph birds have become resident and are breeding.

3 **Jackal Buzzard** *Buteo rufofuscus*

A beautiful raptor with broad wings and short tail. Upperparts and head sooty black. Underpart coloration extremely variable. Breast typically rufous, edged with white above. Belly black with variable white barring. Can have white breast or mostly white underparts. Rarely, almost completely black. Tail plain rufous, often with subterminal dark bar or spots. In flight, underwing coverts are black, flight feathers white with broad, black trailing edge. Eyes dark brown. Bill dark grey; cere and gape yellow. Juveniles and immatures variable, largely warm brown overall with plain light brown underparts and pale eyes. Told from adult Common Buzzard by pale eye and underparts that are not barred or boldly streaked. Common Buzzard is smaller, with narrower wings. **Size** 55–62cm; 900–1,700g. **Call** A nasal *keoo, keoo, keoo*, reminiscent of the yelping of a Black-backed Jackal. **Endemism** Southern Africa. **Status and Habitat** Common resident found throughout the Fynbos Biome, with a preference for mountainous areas.

Falcons   Family Falconidae

Diurnal, small to medium-sized birds of prey. They have long pointed wings, a strong, hooked bill and powerful talons. Several species are long-distance migrants. Four species occur in the Fynbos Biome. They occur in a wide range of habitats, typically favouring open country.

4 **Lesser Kestrel** *Falco naumanni*

Highly gregarious, migratory; breeds in Palearctic. Head blue-grey in male. Mantle and back rufous, not spotted. Greater coverts blue-grey. Tail pale grey, white-tipped, with broad subterminal black bar. Underparts pale buff and scantly marked with dark spots. Bill pale grey with a dark tip. Eye-ring and cere yellow. Legs and feet yellow; claws pale (Rock Kestrel has black claws). Female rufous above and heavily barred. Rump greyish, tail rufous-brown and barred, with broad subterminal black bar. Underparts pale buff, heavily streaked with broad blotches. Grey-streaked malar stripe present. Juvenile similar to female, with more rufous upperparts and rump. **Size** 26–32cm; 110–180g. **Call** Variety of chattering calls and ringing *teee, teee, teee* at roost sites. **Status and Habitat** Uncommon summer visitor. Roosts communally in large alien trees. Radiates into neighbouring habitats, often agricultural areas, to feed.

1 **Rock Kestrel** *Falco rupicolus*

Upperparts orange-chestnut with numerous black spots. Head grey with many fine, dark grey streaks. Dark eye surrounded by fleshy yellow ring. Throat pale buff with limited light streaking. Chest and belly chestnut with variety of spots and streaks. Vent and leggings pale buff. Male's tail grey above, with fine black barring and prominent subterminal black band. Female has more defined fine black tail barring. Bill blueish grey and dark-tipped. Cere bright yellow. Legs and feet yellow; claws black. Juvenile has streaked grey-brown head; flight feathers buff-tipped. Eye-ring and cere dull greenish yellow. **Size** 30–34cm; 185–275g. **Call** Series of sharp *ki, ki, ki, ki* notes. Also produces a quivering *kirrrr, kirrrr* call. **Status and Habitat** Common resident. Primarily a cliff nester, but will also utilise suitable buildings.

2 **Lanner Falcon** *Falco biarmicus* VU

A large, powerful falcon with long, pointed wings. Upperparts slate to brownish grey; feathers with fine pale edges. Frons buff with forecrown black and streaked. Hind crown and nape rufous. Long, bold, black malar stripes present. Cheeks pale buff. Underparts pale buff, occasionally with some dark makings, especially on flanks. Eye-ring and cere yellow. Bill grey with black tip. Female far larger than male. Juvenile browner overall with pale crown and nape. Underparts heavily streaked. Juvenile separated from Peregrine Falcon by underwing coverts being darker than flight feathers. **Size** 36–48cm; 420–800g. **Call** Series of harsh *kak, kak, kak* notes. Also produces a variety of high-pitched whining calls. **Status and Habitat** Uncommon resident with additional birds moving into the region in summer. Most common in lowland agricultural areas. **Conservation Status** Vulnerable. Primarily threatened by habitat loss in Grassland Biome.

3 **Peregrine Falcon** *Falco peregrinus*

Well known, famous for its dashing demeanour and ability to reach incredible speeds. Upperparts dark slate-grey with a slightly paler rump. Dark hood continues into very broad malar stripes. Underparts usually pale buff, but can range from white to beige. Upper breast with variable fine streaking. Remainder of underparts barred. In flight, underwings show no contrast between wing coverts and flight feathers. Eye-ring and cere yellow to orange. Bill dark grey with paler base. Female much larger. Juvenile blackish brown above with pale-edged feathers. Pale buff patches on nape. Underparts heavily streaked, not barred. **Size** 34–44cm; 500–850g. **Call** Similar to Lanner Falcon. A rapid series of harsh *kha, kha, kha* notes and various high-pitched whining calls. **Status and Habitat** Local subspecies *F. p. minor* is a fairly common resident. Mainly associated with mountainous areas but also frequent urban areas where it readily breeds on buildings.

Barn owls   Family Tytonidae

Characteristic heart-shaped face serves to amplify the noises made by their prey. They are extremely important in controlling rodent pests and their populations fluctuate in response to prey availability. There are two species in the Fynbos Biome. Western Barn Owls have adapted to breeding in suitable human-made structures, especially abandoned buildings and barns.

4 **Western Barn Owl** *Tyto alba*

A classically beautiful owl. Upperparts a mosaic of pale grey and yellowish buff with numerous fine black and white spots. Prominent white, heart-shaped facial disk present. Underparts pearly white to light buff, finely speckled with black. Eyes black. Bill pale whitish pink. Recently fledged juveniles are slightly darker above and more buff below. Best told from rare African Grass Owl by much paler back. **Size** 30–35cm; 270–500g. **Call** Several harsh chilling screams. **Status and Habitat** Fairly common resident, found in a variety of habitats but always dependent on the availability of suitable roosting and nesting sites. Most nest sites are in human-made structures.

1 **African Grass Owl** *Tyto capensis* VU

Superficially similar to Western Barn Owl but much darker above. Upperparts dark brown with fine pale speckling. White, or sometimes brownish, heart-shaped facial disk present. Underparts pale buff with numerous brown spots. Pale underparts contrast sharply with dark upperparts. Juvenile has more buff-coloured facial disk. Unlike Marsh Owl, which utilises similar habitat, feet extend well past tail in flight. **Size** 34–37cm; 355–520g. **Call** Similar to Barn Owl, but not as long or harsh. Also produces a fast-clicking flight call. **Status and Habitat** Very rare resident of treeless marshy areas (not dense reedbeds). Historically a bird of the lowlands from Cape Town eastwards, now only persisting in the Overberg area in very low numbers. **Conservation Status** Vulnerable owing to habitat loss. Habitat degradation from heavy grazing pressure and too frequent fires is also a significant threat.

Typical owls   Family Strigidae

Small to large nocturnal birds of prey. Owls sit with an upright posture and are cryptically coloured. They have a large head, huge forward-facing eyes, and can rotate their head up to 270 degrees. The flat facial disk concentrates sound, enabling the bird to locate and pinpoint prey. Several adaptions enable them to fly silently. Three species occur in the Fynbos Biome. The African Wood Owl (*Strix woodfordii*) occurs in the region but does not use Fynbos Biome habitats.

2 **Cape Eagle-Owl** *Bubo capensis*

A rarely encountered owl that inhabits mountainous areas. Larger and more powerful than the far more common Spotted Eagle-Owl. Upperparts dark brown with tawny and buff blotching. Prominent long ear tufts present. Chest and upper belly heavily blotched with chocolate-brown and buff. Flanks and belly coarsely barred. Eyes large and orange. Feet and claws large and powerful. Female larger. Recently fledged juveniles lack ear tufts and have yellower eyes. Best told from Spotted Eagle-Owl by having far less, and wider spaced, barring on underparts. **Size** 48–54cm; 910–1,400g. **Call** Deep guttural *hooo – hu*. **Status and Habitat** Rare resident, confined to mountainous regions of Fynbos Biome. Absent from Cape Peninsula.

3 **Spotted Eagle-Owl** *Bubo africanus*

The most frequently encountered owl in the Fynbos Biome. Smaller and usually greyer overall than rare Cape Eagle-Owl. Upperparts greyish brown with many paler spots. Prominent ear tufts present. Eyes yellow, occasionally orange. Underparts off-white, well marked with fine barring. Brown blotching on breast. Juvenile browner than adult with shorter ear tufts. Feet and claws smaller than those of Cape Eagle-Owl. Best told from Cape Eagle-Owl by finer barred underparts. **Size** 43–50cm; 500–1,100g. **Call** Classic owl hooting: *hoooo-hoo* or *whooo – wooo-who*. Pairs often duet. **Status and Habitat** Common resident, found throughout the Fynbos Biome in all habitat types, including urban areas.

4 **Marsh Owl** *Asio capensis*

A medium-sized owl with small ear-tufts that are often not evident. Dark brown above. Obvious facial disk buff or greyish with blackish rim. Eyes dark brown. Upper breast uniform brown. Lower breast and belly mottled brown and pale buff. Vent white. Flight feathers barred. Buff windows present in primaries. Juvenile has darker dusky facial disk. African Grass Owl has white facial disc and is pale buff below. When flushed, Marsh Owl's feet do not extend past tail in flight. **Size** 35–38cm; 230–370g. **Call** Well-spaced harsh *kraak* in flight or on ground. **Status and Habitat** Rare resident within the Fynbos Biome, appears to have some local movements which are not well understood. Favours extensive wetland edges and marshy areas dominated by grasses, restios and sedges.

Nightjars   Family Caprimulgidae

Characterised by their short legs, long wings and extremely short bill. They are cryptically coloured with beautifully patterned plumage. Mainly nocturnal insectivores, catching their prey on the wing. The Old World species have rictal bristles around the gape. Identification can be very difficult when not calling. In hand, the extent and positioning of the white wing spots are important for identification. Three species occur in the Fynbos Biome. The Rufous-cheeked Nightjar (*Caprimulgus rufigena*) is mostly associated with karroid vegetation, and is not incuded.

1 Fiery-necked Nightjar *Caprimulgus pectoralis*

The most common nightjar in the Fynbos, readily identified by its diagnostic call. Richly marked with grey, brown, black, buff and rufous. Rufous collar present. Male has extensive white tips to outer tail feathers. Female similar, but with less white in tail. Juveniles have buffy, not white, wing spots and outer tail feathers. Rictal bristles characteristically pale-based, best seen at very close range. Lacks thin off-white eyebrow usually present in Rufous-cheeked Nightjar. **Size** 23–25cm; 48–65g. **Call** One of Africa's most classic and easily recognised bird calls. The whistled call can be likened to 'good Lord, deliver us'. **Status and Habitat** Common resident. Found in a diverse array of habitats, but needs some wooded or thicket habitat in which to roost and breed.

2 Freckled Nightjar *Caprimulgus tristigma*

Larger, darker and more uniform than the more common Fiery-necked Nightjar. Upperparts, neck and chest plain sooty grey with fine speckling and vermiculations. No rufous coloration on head, neck or back. Belly and underwings buff with fine brown barring. Female similar to male but lacks any white in tail. Juvenile resembles female but lacks white spots in primaries. **Size** 26–28cm; 70–90g. **Call** A clear and distinctive *pow-wow*. **Status and Habitat** Uncommon resident. Confined to rocky mountainous areas. Within the Fynbos Biome, most prevalent in the western mountain ranges.

Swifts   Family Apodidae

Highly specialised aerial feeders. Some are considered to be the most aerial of all lifeforms. Common Swifts can stay airborne for up to 10 months without landing. Swifts are also some of the fastest birds in the world and several species are migratory. They are insectivores and all prey is caught on the wing. Six species occur in the Fynbos.

Aerial feeders: swifts versus swallows

Swifts and swallows can be confusing and the term swift or swallow is often, and incorrectly, used interchangeably. The two groups are not closely related and belong to different taxonomic orders. They are also very different to the trained eye, with the only real similarity that they are specialist aerial feeders. Often seen in mixed species flocks where there is an abundance of flying insects. Swifts have a characteristic shape with long, crescent-shaped wings. They usually fly high and directly. Swallows and martins (Hirundinidae) have smaller, more rounded wings and a dynamic darting and gliding flight, often at a low level. Swallows, unlike swifts, are often seen sitting on exposed perches such as branches or telephone lines. Swifts only alight at their nesting or roosting sites.

3 Alpine Swift *Tachymarptis melba*

The largest swift species in the Fynbos Biome. Powerful and extremely fast. Dark brown with diagnostic white belly. Throat white, resulting in dark breast band. No white rump. Juvenile similar, but with pale-edged feathers. **Size** 20–22cm; 68–90g. **Call** Rapid series of high-pitched *ti, ti, ti, ti* or *pi, pi, pi, pi* notes. **Status and Habitat** Common, widespread resident and summer migrant. Breeds on cliffs, but forages widely. Can occur over any habitat.

1 **Common Swift** *Apus apus*

This amazing bird is airborne for up to 10 months continuously each year. Blackish brown in appearance with pale greyish throat patch, forehead and thin eyebrow. From above, there is little contrast between back and secondaries. This separates it from the very similar African Black Swift, where paler secondaries contrast with darker back. Juvenile has larger white throat patch and pale-edged body feathers. The subspecies *A. a. pekinensis* also appears to be a regular in the Fynbos Biome. It differs from the nominate by being paler overall and having a larger, whiter throat patch. **Size** 17cm; 30–44g. **Call** Strident screaming *shreeee*, generally silent in its non-breeding grounds. **Status and Habitat** Fairly common, non-breeding summer visitor from Eurasia. Completely aerial when in the Southern Hemisphere and can be found over any terrain.

2 **African Black Swift** *Apus barbatus*

More frequently encountered than Common Swift in the region. Blackish brown with pale greyish-brown forehead and eyebrow. Throat off-white. Rest of underparts blackish brown. When freshly moulted, body feathers are white-edged, resulting in scaled appearance. From above, paler secondaries contrast with darker back. In very similar Common Swift, back and upper wings are uniform in colour, showing little contrast. Juvenile has paler forehead and crown. **Size** 18cm; 35–50g. **Call** Long, nasal, sizzling *tshreeeeeeeee*. Engages in highly vocal social interactions. **Status and Habitat** Common summer visitor and resident. While breeding sites are limited to cliffs, they forage widely and can be seen over any habitat. Often occurs in very large flocks, alongside other swifts and swallows.

3 **Little Swift** *Apus affinis*

The smallest swift in the Fynbos Biome. Easily told from all other swifts by the square-ending tail and large white rump. Remainder of plumage brownish black except for white throat and narrow, pale-buff eyebrow. Juvenile is similar but has pale-edged feathers. **Size** 12cm; 20–30g. **Call** Very vocal. High-pitched trilling *ti-ti-ti-triiiiiiiiiiiiiii*. **Status and Habitat** Common, widespread resident and breeding summer visitor. Natural breeding sites are on cliffs but most colonies are invariably on human-made structures, especially under bridges, the eaves of tall buildings and on water tanks. Often seen close to their colonies but also forage widely and can be seen above any habitat.

4 **Horus Swift** *Apus horus*

The scarcest of the local swifts and intermediate between White-rumped Swift and Little Swift in appearance. Brownish black, with white throat and large white rump that wraps around onto flanks. Short eye stripe and forehead greyish. Tail has shallow fork, which separates it from square-tailed Little Swift. White-rumped Swift is less stocky, has deeper forked tail and narrower white rump. Juvenile similar to adult but has pale-edged body feathers. **Size** 14cm; 20–34g. **Call** Mostly silent. Buzzing *tchew, chip-chip* and longer *prreeoooo*. **Status and Habitat** Localised and rare summer visitor. Nests in burrows in sand banks. Usually seen in close proximity to their colonies. Most regularly seen from Gansbaai eastwards.

5 **White-rumped Swift** *Apus caffer*

Lighter and more elegant than Little and Horus Swift. Brownish black, with white throat and narrow U-shaped white rump band. Forehead and thin eyebrow greyish. Upper side of secondaries tipped with greyish white. When long tail is fanned, it shows a deep fork, which separates it from the square-tailed Little Swift. Horus Swift has large white rump and shallow forked tail. Sexes alike. Juvenile similar to adult. **Size** 14–16cm; 18–20g. **Call** Nasal, trilling *sneeew* and fast chirping. **Status and Habitat** A common, breeding summer visitor. In the Fynbos Biome, it usually breeds in the nests of Greater Striped Swallows or Little Swifts, but will also build their own nests on a building or cliff. Forages widely and can be seen above any habitat.

Mousebirds Family Coliidae

The six species of mousebird are so unique that they form their own family and order. Medium-sized, slender birds with long, stiff, graduated tails. They have a short crest, thick, stubby bill and hair-like body feathers. Adept at climbing, mouse-like, in thick vegetation. Strongly social, found in small to medium-sized flocks. Three species occur in the Fynbos Biome.

1 Speckled Mousebird *Colius striatus*

The brownest and most nondescript of the local mousebirds. Back brown with fine inconspicuous barring on mantle and rump. Head and crest paler greyish brown. Black lores and black ring around eye create impression of dark face. Bill bicoloured; upper mandible black and lower off-white. Throat and breast brown with inconspicuous fine darker barring. Belly, vent and undertail warm tawny brown. Feet and legs dark reddish black. Juvenile similar to adult but lacks black face markings and has pale upper mandible and dark lower mandible. **Size** 32cm; 35–65g. **Call** Harsh, short, scolding and chittering notes, including *cheet, chee, chee* calls. **Status and Habitat** Common resident in dense thickets. Very common in coastal thickets of the southern Cape. Uncommon on the western coastal plain.

2 White-backed Mousebird *Colius colius*

Upperparts and tail grey. Lower back and upper rump have white bar bordered by black. Rump dark maroon, usually appears black. Crest, head, throat and upper breast grey. Lores and chin blackish; narrow black ring around eye. Belly and vent buff. Bill off-white with back tip. Feet and legs pinkish red. Juvenile has shorter tail; upper mandible cream; lower mandible black. **Size** 31cm; 30–55g. **Call** Series of very rapid *ti, ti, ti* notes and rapid *tzwee, zit, zit, zit*. **Endemism** Southern Africa. **Status and Habitat** Common resident. Favours drier habitats than the other two mousebird species. Most common in the Strandveld of the western coastal plain.

3 Red-faced Mousebird *Urocolius indicus*

The only local mousebird with red on its face and bill. Back, head and crest grey with blueish-green tinge. Tail long, narrow, pointed and blue-green above. Bill black, with red base. Bare red skin of lores and large eye-ring create distinct red-faced appearance. Frons and chin buff. Vent grey. Chest and belly greyish with warm buff hue. Juvenile has dull greenish-yellow base to bill and eye-ring. **Size** 34cm; 40–70g. **Call** Melodious, high-pitched whistled *tchi, vu, vu* or a series of *theeu* notes often given in flight. **Status and Habitat** Common resident, but nomadic with significant local movements. Does not readily utilise mountain Fynbos habitats, probably owing to a lack of fruiting shrubs. Common in urban gardens.

Cuckoos Family Cuculidae

Most are medium-sized inhabitants of forest or woodland. They feed predominantly on insects, with a preference for caterpillars. Famous for being brood parasites, but most species are not parasitic. Typically shy and retiring, more often heard then seen. Three species are often encountered in the Fynbos. Three more occur in the CFR, but only in forests or plantations.

4 Burchell's Coucal *Centropus burchellii*

Large and distinctive. Head and nape black. Eyes red. Bill black, heavy and decurved. Wings, mantle and upper back rufous. Lower back and rump dark brown with fine buff barring. Long black tail has narrow buff barring at base. Sides of neck and underparts light cream. Juvenile has thin white eyebrow and streaked crown; upperparts finely barred with dark brown. **Size** 41cm; 160–210g. **Call** Clear musical series of *du-du-du-du-du* notes. Alarm call is harsh *kek, kek, kek*. **Status and Habitat** Fairly common resident. Confined to southern coastal plain, inhabiting dense tangled vegetation usually associated with water. Decreased locally in Cape Town in recent years.

Mousebirds fluff up their feathers and sun their bellies to aid with the digestion of their plant-based diet.

1 Diederik Cuckoo *Chrysococcyx caprius*

This small, attractive cuckoo always has some white in the folded wing. Male has red eye and fleshy red eye-ring. White patch in front of eye and long white stripe behind eye. Upperparts bright, iridescent green, often with reddish-bronze sheen. Underparts white with green barring on flanks. Bill black. Female duller overall and lacks red eye. White throat and upper breast washed brown. Course barring on flanks and white wing spots not found in female Klaas's Cuckoo. Juvenile has pale eye and distinctive orange bill. **Size** 17–20cm; 22–42g. **Call** Characteristic plaintive onomatopoeic whistle *dee, dee, dee, dee-derik*. **Status and Habitat** A common spring and summer visitor. Widespread but avoids treeless habitats. Parasitises a diverse array of species but favoured local hosts are bishops, weavers and Cape Sparrow.

2 Klaas's Cuckoo *Chrysococcyx klaas*

A beautiful cuckoo with no white in the folded wing. Upperparts of male metallic green, often with bronze sheen. Has white patch behind eye. Green on neck continues onto sides of upper breast, forming partial collar. Underparts white, sometimes with fine scaling on flanks. Bill greenish grey. Eyes dark brown with thin pale green eye-ring. Female has greyish-brown head with small pale patch behind eye. Back barred, metallic green and brown. White underparts finely barred with greyish brown. Juvenile white below with brown or greenish-brown barring. **Size** 16–18cm; 24–34g. **Call** Plaintive repetitive whistled *meitjie*. **Status and Habitat** Common resident, though not a pure denizen of Fynbos habitats, requiring some trees or thickets. However, widespread in the Fynbos Biome where its favoured host is Cape Batis.

Pigeons and doves   Family Columbidae

Medium-sized to large, most being medium-sized. They have a short bill and fleshy cere. The body feathers have fluffy bases and are easily extracted, presumably aiding them in escaping from predators. A unique feature of this order and family is that both parents feed their young with a fat- and protein-rich substance produced in their crop, known as crop milk. The Rock Dove (*Columba livia*) is one of the most familiar birds in the world, being established in every major city. Nine species occur in the CFR with five occurring in Fynbos Biome habitats.

3 Speckled Pigeon *Columba guinea*

Large and distinctive. Head grey. Eyes yellow with very large, naked, fleshy red eye-ring. Bill black, cere grey. Throat and sides of neck have narrow, slightly elongated pale grey and rufous feathers. Back brick-red with numerous white spots. Underparts dark grey. Legs and feet dull red. Tail has broad, black terminal band. Juvenile much duller overall, lacks red eye-ring; eye brown. **Size** 30–34cm; 280–400g. **Call** Rapid series of notes increasing in intensity: *hu, hu, hu, hu, hu, hu....* . Also produces a *whu-hu-hu*. **Status and Habitat** Very common resident. Historically confined to mountainous regions owing to dependence on cliffs for breeding. However, they have adapted to breeding on buildings and are now very common in towns and cities.

4 Red-eyed Dove *Streptopelia semitorquata*

Superficially similar to Cape Turtle Dove but larger, darker and more colourful. Head pale pinkish grey; forehead very pale grey. Eye reddish brown to orange with inconspicuous broad, dark red, fleshy eye-ring. Black collar present. Back greyish brown. Underparts pinkish grey. In flight, tail has broad, pale grey, terminal bar. Juvenile darker overall, has less obvious collar, with buff-edged upperpart feathers. **Size** 32–34cm; 190–300g. **Call** Regular song is five-note call *du, du, du-du-du*, that can be rendered as 'I am, a Red-eyed Dove'. **Status and Habitat** A very common resident. Dependent on trees and not found in treeless shrublands. Tree planting across the Fynbos Biome has greatly benefited this species.

1 Cape Turtle (Ring-necked) Dove *Streptopelia capicola*

Rather pale overall. Head soft pale grey; nape and mantle with pinkish hue. Thin black line runs from dark eye to base of blackish bill. Broad, black collar present on hindneck with thin white border. Upperparts light tan with pale blueish-grey coverts. Chest pale rose-grey. Underparts pale grey with pinkish hue. In flight, tail has large white outer tips. Smaller and much paler than Red-eyed Dove, which also has dark red eye-ring. Juvenile similar but duller overall, with pale, buff-edged feathers on upperparts. **Size** 25–27cm; 100–160g. **Call** Regularly repeated *toet, kur, kirrrr*. **Status and Habitat** A very common resident, utilising all available habitat types. Not dependent on the presence of trees. Inexplicably rare in many suburbs of Cape Town.

2 Laughing Dove *Spilopelia senegalensis*

An attractive little dove. Head and nape plain pinkish grey, with no collar on nape. Bill black, eye dark brown without an eye-ring. Upperparts soft pinkish tan and greyish blue. Upper breast rich rufous with black flecking. Lower breast pink; belly off-white. Female slightly paler than male. Juvenile much duller and greyer overall. Feathers pale buff-edged; speckled upper breast band patchy. **Size** 22–24cm; 80–130g. **Call** Muffled bubbling, *who hu hu hu hu*, reminiscent of subdued laugh. **Status and Habitat** A very common resident, widespread and found in most habitat types. Very common in urban areas. Not common in mountain Fynbos.

3 Namaqua Dove *Oena capensis*

A small, elegant dove. Exhibits marked sexual dimorphism. Male greyish brown above with metallic purple wing spots. Face, throat and breast black, forming diagnostic bib. Bill yellow with dark red to purplish base. Two black bars on back separated by off-white bar. Long, pointed tail dark grey. Flight feathers rufous with dark tips. Female has all-black bill and no black on face or breast. Juvenile like female, but feathers on underparts are pale-tipped. **Size** 28cm; 30–40g. **Call** Plaintive cooing *who-woooo*. **Status and Habitat** Common resident and summer visitor. Occurs in most natural habitats, most common in West Coast Strandveld. Absent from suburbia.

Hoopoes   Family Upupidae

Colourful, charming birds with an elaborate crest and long, thin bill. They forage on the ground, feeding on invertebrates and occasionally small vertebrates, and require open habitats. One species occurs in the Fynbos Biome.

4 African Hoopoe *Upupa africana*

Distinctive and easily identified. Male rich orange-rufous overall. Back and wings strongly patterned with broad white, pale orange and black bars. Crest of very long, black-tipped feathers, which can be erected (inset). Bill very long and decurved. Female duller rufous overall with grey tones to face, chest and back. In flight, female also has less white in wing. Juvenile has shorter crest and bill, duller in colour overall. **Size** 25–28cm; 40–60g. **Call** Song is a repetitive *hooop, hooop, hooop*. **Status and Habitat** Common resident, found throughout the Fynbos Biome but absent from mountain Fynbos. Prefers disturbed sites that have open ground. Especially fond of short mowed or grazed lawns.

Kingfishers
Family Alcedinidae

Small to medium-sized, colourful birds. They have a large head, a long, heavy bill that tapers to a sharp point, and stubby legs. They feed on invertebrates and small vertebrates. Many species are not closely associated with water. Five species are resident in the CFR. Four are waterbirds. One of these, the Giant Kingfisher, is regularly seen in relatively small mountain streams in the Fynbos. The only terrestrial kingfisher in the Fynbos Biome is the Brown-hooded Kingfisher.

1 Brown-hooded Kingfisher *Halcyon albiventris*

Male has black back and bright turquoise blue wing feathers and tail. Head brown, heavily streaked with darker brown. Heavy, long, pointed bill red with black tip. Diffuse white eyebrow present. Underparts off-white to tawny with variable dark brown streaking, particularly across breast and on flanks. Female has dark brown back. Juvenile duller overall. **Size** 20–22cm; 50–75g. **Call** A loud ringing *pli-pli-pli-pli* or *klee-klee-klee*. **Status and Habitat** Fairly common resident. Terrestrial, hunting insects and small vertebrates from an exposed perch. Largely restricted to southern and eastern parts of the Fynbos Biome. Associated with trees and absent from treeless habitats such as mountain Fynbos.

2 Giant Kingfisher *Megaceryle maxima*

A huge kingfisher with a massive black bill. Head black with fine white streaking. Crown and nape feathers long, forming shaggy crest. Sides of neck and throat white, often with black streaking. Upperparts black with numerous small, white spots. Male has rich chestnut breast; remainder of underparts white with black spots and bars. Female has white chest with heavy black spotting. Rest of underparts chestnut. Juvenile male has mottled black and chestnut breast. Juvenile female has chestnut belly and underwings. **Size** 40–45cm; 320–440g. **Call** Loud and raucous series of *ka-ka-ka* notes, often given in flight. **Status and Habitat** Fairly common resident. An aquatic kingfisher with a preference for streams and rivers. Occasionally hunts along the rocky seashore.

Bee-eaters
Family Meropidae

All bee-eaters are morphologically similar, being slender and colourful. They have a long, slender, decurved bill and short legs. Bee-eaters are insectivores, hunting from an exposed perch and catching flying insects on the wing. Most are gregarious and breed colonially in burrows in vertical banks. Only one species regularly occurs in the Fynbos Biome. However, as bee-eaters are prone to wander, many species occur as vagrants.

3 European Bee-eater *Merops apiaster*

Upperparts shades of chestnut, orange and yellow. Frons white. Broad black line runs through eye. Thin black line separates bright yellow throat from turquoise-blue underparts. Tail dark green above. Central tail feathers pointed and extending about 3cm beyond tail tip. Told from all potential vagrant bee-eaters by yellow throat and turquoise underparts. Juvenile greener above and lacks elongated tail feathers. **Size** 28cm; 40–66g. **Call** Rather vocal. Most commonly uttered call is a throaty *preeup, preeup*. **Status and Habitat** A common spring and summer visitor, primarily to the western areas of the Fynbos Biome. Rare in the Overberg and eastern parts of the region. Birds that visit and breed in the Fynbos Biome are not from Europe but are inter-Africa breeding migrants.

African barbets   Family Lybiidae

Small to medium-sized, robust birds that occur in a wide variety of habitats, but are mainly found in forest and woodland. The heavy, pointed bill is often notched. They feed on fruit and invertebrates. Only one species occurs in the Fynbos.

1 Acacia Pied Barbet *Tricholaema leucomelas*

A stocky bird with a heavy black bill. Upperparts black with pale-yellow flecks and streaks. Forehead bright red. Very broad and long tapering eyebrow present. Eyebrow white, but pale yellow in front of eye. Throat and upper breast black. Underparts pale grey with dark blotching and streaking, especially on flanks. Juvenile lacks red forehead. **Size** 16–18cm; 25–36g. **Call** Series of low hooting notes *hoop, hoop, hoop, hoop* and nasal *nehh* notes. **Status and Habitat** Common resident but absent from treeless habitats such as mountain Fynbos. Dependent on trees that are large enough to excavate nests. Establishment of alien trees has allowed expansion of its range within the Fynbos Biome.

Woodpeckers   Family Picidae

Morphologically all quite similar, but range in size from small to large. Most species are associated with trees and are therefore found in forests or woodland. Woodpeckers are well known for their characteristic behaviour of clinging to trunks and branches and hammering with their strong, pointed bill. They feed on invertebrates, mainly insect larvae. Four species occur in the CFR, two that frequent Fynbos habitats.

2 Ground Woodpecker *Geocolaptes olivaceus*

Large, beautiful and highly specialised. Back and mantle olive-brown with numerous pale yellow flecks. Wings heavily spotted with pale yellow. Rump red and tail olive with yellow barring. Head grey with pale yellowish eyes. Bill black, strong, and dagger-like. Male has dark grey malar stripe infused with red. Throat pale grey. Upper breast olive-buff, gradually merging with red lower breast and belly. Flanks and vent olive, barred with dull yellow. Juvenile has duller red coloration and grey eyes. **Size** 23–30cm; 110–130g. **Call** High pitched and far carrying *tchee-aar* and a series of *tchic-pee* notes. **Endemism** Southern Africa. **Status and Habitat** Fairly common resident. Family groups inhabit treeless mountainous areas, most common in mountain Fynbos. Will also utilise isolated rocky environments away from mountains. Feeds on the ground, mainly on ants.

3 Cardinal Woodpecker *Dendropicos fuscescens*

Diminutive woodpecker. Male has brown forecrown and bright red hind crown. Cheeks and sides of neck pale grey with fine, dark grey streaking. Back and wing feathers brown, strongly barred creamy white, tinged with yellow. Tail brown, strongly barred with pale yellow, the central shafts golden yellow. Dark brown malar stripes present. Underparts pale grey, heavily streaked with dark brown. Female similar but hind-crown black, not red. Juvenile duller and greyer and both sexes have red patch in the centre of the crown. **Size** 14–16cm; 20–36g. **Call** Harsh rattling *tche-che-che-che* call and scolding *kreee, kreee, kreee* notes. **Status and Habitat** Fairly common resident. Usually associated with trees and thickets. Utilises natural thickets but has benefited from the spread of alien trees.

Wattle-eyes and batises

Family Platysteiridae

Small, compact birds. They are specialist insect eaters and have a broad, flat bill with a hooked tip. One species occurs in the Fynbos Biome.

1 Cape Batis *Batis capensis*

Inquisitive and confiding. Male has slate-grey crown with broad black face mask. Eyes bright yellow. Upperparts olive-brown with rufous wing bars. Broad, black bar across breast. Throat and sides of neck white. Flanks rufous. Belly and vent white. Female has rufous breast band, rufous patch under throat and red eyes. Juvenile similar to female, but the face mask brown and the eyes dark brown. Separated from Pririt Batis (*B. pririt*) by rufous, not white, wing bars. **Size** 13cm; 12g. **Call** A very vocal species. Song is a three-note strident whistled *tchew, tchew, tchew*. Social call is a slurred churring. **Status and Habitat** Common resident. Favours forest and thicket habitats but will readily utilise dense, wooded gardens and alien thickets. Also utilises tall Fynbos habitats, usually near forest patches or riparian thickets.

Bushshrikes

Family Malaconotidae

These small to medium-sized birds are similar to shrikes (Laniidae) in that they are carnivorous with a heavy, hooked bill. However, bushshrikes are often more colourful and many are more skulking in habit. Three species occur in the Fynbos Biome.

2 Bokmakierie *Telophorus zeylonus*

A very familiar and striking bird. Back and wings olive-green. Crown and nape grey. Central tail feathers olive-green; remaining tail feathers black with broad yellow tips. Bright yellow eyebrow present. Broad, black breast band joins black lores below eye. Throat bright yellow. Belly yellow with greenish flanks. Upper flanks grey. Bill black. Juvenile dull olive above and pale yellow below. Lacks black collar and grey hood. **Size** 23cm; 60–66g. **Call** Complex array of ringing melodious calls. Male and female duet. Classic call includes onomatopoeic *bok, bok, ta-jie* or variations. **Status and Habitat** Common resident, found throughout the Fynbos Biome. **Endemism** Southern Africa.

3 Southern Boubou *Laniarius ferrugineus*

Male all glossy black above with narrow, white bar running across wing coverts. Tail all black. Throat white, gradually merging with rich rufous flanks, lower belly, and vent. Female a duller black above and rufous-buff below, including the throat and breast. Bill black. Juvenile upperparts mottled buff and underparts lightly barred rufous. **Size** 22cm; 59g. **Call** Very vocal. A variety of beautiful liquid whistles. Pairs sing in duets. Calls include a plaintive *tchwoooo, bou-bou-bou* and *wiet-weeo*. A harsh grating call is produced when alarmed. **Status and Habitat** Common resident that requires thick cover. Inhabits dense Fynbos, coastal thickets, forest edge and gardens. Rare along the western coastal strip and largely absent from the extensive agricultural areas. **Endemism** Southern Africa.

4 Southern Tchagra *Tchagra tchagra*

Crown, mantle and back brown. Wing coverts and outer edge of flight feathers rich rufous. Tail blackish brown, each feather white tipped. Long, bold, white eyebrow present, bordered below by long black stripe that runs through eye. Thin, black line separates white eyebrow from brown crown. Underparts grey, palest on throat. Bill black, long. Juvenile has brown bill and buff tail spots. **Size** 21cm; 47g. **Call** Can be cryptic when not calling. Display song a decelerating series of *chia, chia, cheea, cheeeyu, cheeyu, cheeyuu* notes. Alarm call is a series of scolding nasal *tzeee* notes. **Status and Habitat** Fairly common resident. Favours riverine and coastal thickets. **Endemism** Southern Africa.

Shrikes   Family Laniidae

These medium-sized, predatory birds have a strong, hooked bill. They prey on invertebrates and a variety of small vertebrates. Only one species occurs in the Fynbos Biome.

1 Southern Fiscal *Lanius collaris*

Male all black above with white scapulars that form bold V on back. Small white spot visible on folded primaries. Tail black, long, slender, with white outer feathers. Underparts white. Bill black, stout and hooked. Female duller with chestnut patches on flanks; patches largely hidden when perched. Juvenile brown above with fine, dark barring; underparts off-white, finely scaled grey. Separated from Fiscal Flycatcher by heavier bill, longer tail and white patches on scapulars, not secondaries. **Size** 21–23cm; 25–50g. **Call** Typical call is harsh *tcher, tcher*. Song is rich melodious warble, including harsh grating phrases and mimicry of other species. **Status and Habitat** Abundant resident, found in diverse habitat types.

Crows   Family Corvidae

Medium-sized to large birds with strong legs and a heavy bill. Corvids are among the most intelligent of all animals. They have a high brain-to-body mass ratio, comparable to some of the great apes. Highly varied omnivorous diet, scavenging readily. Four species occur in the Fynbos Biome, but the introduced House Crow (*Corvus splendens*) occurs only in the urban sprawl of the Cape Flats.

2 Cape Crow *Corvus capensis*

The only all-black corvid in the region. No white plumage. Bill long and slender. Juvenile duller with brown tones. **Size** 45–50cm; 410–630g. **Call** Deep, crow-like cawing. Also produces a bewildering array of buzzing and gargling sounds. **Status and Habitat** Common resident throughout most of the Fynbos Biome. Especially common in low-lying agricultural areas in the southern part of the Biome. Largely absent from Cape Peninsula, Cape Flats and West Coast lowlands. Reason for rarity on West Coast not clear. More insectivorous than Pied Crow and White-necked Raven.

3 Pied Crow *Corvus albus*

A familiar and distinctive black-and-white crow. All glossy black with broad, white collar that merges with all-white breast and upper belly. Vent and lower belly black. Only local crow species with white on belly. Juvenile duller overall; border between black and white diffuse, especially on belly. **Size** 46–50cm; 410–610g. **Call** Typical harsh, crow-like cawing. Also produces various other harsh rattling calls. **Status and Habitat** Very common resident, found throughout the region but particularly abundant on Cape Flats and western coastal plain. Least common in mountainous regions of southern Cape and less common than Cape Crow in parts of the Overberg.

4 White-necked Raven *Corvus albicollis*

All black with white collar, which is restricted to nape. Bill massive, black with white tip. In flight easily recognised by very broad wings and relatively short, fan-shaped tail. Female marginally larger. Juvenile with browner plumage, especially on head. **Size** 50–56cm; 750–880g. **Call** Series of short squawks, *kraak, kraak, kraak*. **Status and Habitat** Common resident. Dependent on cliffs for breeding and very common in mountainous areas. Forages over large distances and can be seen in all habitats. Regularly scavenges in urban areas.

Rockjumpers   Family Chaetopidae

Boldly coloured and found on open, rocky mountain slopes. An enigmatic family comprising two species endemic to South Africa and Lesotho. Feed on arthropods and occasionally small reptiles and frogs. One species occurs in the Fynbos Biome.

1 Cape Rockjumper *Chaetops frenatus* NT

An iconic mountain Fynbos bird. Male has black head and back, heavily streaked with silver-grey. Bold, white malar stripe runs to shoulders. Throat and breast black. Rump rich chestnut. Tail long, black with white outer tips. Belly rich chestnut. Eyes orange-red. Female duller overall; head grey and heavily streaked. Juvenile similar to female. **Size** 23–25cm; 50–70g. **Call** Series of loud, high-pitched whistles, *pee-pee-pee-pee-pee-pee*, falling in pitch. **Status and Habitat** Fairly common habitat specialist, occurring in rocky mountain Fynbos of Cape Fold Mountains from around Clanwilliam in north to Gqeberha in east. **Endemism** Fynbos Biome. **Conservation Status** Near Threatened owing to apparent recent population decline. Could be vulnerable to future climate change.

Fairy Flycatcher and allies   Family Stenostiridae

A recently recognised, very small family of small, insectivorous, flycatcher-like birds. One species occurs in the Fynbos Biome.

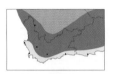

2 Fairy Flycatcher *Stenostira scita*

A charming, dainty little bird. Dark blue-grey above with black face mask. White eyebrow and malar stripes present. Short, thin white line below eye. Wings black with bold white bar. Breast pale blue-grey. Slight pink hue across lower breast and belly. Tail black with white outer tail feathers. Juvenile similar but browner above and lacks pinkish tones on underparts. **Size** 11cm; 6g. **Call** High-pitched wispy *tisee-tchee-tchee* reminiscent of sunbird song. **Status and Habitat** Fairly common resident, found primarily in more arid habitats. Common in the Succulent Karoo and drier fringes of Fynbos Biome. Subject to local movements, and single birds can turn up anywhere in winter. **Endemism** Southern Africa.

Tits   Family Paridae

Small, stocky woodland birds. They have a short, stout bill. They have mixed diets, feeding on seeds and insects. One species occurs in the Fynbos.

3 Grey Tit *Melaniparus cinerascens*

A compact, dapper little bird. Back greyish brown. Crown and nape black with small buff spot on nape. Broad, white line runs from below eye to sides of neck and then onto sides of breast. Throat and breast black. Black bib tapers down to a point on belly. Remainder of underparts buff-grey. Bill black. Juvenile has browner head and throat; wing feathers pale-edged. **Size** 15cm; 18–22g. **Call** Song includes harsh scolding *cher-chre-chre* and melodious whistled *piet-tjou-tjou* phrases. **Status and Habitat** Fairly common resident. Avoids wet mountain Fynbos, urban areas, and extensive transformed agricultural areas. Most common in Strandveld in West Coast lowlands. **Endemism** Southern Africa.

Penduline tits — Family Remiidae

Very small birds with a fine pointed bill. Feed mainly on insects. One species occurs in the region.

1 Cape Penduline Tit *Anthoscopus minutus*
Smallest bird in region. Upperparts brownish grey. Crown grey; frons scaled black and white. Short white eyebrow present. Lores black, extending into short dark line behind eye. Cheeks and throat off-white. Underparts yellowish buff. Very sharp, conical bill dark grey. Juvenile browner above, paler below. **Size** 8cm; 7–9g. **Call** High-pitched plaintive *ptseee, ptseee, ptseee*. Contact call is various short notes, including *tsi, tsi, tsi*. **Status and Habitat** Fairly common but easily overlooked, best noticed by call. Confined mainly to Strandveld and karroid vegetation.

Larks — Family Alaudidae

Cryptically coloured ground-dwelling birds. Primarily seedeaters. Five species occur in the region.

2 Cape Long-billed Lark *Certhilauda curvirostris*
Large, with impressively long, decurved bill. Upperparts greyish brown and streaked. Long off-white to buff eyebrow present. Underparts off-white and extensively streaked, especially on breast. Female has shorter bill. Juvenile upperpart feathers buff-tipped; spots on underparts more rounded. To be lumped with Agulhas Long-billed Lark. **Size** 20–24cm; 40–60g. **Call** Loud, plaintive, descending whistle, *whit, pseeuuuuuu*. **Status and Habitat** Fairly common localised resident. Utilises vegetation remnants and neighbouring agricultural fields. **Endemism** South Africa.

3 Agulhas Long-billed Lark *Certhilauda brevirostris* NT
Soon to be lumped with larger and longer-billed Cape Long-billed Lark. Upperparts brown and streaked. Buff eyebrow present. Underparts cream to buff, extensively streaked. Long decurved bill, shorter than Cape Long-billed Lark. Juvenile upperpart feathers buff-tipped; spots on underparts more rounded. **Size** 18–20cm; 35–48g. **Call** Plaintive *pseeu, pseeuuuuuu*. **Status and Habitat** Common resident. Confined to the Overberg to just east of Mossel Bay. Utilises fallow fields, croplands and Renosterveld and Fynbos remnants. Favours stony ground. **Endemism** Fynbos Biome. **Conservation Status** Near Threatened owing to small global population and distribution range.

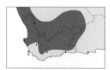

4 Karoo Lark *Calendulauda albescens*
Upperparts greyish brown; mantle and back streaked. Face boldly marked. Prominent eyebrow present; white ring below eye. Thin dark line through eye. Cheek and ear covert patch uniform brown, usually with rufous tinge. Underparts white to off-white. Throat, breast and flanks heavily streaked. Decurved, slender bill dark grey, slightly paler at base. Juvenile has spotted upperparts. **Size** 16–17cm; 25–33g. **Call** Song: *tip, tip, twizerrrrr*. Variety of similar phrases and trilling alarm calls. **Status and Habitat** Fairly common resident. Most common in West Coast Strandveld. Scarce in sand Fynbos, absent from mountain Fynbos and extensive areas of cultivation. **Endemism** Southern Africa.

5 Cape Clapper Lark *Mirafra apiata*
Upperparts grey, richly marked with buff, grey and black spots and bars. Crown rufous, streaked with grey and black, can be raised into short crest. Indistinct streaky, buff eyebrow present. Underparts rich buff to orange. Dark spotting on throat and breast fades to mottling on flanks. Juvenile browner overall, with pale-edged feathers above. Subspecies from southern coastal plain, *M. a. marjoriae*, greyer above and darker overall. **Size** 15cm; 23–38g. **Call** Characteristic aerial display of accelerated clapping of the wings. *M. a. apiata* gives ascending whistle as it drops down to ground, *M. a. marjoriae* gives two descending whistles. **Status and Habitat** Fairly common. Inconspicuous when not displaying. Occurs in Fynbos and Renosterveld; scarce in Strandveld. **Endemism** South Africa.

1 Large-billed Lark *Galerida magnirostris*

Heavyset, boldly marked lark with thick, dark bill with yellow base. Upperparts brown, heavily streaked with dark brown. Crown, brown with fine black streaking, can be raised to form short crest. Buff eyebrow present; large pale ring around eye. Underparts off-white; chest heavily streaked. Upper belly and flanks with light streaking. Juvenile upperparts have pale buff tips to feathers, creating spotted appearance. **Size** 18cm; 35–48g. **Call** Melodious fluty *tup, tup, tree-eeleo*, often compared to squeaky gate being opened. **Status and Habitat** Common resident with a preference for disturbed open areas. Common in agricultural lands. Utilises remnant patches of Renosterveld, Strandveld and open arid Fynbos habitats. **Endemism** Southern Africa.

Bulbuls
Family Pycnonotidae

Medium-sized, slender and long-tailed. Many have an elongated, slightly hooked bill and several species have a crest. Primarily frugivores, they occur in forests, woodlands, scrub and thickets. Highly vocal. Two species occur in the Fynbos Biome.

2 Sombre Greenbul *Andropadus importunus*

This highly vocal bird is indeed sombre in coloration. Upperparts dull olive-green, with yellow-edged flight feathers that form pale yellow panel in folded wing. Underparts paler greyish olive. Bill black, relatively long and heavy. Eye striking, white to pale blueish grey. Juvenile has dark eye and yellow gape. **Size** 18cm; 30–39g. **Call** Regularly whistled *theee-oo*. Song a loud melody of whistled phrases, often rendered as 'Willie. Come and fight, or are you scaaaaared'. **Status and Habitat** Locally common resident in riparian and coastal thickets. Favours localised forest patches. Largely absent from the western parts of the Fynbos Biome, occurring only as far north as the Tulbagh area.

3 Cape Bulbul *Pycnonotus capensis*

Chocolate-brown all over, darkest on face. Crown has short, pointed crest. Dark reddish-brown eye encircled by thick, fleshy, white eye-ring, which is broadest in front of eye. Bill fairly long and black. Vent bright yellow. Juvenile has grey to reddish-purple eye-ring, which whitens soon after fledging. **Size** 21cm; 30–46g. **Call** Short but melodious whistle, *choep-cheee-toodley*. **Status and Habitat** Very common in variety of habitats, but least common in Fynbos, where there are few fruiting shrubs. Especially common in Strandveld and gardens. **Endemism** CFR (in South Africa).

Swallows and martins
Family Hirundinidae

They occupy a wide range of habitats, often near water. Specialist aerial feeders with a distinct appearance. Nine species occur in the Fynbos Biome.

4 Black Saw-wing *Psalidoprocne pristoptera*

A glossy black swallow with a long, deeply forked tail. No other swallow in the region is all black. Juvenile plumage duller with shorter tail. Easily separated from swifts which have long crescent-shaped wings and usually fly high and directly. Swallows have smaller, more rounded wings and a dynamic darting and gliding flight, often at a low level. Swallows, unlike swifts, are often seen sitting on exposed perches. **Size** 14cm; 11–13g. **Call** Buzzy, canary-like chirps in flight or from perch. **Status and Habitat** A fairly common summer migrant. Most common in the southern part of the region. Utilises trees and frequents the edges of forest, plantations and alien stands where they forage over the surrounding Fynbos.

1 Brown-throated Martin *Riparia paludicola*

A small, greyish-brown martin, usually with a white belly. Extent of white variable and many birds are uniform brown overall. Pale-bellied birds easily separated from Banded Martin and Sand Martin by brown throat. All-brown birds are told from Rock Martin by their smaller size, darker underwing coverts and lack of any pale spots in tail. Juvenile has pale, buff-edged feathers on upperparts. **Size** 12cm; 10–16g. **Call** Jumbled soft twittering. Contact call is harsh *tcheeee*. **Status and Habitat** A very common resident, with some movement out of the area in midwinter. Closely associated with wetlands and feeds over the water or neighbouring open areas.

2 Banded Martin *Riparia cincta*

A large, distinctive martin. Upperparts dark brown. Short white eyebrow, ending above eye. Underparts white, except for narrow, but bold, breast band. Variable, dark band across vent may be present. Juvenile dark chocolate-brown above with rufous-edged feathers. Easily separated from Brown-throated Martin by white throat. Differentiated from rare summer-visiting Sand Martin (*R. riparia*) by much larger size, small white eyebrow, and off-white underwing coverts. **Size** 17cm; 23–29g. **Call** Melodious series of squeaky notes. **Status and Habitat** Fairly common but localised spring and summer visitor. Most common in western coastal lowlands but also frequently recorded along southern coastal plain, especially around Jeffreys Bay. Prefers areas with short vegetation.

3 Barn Swallow *Hirundo rustica*

The most abundant swallow in the Fynbos Biome. Non-breeding birds glossy dark blue above. Tail black with blueish sheen and white windows. Frons and throat dull chestnut. Broad blue-black breast band encircles chestnut throat patch. Belly off-white, occasionally warm buff. Breeding birds brighter overall and have long tail streamers. Female has slightly shorter tail streamers. Can be seen in breeding plumage just before they depart in autumn. Juvenile browner and duller overall with pale buff throat and frons. **Size** 15–20cm; 16–24g. **Call** Song is a jumbled series of high-pitched twittering phrases. **Status and Habitat** Abundant, non-breeding, summer visitor. Feeds over a variety of habitats, including beaches. Sometimes roosts in massive flocks.

4 White-throated Swallow *Hirundo albigularis*

A dark blue-and-white swallow with a white throat and dark blue breast band. Upperparts uniform dark metallic blue, except for dark chestnut frons. Throat white, belly off-white to pale brownish grey. Breast band metallic blue-black, narrowest in middle but usually complete. Tail has white windows in all but central tail feathers, seen only when tail is fanned. Juvenile duller overall with dull black breast band and yellow gape. **Size** 15cm; 18–28g. **Call** Song is short high-pitched series of twittering notes. Also produces a series of *chip-chip-chip* notes. **Status and Habitat** Common spring- and summer-breeding visitor; closely associated with water.

5 Pearl-breasted Swallow *Hirundo dimidiata*

A small, dainty swallow. Upperparts, including rump, uniform blue-black with blue gloss. Lores and cheeks dull black. Tail has shallow fork without any tail streamers. Underparts white to off-white. No red or chestnut colouring whatsoever. Juvenile duller and less glossy. Similar Common House Martin is easily separated by its white rump. **Size** 13cm; 10–15g. **Call** Series of sharp nasal *cheep* or *chip* notes. **Status and Habitat** Fairly common spring- and summer-breeding visitor. Found in a variety of habitats but avoids mountain Fynbos areas.

1 Rock Martin *Ptyonoprogne fuligula*

A common martin with a series of distinctive off-white windows towards tip of tail. These spots are best seen when the tail is fanned. Upperparts dark brown, contrasting with paler buffy underparts. Buff coloration richest on throat. Best separated from all-brown Brown-throated Martin by larger size and diagnostic pale tail spots. Juvenile has pale buff-edged feathers on upperparts. **Size** 14cm; 14–16g. **Call** Short, nasal twittering song and high-pitched *teet, teet, teet* notes. **Status and Habitat** Common resident, found throughout the Fynbos Biome. Prefers rocky areas where it nests on cliffs. Also nests on human-made structures away from mountainous areas. There is some movement away from high altitudes during cold periods.

2 Common House Martin *Delichon urbicum*

A dark blue-and-white martin with a distinctive white rump. Upperparts dark glossy blue. Wings and shallow forked tail dull black. Underparts snowy white. Feet and legs covered with white feathers, though difficult to see. Juvenile duller and less glossy above, with grey smudged breast. **Size** 14cm; 10–16g. **Call** Short, squeaky chirps and swizzling noises. **Status and Habitat** Uncommon, non-breeding summer visitor from Europe and western Asia. Primarily feeds at high altitudes, often with other aerial feeders. Not fussy about underlying habitat.

3 Greater Striped Swallow *Cecropis cucullata*

Crown and nape dark rufous. Rump pale rufous, can appear very pale in strong light. Back dark metalic blue-black. Tail and wings dull black. Tail deeply forked, with white windows and elongated outer tail feathers. Underwing coverts white. Ear coverts, chin and throat pale buff, densely marked with fine streaking. Underparts pale beige to buff with dense fine streaking, which is not always visible, especially at distance. Juvenile duller, with less glossy back and shorter outer tail feathers. Lesser-striped Swallow (*C. abyssinica*) is rare visitor, smaller, with heavier streaking below and rich rufous ear coverts. **Size** 16–20cm; 20–35g. **Call** A vocal species producing regular squeaky *chirrup, chirrup* and a variety of other notes and phrases. **Status and Habitat** A very common, breeding spring and summer visitor. Widespread throughout the region in a variety of habitats. Breeds on overhanging cliffs, in buildings, under bridges or in culverts.

Crombecs and allies Family Macrosphenidae

Also known as the African warblers. Small to medium-sized insectivores that occur in a variety of habitats. Three species occur in the Fynbos Biome.

4 Cape Grassbird *Sphenoeacus afer*

Upperparts richly marked with black, rufous and buff. Crown bright rufous. Buffy eyebrow present. Belly pale buff and heavily streaked with black. Throat cream; black malar stripe present. Bill grey. Rufous tail long, shaggy and pointed. Juvenile duller, with streaked crown. **Size** 17–19cm; 26–34g. **Call** Calls from an exposed perch. Song is repetitive but pleasant burst of notes that builds in volume, pace and pitch. Alarm call is high-pitched mewing *peeeee*. **Status and Habitat** A common resident in well-vegetated areas. Prefers wetter environments and most common in mountain Fynbos. **Endemism** Southern Africa.

5 Long-billed Crombec *Sylvietta rufescens*

A small warbler that appears almost tailless. Upperparts uniform grey. Underparts pale buff, palest on throat and upper breast. Pale eyebrow present. Lores grey. Bill long, dark grey, with pale base to lower mandible. Juvenile has paler underparts. **Size** 11cm; 9–14g. **Call** Contact call is frequently uttered trill-like *prritt*. Song is wispy *tree-rriit, tree-rriit*. **Status and Habitat** Widespread resident, common in dry, low shrublands, especially Strandveld habitats of the West Coast. Avoids moist mountain Fynbos.

1 **Victorin's Warbler** *Cryptillas victorini*
Unique, the only species in the genus *Cryptillas*. Upperparts brown. Underparts rich rufous-orange. Cheeks grey. Eyes pale orange. Female duller overall. Juvenile has duller grey upperparts and grey eyes. **Size** 16cm; 20g. **Call** Reminiscent of Cape Grassbird. A frantic series of *whit-itty-weeo* notes that increase in intensity and volume. Can be likened to *Mis-sis-sippi, Mis-sis-sippi, Mis-sis-sippi*. Bouts of song interspersed with series of *chew-chew-chew* notes. **Status and Habitat** Common localised resident, but can be very cryptic and difficult to observe. Found only in dense mountain Fynbos associated with seeps and streams. Absent from the Cape Peninsula. **Endemism** Fynbos Biome.

Reed warblers — Family Acrocephalidae

Plainly coloured insectivores. These birds are accomplished songsters. Most species inhabit marshes and reedbeds. Several are long-distance migrants. Two species occur in the Fynbos.

2 **Lesser Swamp Warbler** *Acrocephalus gracilirostris*
A large, relatively conspicuous warbler that is easily identified by its call. Upperparts warm brown. Distinct white eyebrow present. Underparts off-white with buff flanks. Legs and feet appear black. Long, thin bill dark grey with yellow base to lower mandible. **Size** 14–16cm; 12–20g. **Call** Very vocal. Pleasant, melodious, warbling call including *cheerup-chee-chiree-chiree* and variations of these notes. **Status and Habitat** A common resident that is strictly associated with reedbeds. Will utilise relatively small patches of reed at any perennial wetland.

3 **Common Reed Warbler** *Acrocephalus scirpaceus*
African Reed Warbler has been lumped with Eurasian Reed Warbler and is now known as Common Reed Warbler. Noticeably smaller than Lesser Swamp Warbler. Upperparts warm brown. Throat and belly off-white. Breast, flanks and vent washed with buff. Indistinct short buff eyebrow present. Legs and feet greenish yellow to brown. Bill bicoloured; upper mandible grey and lower mandible dull yellow. Juvenile has brighter rufous tones. Very similar to vagrant Marsh Warbler (*A. palustris*), which has greyish-brown (not warm brown) back and longer primaries. Marsh Warbler regularly utters a soft *tuk* contact call, not given by Common Reed Warbler. **Size** 12–13cm; 8–14g. **Call** Long rambling series of harsh but rhythmic grating notes, churs and chips. **Status and Habitat** Fairly common inter-Africa spring and summer visitor. Associated with wetland vegetation, preferring edges where reedbeds merge with tangles of riparian vegetation.

Grasshopper warblers and grassbirds — Family Locustellidae

Relatively small, with a long, pointed tail. All are brown and drab, some with heavy streaking. Insectivorous and occur in a variety of habitats, but most species inhabit reedbeds or grasslands. Many species are cryptic and hard to observe. One species is resident in the Fynbos.

4 **Little Rush Warbler** *Bradypterus baboecala*
Upperparts dark brown. Underparts pale grey; flanks and vent tawny. Throat and upper breast off-white with diffuse streaking that is not always evident. Pale eyebrow present. Juvenile has yellow-tinted underparts. **Size** 15–17cm; 12–18g. **Call** Series of *tchup* notes accelerating in frequency, a familiar call in most wetland habitats in the region. Calling often associated with short flights and intense wing fluttering. Alarm call is nasal *wheeaaa*. **Status and Habitat** A common resident inhabiting reedbed and dense waterside vegetation. Often remains concealed in thick vegetation.

Cisticolas and allies   Family Cisticolidae

Most species are small and cryptically coloured insectivores. Call, habitat, behaviour and distribution are important for identification. Nine species are known to occur in the Fynbos Biome.

1 Lazy Cisticola *Cisticola aberrans*

A plain-backed cisticola, similar to Neddicky. The palest subspecies in southern Africa (*C. a. minor*) occurs in the Fynbos. Upperparts plain greyish brown. Tail plain brown, often held in cocked position. Crown and nape russet. Long, diffuse eyebrow present. Underparts off-white with buff to light grey flanks. Separated from Neddicky by longer tail, buffy eyebrow and call. In the Fynbos Biome, Neddicky has darker grey underparts. **Size** 14cm; 13–15g. **Call** Variety of nasal mewing and whining notes. Common call is high-pitched *tsweeee*. Lacks elaborate displays characterised by many cisticolas, hence common name. **Status and Habitat** Uncommon and localised in the region, occurring in coastal Fynbos and grassy areas, usually with scattered rocks. Found on the coastal plain east of Knysna and in the Baviaanskloof.

2 Grey-backed Cisticola *Cisticola subruficapilla*

Back grey with dark grey streaking. Flight feathers form dull, reddish-brown panel in folded wing. Crown dull rufous-brown. Tail rufous-brown with darker subterminal bar and white tips. Underparts pale grey, often with some streaking on breast. Juvenile has yellow bill and yellow tone to underparts. Best told from larger Wailing Cisticola by colder tones, especially on underparts, mantle and crown. **Size** 12cm; 10–12g. **Call** Piercing *trrreee-tee-tee-tee*, one of the characteristic calls in much of the Biome. Call similar to Wailing Cisticola but slower and deeper. **Status and Habitat** Abundant resident, occurring in almost all shrubland habitats. One of the most common bush birds in the Fynbos Biome.

3 Wailing Cisticola *Cisticola lais*

Occurs only in eastern coastal parts of the Fynbos Biome. Similar to Grey-backed Cisticola. Back greyish brown with heavy, dark grey streaking. Flight feathers form reddish-brown panel in folded wing. Crown rufous-brown. Tail rufous, underparts warm buff. Local race (*C. l. maculatus*) can show streaking on breast. Juvenile washed yellow below. Best told from smaller Grey-backed Cisticola by warmer tones, especially on underparts, mantle and crown. **Size** 14cm; 15g. **Call** Rattled *t-trrrrrreee*, usually followed by several piping *t-pee t-pee t-pee* notes. Similar to Grey-backed Cisticola but faster and higher pitched. **Status and Habitat** Uncommon and localised. Inhabits grassy Fynbos slopes, usually with some rocks. Occurs patchily from Mossel Bay eastwards along the coast.

4 Levaillant's Cisticola *Cisticola tinniens*

A long-tailed wetland cisticola. Back black with greyish streaks. Rufous wing panel evident. Crown bright rufous. Diffuse, buffy eyebrow present. Underparts pale grey to white. There can be some streaking on flanks. Non-breeding birds have buff-brown streaking on back. Juvenile duller with less rufous crown. **Size** 13cm; 11g. **Call** Very vocal and conspicuous. Song is short, melodious *tsi tsiororee*. Alarm call is high-pitched *tee tee tee*. **Status and Habitat** Common resident, always associated with wetlands. The only cisticola in the Fynbos Biome that inhabits reedbeds and other dense riparian habitats.

5 Neddicky *Cisticola fulvicapilla*

A plain cisticola with no streaking or other obvious markings. Upperparts uniform grey-brown. Crown rufous-brown. Lores pale. Diffuse pale ring around light brown eye. Fynbos Biome subspecies (*C. f. silberbauer*) has grey underparts. Juvenile has yellow base to bill and darker eyes. **Size** 11cm; 9g. **Call** Monotonous, high-pitched *tseep tseep tseep* song by male from exposed perch. Alarm call is fast succession of *tic* notes. **Status and Habitat** Common resident but largely restricted to mountain Fynbos. Absent from lowland Fynbos and Strandveld.

1 Zitting Cisticola *Cisticola juncidis*

Upperparts tawny-buff with extensive dark streaking. Underparts buff with rich, tawny flanks. Short, white-tipped tail has darker subterminal bar. Rump rufous and unstreaked. Breeding birds have darker brown crown with limited streaking. Larger and longer tailed than Cloud Cisticola with no streaking on breast. Juvenile with yellower underparts. **Size** 11cm; 9g. **Call** Monotonous *zit* note uttered about once per second by male while in diagnostic undulating display flight performed at up to 20m above the ground. May also call from a prominent perch. **Status and Habitat** Very common resident. Favours transformed habitats where grasses or crops (such as lucerne) dominate, but can be seen in open natural areas. Easily detected when displaying.

2 Cloud Cisticola *Cisticola textrix*

A tiny bird with an extremely short tail. Cryptically coloured but intricately marked. Tail dark and white-tipped. Legs very long and pinkish. Difficult to see well but easily identified by display and call. Local subspecies (*C. t. textrix*) characterised by heavily streaked breast and flanks. Juvenile duller, tinted yellow below. **Size** 10cm; 11g. **Call** Male circles and calls for long periods during diagnostic aerial display, at an impressive height of up to about 50m. Call is plaintive *tsoe-si-si-si* followed by series of clicks. Descent to ground steep and rapid while uttering rapid series of clicks. Does not snap wings. **Status and Habitat** A common resident on the coastal plains, preferring short, wet grasslands. Utilises wheat and other crops. Also occurs in low, open Renosterveld and Fynbos habitats.

3 Karoo Prinia *Prinia maculosa*

Abundant, small bush bird. Upperparts mouse-brown. Crown finely streaked with black. Broad off-white eyebrow present. Underparts pale buff, heavily streaked on throat, chest and flanks. Tail long and narrow, often held in cocked position. Eyes pale brown. Bill black. Juvenile more buff below, with faint streaking. **Size** 14cm; 9g. **Call** Very vocal, producing various clicking and ringing notes. Regular call is series of *klip, klip, klip* notes. Speed of delivery and tone of notes can vary. **Status and Habitat** One of the most common birds in the Fynbos Biome, occurring in all shrubland habitats. **Endemism** Southern Africa.

4 Bar-throated Apalis *Apalis thoracica*

A very variable species across its large range. Local races: upperparts slate-grey. Pale eye contrasts strongly with grey face and cheeks. Throat white with bold, narrow, black breast band. Belly white to off-white with pale buff to grey flanks. Bill black. Feet and legs orange to pink. Tail long and narrow. In juvenile, breast band often incomplete. **Size** 13cm; 11g. **Call** Series of loud, rhythmic *tup, tup, tup, tup* notes by male. Female responds with fast *ti, ti ti, ti*. **Status and Habitat** Common resident with a preference for Strandveld and riparian thickets.

Sylviid babblers   Family Sylviidae

Historically a dumping ground for various species with unresolved affinities. Now known to be more closely related to Old World babblers than to the warblers. Two species occur in the Fynbos.

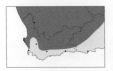

5 Layard's Warbler *Curruca layardi*

Overall blue-grey with striking pale eyes. Underparts paler grey with white vent. Throat pale with fine streaking. Tail black with white tip and outer edges. Female has slightly browner tones. Juvenile has slate-brown upperparts and slightly buffy underparts; throat lacks streaking. **Size** 14cm; 14–16g. **Call** Similar to Chestnut-vented Warbler but lacks characteristic *cher-eeetr tik-tik-tik* phrase of that species. Alarm call is long *tit-trt-trt-trt-trt*. **Status and Habitat** Fairly common resident, favouring drier, bushy environments, particularly on arid edges of the Fynbos Biome. Absent from the Overberg and from moist mountain Fynbos. Occurs in coastal Strandveld on the West Coast, from Blaauwberg northwards. **Endemism** Southern Africa.

1 Chestnut-vented Warbler *Curruca subcaerulea*
A slate-grey, warbler-like bird with striking pale eyes. Underparts grey with diagnostic chestnut vent. Throat pale grey with heavy streaking. Tail black with white tip and outer edges. Juvenile lacks obvious throat streaking; vent paler chestnut. **Size** 15cm; 12–18g. **Call** Typical call is harsh *cher-eeetr tik-tik-tik*. Song is pleasant melodious series of whistled phrases, often including mimicry of other species. **Status and Habitat** A common resident in thick shrubby areas. Favours coastal Strandveld on West Coast and arid thicket across rest of Fynbos Biome. Absent from Fynbos vegetation types and largely absent from coastal lowlands east of Cape Town.

White-eyes   Family Zosteropidae
Small, social birds that eat insects, fruit and nectar. Most species are shades of green, grey or olive. Many with a conspicuous ring of small white feathers around eyes. One species in Biome.

2 Cape White-eye *Zosterops virens*
A charming and often confiding little bird. Upperparts greenish olive. Chin and throat yellow. Underparts grey with variable buff shading on flanks. Narrow, but bright and conspicuous, white eye-ring present, broken by small, black loral spot. Bill dark grey, paler grey towards base. Juvenile duller with narrower white eye-ring. **Size** 11cm; 11g. **Call** Very vocal, with twittering contact calls. Song is rambling warble containing various phrases. **Endemism** Southern Africa. **Status and Habitat** A very common, widespread resident throughout the Fynbos Biome. Favours moist environments with trees or larger shrubs. Abundant in gardens.

Sugarbirds   Family Promeropidae
Nectivores with a long tail and decurved bill. Strongly associated with proteas. No iridescence, unlike sunbirds. Endemic to southern Africa and comprises two species. One species occurs in the Biome.

3 Cape Sugarbird *Promerops cafer*
An iconic Fynbos bird. Brown above and largely buff to white below, with numerous brown streaks. Distinctive malar strip present. Vent bright yellow. Long, brown tail can be up to three times body length in male. Bill black, long and decurved. **Size** 28–48cm; 25–50g. **Call** Various harsh chirps, whistles and grating notes. **Status and Habitat** A common endemic found primarily in Fynbos habitats that contain proteas. Movements occur in response to food availability, and are often dictated by fire events. **Endemism** Fynbos Biome.

Starlings   Family Sturnidae
Most species have some iridescent plumage. Social, often forming flocks. Omnivorous. Cavity nesters, some breeding communally. Four species occur in the Fynbos, one of which is introduced.

4 Common Starling *Sturnus vulgaris* Ⓐ
Breeding male black with metallic green to purple lustre. Feathers pale-tipped, producing finely spotted appearance. Underparts heavily marked with white V-shaped spots. Can appear uniform black when pale tips to feathers abrade away. Bill yellow. Breeding female less metallic. Non-breeding birds have black bill and duller black plumage. Plain grey-brown juvenile separated from Wattled Starling by dark bill and rump. **Size** 21cm; 65–95g. **Call** Rich, warbled song of various high-pitched whines, squeaks and rattles. Regularly includes mimicry of other species. **Status and Habitat** Well-established alien found in all habitats; largely absent from mountain Fynbos.

1 Wattled Starling *Creatophora cinerea*
A small, short-tailed starling with a pale rump and bill. Male pale grey with black flight and tail feathers. Female has dark brown flight and tail feathers. Female and non-breeding male have plain head, with some pale yellow skin behind eye and black malar stripes. Juvenile like female but bill yellower. Breeding male develops extensive variable black and bright yellow bare skin and wattles on head. In flight, pale rump is conspicuous. **Size** 21cm; 52–84g. **Call** Song is warbled melody of high-pitched whines, squeaks and cackles, similar to Common Starling. Flight call is series of *skreak-skreak* notes. **Status and Habitat** Fairly common, nomadic visitor. Most common on western coastal plain and the Overberg. Can occur in large flocks, often in the company of Pied Starlings.

2 Pied Starling *Lamprotornis bicolor*
A large, blackish-brown starling with limited metallic green sheen and striking white eyes. Lower mandible yellow with black tip. Gape fleshy and bright yellow. Vent white. Juvenile matt-black with dark eyes; bill all black with dull yellow gape. **Size** 27cm; 94–112g. **Call** Nasal *skeer-kerrra-kerrra*, often given in flight. **Status and Habitat** Very common resident, particularly on western coastal plain and in Overberg. Rare in mountain Fynbos habitat and absent from Cape Peninsula. Roosts and breeds communally in sand banks and road cuttings. **Endemism** Southern Africa.

3 Red-winged Starling *Onychognathus morio*
A large, long-tailed, social starling. All black with glossy sheen. Brick-red primary feathers form obvious leading edge to folded wing. Primaries dark-tipped. Female has grey hood which merges with black feathers on upper breast and nape. Juvenile like male, but with dull, matt-black plumage. Dark eyes, longer tail and rufous flight feathers separate this species from similar Pale-winged Starling, which occurs in rocky Succulent Karoo habitats neighbouring the Fynbos Biome. **Size** 28cm; 120–155g. **Call** Loud, melodious *cher-leeeeooo* whistle. Alarm call is grating *garrrr*. **Status and Habitat** A common resident and cliff nester, closely associated with mountainous areas. Readily nests on buildings and very common in urban areas.

Chats and Old World flycatchers   Family Muscicapidae
Small to medium-sized insectivorous birds. Many are very vocal and some are good songsters. The juvenile plumage is usually heavily mottled or spotted. There are 11 species in the Biome.

4 Karoo Scrub Robin *Cercotrichas coryphoeus*
Greyish brown overall. Short, white eyebrow present. Thin white line below eye. Small white to grey moustachial stripes present. Throat pale. Small, but prominent, white outer tail tips to the dark tail. Juvenile has pale-edged back feathers and mottled underparts. **Size** 14–16cm; 18–23g. **Call** Very vocal. Song is variable mixture of harsh chittering and sizzling notes and whistles. **Status and Habitat** A common and conspicuous resident. Occurs in most bushy environments but absent from mountain Fynbos and urban areas. Rare or absent from extensive cultivated agricultural areas. **Endemism** Southern Africa.

5 Chat Flycatcher *Melaenornis infuscatus*
Very plain and nondescript, with no obvious markings. Plain brown all over with darker brown wing feathers and coverts, which are narrowly edged in pale buff. Juvenile darker brown above with pale buff spotting. Pale below with heavy streaking on breast and flanks. Gape yellow. Separated from chats by longer, plain tail and unmarked rump. **Size** 20cm; 39g. **Call** Song is collection of harsh churring and grating notes. **Status and Habitat** Conspicuous resident, readily perching on telephone poles and wires. Found in coastal lowlands north of the Berg River; common only from Lambert's Bay northwards. Range in Biome has contracted owing to habitat transformation.

1 Fiscal Flycatcher *Melaenornis silens*

A distinctly pied bird. Male all black above with white panel in wing. Underparts pale grey, sometimes appearing almost white. Upper two-thirds of outer tail have large white patches. Female dusky above with reduced, white tail patches. Underparts more greyish. Juvenile has dark grey-brown upperparts with heavy buff spotting. Underparts pale grey and mottled. Separated from Southern Fiscal by shorter tail, much finer bill and white patches in wing being limited to secondaries. **Size** 18–20cm; 22–36g. **Call** Long series of thin, high-pitched notes. **Status and Habitat** Common resident, associated with trees and absent from extensive areas of low indigenous vegetation. Readily uses alien trees. **Endemism** Southern Africa.

2 Cape Robin-Chat *Cossypha caffra*

Upperparts grey with brown tinge. Conspicuous white eyebrow present. Black face mask runs from lores to cheeks. Throat and breast orange. Belly pale grey. Vent and flanks pale orange. Rump and outer tail feathers rufous. Juvenile lacks eyebrow; browner overall with heavy buff mottling. **Size** 17cm; 23–38g. **Call** Song is short series of whistles. Regularly mimics a variety of other species. Alarm call is nasal *chur-der-durrr*. **Status and Habitat** A common resident wherever there is suitable bushy cover.

3 Cape Rock Thrush *Monticola rupestris*

A large, robust rock thrush. Male has diagnostic orange-brown back. Head uniform blue-grey. Underparts, including upper breast, dark orange. Female has mottled brown head; orange underparts with some inconspicuous brown scaling. Juvenile like female, but heavily spotted with buff. Female separated from female Sentinel Rock Thrush by darker orange underparts, especially on breast. Male easily distinguished by brown, not blue, back and orange upper breast. **Size** 20–22cm; 50–65g. **Call** Loud melodious whistled song. **Status and Habitat** Common resident. Occurs in rocky areas and largely confined to mountain Fynbos. **Endemism** Southern Africa.

4 Sentinel Rock Thrush *Monticola explorator*

Smaller than Cape Rock Thrush. Male has uniform blue-grey back, head and breast. Underparts orange. Female brown above with pale buff to orange underparts. Breast and throat paler with extensive brown and white mottling. Juvenile like female, with extensive buff spotting. **Size** 18–20cm; 44–51g. **Call** Whistled song similar to but softer and more varied than Cape Rock Thrush. Can include mimicry of other species. **Status and Habitat** Uncommon, localised resident with some seasonal altitudinal movements. Found almost exclusively in rocky mountain Fynbos. In winter, birds may pitch up far away from these habitats. **Endemism** Southern Africa.

5 African Stonechat *Saxicola torquatus*

Striking and conspicuous. Male has all-black head. Feathers on back and mantle black, sometimes edged brown. White patch on wing coverts. Large white neck patch on side of head. Breast, chest and flanks rich orange to chestnut. Belly white. Female duller, with grey-brown head and faint eyebrow. Chest and flanks duller orange-brown. Juvenile like female; spotted buff above, with mottled chest. **Size** 13cm; 12–17g. **Call** *Weet-weet* and harsh *chak*. Song is high-pitched series of fast whistles. **Status and Habitat** Common resident in almost all habitat types; avoids suburbia.

6 Sickle-winged Chat *Emarginata sinuata*

Brown-grey overall. Upperparts darker and contrasting with pale grey underparts. Thin white eye-ring present. Rump and outer tail feathers dull orange. Central tail black, forming dark V-shape. Juvenile buff-spotted above and mottled below. Wing-flicks on landing, but not as regularly or prodigiously as Familiar Chat. More slender and longer legged in appearance than far more common Familiar Chat. **Size** 15cm; 17–24g. **Call** Soft *tree-tree* or buzzy *brrr-brrr*. Not very vocal. **Status and Habitat** Locally common resident, but rare or absent from much of the Fynbos Biome. Common on the West Coast, particularly in Vredenburg and St Helena Bay area. **Endemism** Southern Africa.

1 **Familiar Chat** *Oenanthe familiaris*

Greyish brown overall. Upperparts slightly darker than underparts, but no sharp contrast. Thin white eye-ring and orange-brown cheek patch (often indistinct) present. Rump and outer tail feathers rusty-orange. Central tail and tail tip black, forming T-shape. Juvenile mottled below. Characteristically flicks wings on landing. Similar to Sickle-winged Chat, which also habitually flicks wings. Familiar Chat best separated by not showing marked contrast between upper- and underparts. **Size** 15cm; 14–26g. **Call** Variety of squeaky and grating call notes and sharp whistles. Alarm call is harsh *shek-shek*. **Status and Habitat** A common, conspicuous resident. Favours rocky and mountainous areas. Away from rocky areas, strongly associated with buildings and other artificial structures, but absent from urban areas.

2 **Capped Wheatear** *Oenanthe pileata*

Adult has rich brown back, black head and broad black breast band. Very large white eyebrows meet on frons. Throat white. Belly white with buff flanks. Juvenile pale brown above, buff below, with variable mottling especially on breast. Often responsible for claims of vagrant migratory wheatears, but juvenile Capped Wheatear has dull yellow base to bill, different tail pattern and shorter wings. **Size** 17cm; 23–32g. **Call** A regularly uttered *chip*. Song is pleasant rambling warble with loud chattering and strident whistles. Can include mimicry of many species. **Status and Habitat** Very common, conspicuous resident with a preference for flat, disturbed agricultural areas or natural vegetation subject to heavy grazing. Not found in mountain Fynbos.

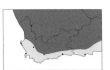

3 **Mountain Wheatear** *Myrmecocichla monticola*

Male with range of colour morphs. Grey morph uniform blue-grey, with or without white shoulder patches. Wings black. Dark morph all black, usually with white shoulder patches and occasionally white or grey crown. Pied form is like dark morph with white belly. Female all sooty brown with paler vent. Both sexes and all forms have white rump and upper outer tail feathers. Juvenile similar to female. **Size** 19cm; 32–45g. **Call** Melodious whistling with various chattering and churring phrases. **Status and Habitat** Rare in coastal lowlands and southern mountain ranges. Common along more arid edges with Succulent Karoo and northern mountain ranges. Always in association with natural or artificial rocky areas. Occasionally found around farm buildings.

Sunbirds   Family Nectariniidae

Beautiful, vocal and active nectivores with a slender, decurved bill. Sexes highly dimorphic in most species. Males usually have striking coloration, almost always with some iridescence. Females are much plainer. The nest is a hanging, intricately weaved, oval ball with a side entrance. Five species are found in the Fynbos, where they are important pollinators for a range of plant species.

4 **Orange-breasted Sunbird** *Anthobaphes violacea*

One of South Africa's most spectacular birds and a true Fynbos endemic. Male has dark green, metallic head and throat. Narrow violet band separates green throat from bright orange breast. Orange fades to yellow on belly. Central tail feathers extended. Female upperparts olive-green to brownish. Yellowish-olive underparts distinguish female from other female sunbirds in the region. Juvenile like female. **Size** 12–15cm; 7–13g. **Call** Very vocal. Frequently uttered nasal *tseep-tseep*. Song is high-pitched warble. **Status and Habitat** Common in all Fynbos habitats that contain ericas and other suitable nectar plants. Resident, but with some movements in response to food availability and may move to lower altitudes in winter. **Endemism** Fynbos Biome.

1 Amethyst Sunbird *Chalcomitra amethystina*

Male black with metallic green crown and purple throat, rump and shoulder patches. Can appear completely black in poor light. Female and juvenile more boldly marked than other female sunbirds in region; upperparts dark greyish brown; underparts pale, heavily streaked, especially on throat. Pale eyebrow and malar stripe present. **Size** 15cm; 11–19g. **Call** High-pitched, twittering song with characteristic regular *cheap* or *chip* notes. Calls for long intervals. **Status and Habitat** Widespread, but usually frequents only Fynbos habitats close to suitable gardens and thickets. A bird of well-wooded, moist habitats that has greatly expanded its range into the Western Cape.

2 Malachite Sunbird *Nectarinia famosa*

The largest sunbird in the Fynbos Biome. Bright metallic green breeding male is highly distinctive. Flight feathers and long central tail feathers sooty black. Yellow pectoral tufts seen only when displaying. Female brownish above, with contrasting paler underparts. Throat and chest faintly mottled. Thin, buff eyebrow and diffuse malar stripe present. Outer tail white. Bill black, long and decurved. Juvenile similar to female. **Size** 14–25cm; 11–25g. **Call** Piercing *seep-seep* notes as well as other sharp notes. Also produces soft but rich warbling song. **Status and Habitat** Common in all Fynbos, Renosterveld and Strandveld habitat types. An important pollinator. Significant movements can occur in response to food availability.

3 Southern Double-collared Sunbird *Cinnyris chalybeus*

Similar to Greater Double-collared Sunbird in coloration, but smaller, with shorter and finer bill and much narrower red breast band. Male head and throat metallic green. Narrow, red breast band bordered above by thin bright blue band. Belly grey. Upper tail coverts iridescent blue. Bright yellow pectoral tufts exposed when male displays. Female and juvenile greyish brown overall. **Size** 12cm; 6–10g. **Call** Regularly repeated *chee-chee* call. Song high-pitched, fast and metallic. **Status and Habitat** Resident. The most common sunbird in the Fynbos Biome, found in all habitats, including gardens. **Endemism** Southern Africa.

4 Greater Double-collared Sunbird *Cinnyris afer*

Head and throat of male metallic green. Broad, bright red breast band more than 15mm wide, notably wider than in smaller Southern Double-collared Sunbird. Red band bordered above by bright blue band. Belly olive-grey. Upper tail coverts iridescent blue. Female and juvenile greyish brown. Decurved bill longer and heavier than in Southern Double-collared Sunbird. **Size** 14cm; 10–18g. **Call** Harsh *tchut-tchut-tchut* calls. Metallic song is slower and deeper than that of Southern Double-collared Sunbird. **Status and Habitat** Primarily a bird of forest edges, thickets and gardens. Can be found in Fynbos habitats close to these habitat types. Occurs throughout the southern Cape as far west as Greyton. **Endemism** Fynbos Biome.

Old World sparrows   Family Passeridae

All are primarily seedeaters that are fond of more open habitats. Most are social, occurring in small to large flocks. Two species occur in the Fynbos Biome. The introduced House Sparrow (*Passer domesticus*) is associated with human development and is seldom seen in natural veld.

1 Cape Sparrow *Passer melanurus*

Male has black face and crown. Broad white mark runs from top of eye through ear coverts to throat, forming distinctive C-shaped marking. Nape grey; back chestnut. Belly white with greyish flanks. Bill stout, black, becoming horn-coloured when not breeding. Female much duller, having grey head with broad white eyebrow that also forms washed-out C-shaped marking. Juvenile duller than female. **Size** 15cm; 26–35g. **Call** Several musical *cheep* and *chip* notes. Frequently utters rattling alarm call. **Status and Habitat** Abundant resident, being found in all habitat types. Scarce in mountain Fynbos. Has responded well to agricultural activities and occurs in very large numbers in these areas.

Weavers   Family Ploceidae

Renowned for their intricately woven nests. Most weavers are social and nest in colonies. The males are generally brightly coloured in the breeding season. Primarily seedeaters but also feeds on insects and nectar. Four species occur in the Fynbos.

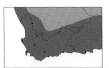

2 Cape Weaver *Ploceus capensis*

A large weaver. Breeding male has golden-yellow head and underparts. Face, frons and throat chestnut to orange, merging with surrounding yellow plumage. Back greenish yellow. Eyes striking pale yellow. Bill black, long and pointed. Non-breeding male much duller, with brown bill. Female and juvenile have olive-green head and back. Underparts dull lemon-yellow. Eyes dark brown. Bill brown. Female and juvenile best told from female Southern Masked Weaver by long, heavy bill and yellow, not whitish, underparts. **Size** 17cm; 28–54g. **Call** Harsh swizzling song. Contact call is *chack*. **Status and Habitat** Abundant resident in all habitat types. Least common in mountain Fynbos. Colonies breed in reedbeds or in trees, preferably overhanging water.

3 Southern Masked Weaver *Ploceus velatus*

Breeding male has black face, throat and forehead. Bill short, thick and black. Crown and underparts bright yellow. Back and mantle greenish yellow with dark streaks. Female and non-breeding male have olive-green upperparts. Throat and breast yellowish, fading to dull white on belly. Eyes red-brown, bill horn-coloured. Juvenile similar to non-breeding female. **Size** 16cm; 30–44g. **Call** Typical swizzling and churring weaver song. Also, sharp *zik, zik* calls. **Status and Habitat** Common resident in most habitat types. Seldom encountered in high-altitude mountain Fynbos. In the non-breeding season, they can form large flocks in agricultural areas.

4 Southern Red Bishop *Euplectes orix*

Breeding male strikingly red and black, easily identifiable. Non-breeding male and female have yellowish to buffy eyebrow; upperparts heavily streaked dark brown. Underparts pale brown to buff, with dark streaking. Female often less heavily streaked on underparts. Juvenile similar to female but with more buff coloration. Female and non-breeding male best told from female Yellow Bishop by lighter streaking below and undertail coverts that almost reach tip of very short tail. **Size** 12cm; 18–29g. **Call** Displaying male has buzzing chirping song. Flight call is *cheet-cheet*. **Status and Habitat** Abundant resident in agricultural areas. Very rare or absent from mountain Fynbos habitat. A colonial breeder favouring *Phragmites* reedbeds.

1 Yellow Bishop *Euplectes capensis*

Breeding male has all-black head and underparts, with bright yellow shoulder patches, rump and lower back. Non-breeding male light brown with very heavy, dark brown streaking. Some yellow patches are retained on shoulders and rump. Female light brown with heavy streaking. Bill thick, conical and horn-coloured. Pale eyebrow present. Juvenile like female, but with buff back and less streaking. Female best told from female southern Red Bishop by being paler below, with more contrasting streaks, and by the longer tail with relatively shorter undertail coverts. **Size** 15–18cm; 25–50g. **Call** Series of high-pitched notes ending in long, buzzing call. **Status and Habitat** Common resident in wide variety of habitats, including mountain Fynbos. Has adapted to cultivated areas where it is very common. Breeds in wet habitats. Does not breed in colonies.

Waxbills   Family Estrildidae

Small birds. Most species are strongly patterned and brightly coloured. They primarily feed on grass seeds. Found in a wide range of habitats. Three species occur in the Fynbos.

2 Swee Waxbill *Coccopygia melanotis*

Charming little birds, usually seen in small flocks. Male has olive back, grey head and greyish underparts. Rump, upper tail coverts and lower back bright red. Black mask below eye, from cheek to throat. Bill bicoloured; upper mandible black, lower bright red. Female lacks black face mask. Juvenile duller with black bill. **Size** 9cm; 5–9g. **Call** Contact call is regularly repeated *swee-swee*. Song is high-pitched series of soft whistles. **Status and Habitat** A bird of moist forest edges and thickets. Has expanded its range in the Western Cape. Occurs in riparian areas, alien thickets and gardens mainly associated with the Cape Fold Mountains. Absent from the western coastal plain. **Endemism** Southern Africa.

3 Common Waxbill *Estrilda astrild*

A small, greyish-brown bird with fine barring on back, underparts and rump. Plumage has pinkish hue, especially on underparts; red belly patch present. Bill bright red and conical. Red mask runs from base of bill through eye. Female has smaller red belly patch than male. Juvenile duller overall with black bill. **Size** 11cm; 7–10g. **Call** Song is nasal *di-di-cheerrr*. Contact and flight call is nasal *tcheek, tcheek, tcheek*. **Status and Habitat** Very common resident. Favours dense vegetation and reedbeds. Radiates out from these moist environments to feed.

4 Quailfinch *Ortygospiza atricollis*

An attractive, compact little bird. Usually only seen when flushed, seldom allowing good views. Male brownish grey above with black face, white chin patch and bright red bill. White, circular line around eye to bill. Breast and flanks barred black and white, belly chestnut. Female lacks black face and much paler overall. Juvenile paler than female with limited barring and darker bill. **Size** 10cm; 9–14g. **Call** Often detected by distinctive squeaky flight call *tchink-tchink*. **Status and Habitat** Uncommon, highly nomadic resident. Occurs most frequently in lowlands of the Overberg and West Coast, with a preference for short grassy areas, particularly around vleis.

Whydahs and indigobirds   Family Viduidae

An interesting family of small finches endemic to sub-Saharan Africa. Specialised brood parasites. Most are species-specific parasites on waxbills, firefinches and twinspots (family Estrildidae). Breeding males are brightly coloured, while females and non-breeding males are cryptically patterned. They feed primarily on seed. Only one widespread species occurs in the Fynbos Biome.

1 Pin-tailed Whydah *Vidua macroura*

Breeding male highly distinctive. White below and black above with white shoulders and white rump. Black tail extremely long. Bill conical, thick and red. Non-breeding male largely brown with heavily black-streaked upperparts. Underparts buff to cream. Head boldly marked with black streaks and pronounced pale eyebrow. Bill remains red. Female similar to non-breeding male, with dark bill. Juvenile with plain brown upperparts and cream underparts. Head plain with pale eyebrow. **Size** 12cm; breeding male 34cm; 13–17g. **Call** Series of sharp *chip-chip-chip* calls. Male calls incessantly during breeding season. **Status and Habitat** Common resident, found in wide range of habitats. Mainly parasitises Common Waxbill, but Swee Waxbill has also been recorded as a host. Extremely pugnacious at feeders, driving away other birds much larger than itself.

Pipits, longclaws and wagtails   Family Motacillidae

Specialised ground dwellers with a preference for open habitats. Most are cryptically coloured, but some species have brightly coloured underparts. All have white outer tail feathers or tips to their tail. Feed on invertebrate prey, very rarely taking small vertebrates. Five species occur in the Fynbos.

2 Cape Wagtail *Motacilla capensis*

The only resident and regularly recorded wagtail in the Fynbos Biome. Upperparts grey-brown with cream eyebrow. Throat creamy white with dark brown, V-shaped breast band. Flanks brown, fading to creamy white on belly. Long, dark brown tail has white outer tail feathers. Bill black, straight and slender. Juvenile browner overall with buff-yellow belly. **Size** 20cm; 21g. **Call** Familiar *tseee-chee-chee* and regularly uttered *tseep* calls. **Status and Habitat** A very common resident, found in diverse habitats, often in association with water.

3 Cape Longclaw *Macronyx capensis*

The only longclaw in the Fynbos Biome. Easily identified by vivid orange throat, encircled by broad black band. Upperparts brown, heavily scalloped with dark brown. Belly bright orange-yellow. Distinct orange eyebrow present. Tail short with bold white outer tips, conspicuous in flight. Female duller with narrower collar. Juvenile lacks orange throat, and collar comprises dull smudges only. **Size** 20cm; 45g. **Call** Cat-like *meew* uttered from perch or in flight. Also utters high-pitched *tsweet* and nasal *skeeaaa* alarm call. **Status and Habitat** Common resident. Has a preference for wetland fringes and seasonally flooded grasslands. **Endemism** Southern Africa.

4 African Pipit *Anthus cinnamomeus*

While pipits can be amongst the most challenging birds to identify, the three species in the Fynbos Biome can be readily separated if seen well. Coloration can be very variable, but relatively small and slender African Pipit has clearly streaked back, yellow base to bill and white outer tail feathers. Facial markings bold; breast well streaked. Belly white to buff. Juvenile darker and more heavily streaked. **Size** 17cm; 25g. **Call** Diagnostic *pli-pli-pli*. Alarm call when flushed is *tshisik*. **Status and Habitat** Common resident of open grassland and very common in agricultural areas, especially in shortly grazed pastures. The default pipit throughout South Africa. Not common in intact Fynbos, Renosterveld or Strandveld, but frequents recently burnt or open disturbed areas.

Cape Longclaw feeding on Clicking Stream Frog

1 Nicholson's Pipit *Anthus nicholsoni*
Superficially similar and often co-occurring with smaller African Pipit. Coloration variable, but breast streaking and facial markings never as bold as in African Pipit. Back streaked, but often rather faintly. Bill with pink or occasionally yellowish base. Tail feathers buff, not white. The local subspecies (*A. n. primarius*) can have very buff to light brown underparts. Juvenile darker and more boldly marked. **Size** 19cm; 30g. **Call** Monotonous, often comprising three distinct notes: *tchreep-tritit-churup*. Alarm call when flushed is *killink*. **Status and Habitat** Uncommon but under-recorded resident with a preference for open, stony or rocky areas. Readily utilises suitable agricultural areas. Exploits recently burnt mountain Fynbos.

2 Plain-backed Pipit *Anthus leucophrys*
Readily distinguished from other local pipits by plain grey-brown back. Breast very lightly streaked. Outer tail feathers buff, not white. Base of bill yellowish. Juvenile darker brown above with more heavily streaked breast. **Size** 17cm; 26g. **Call** Monotonous series of double notes: *thceep-cheroooo*. Alarm call when flushed is *tsissik*. **Status and Habitat** Fairly common nomad, occurring primarily in rocky mountainous Fynbos. Very quick to colonise areas after fire and will move away once the vegetation becomes too dense. Frequently utilises sandy beaches above high-water mark. Rare in agricultural areas.

Finches   Family Fringillidae

These birds have a strong conical bill and feed on seeds. Eight species occur regularly in the Fynbos. The alien Common Chaffinch (*Fringilla coelebs*) is established in the vicinity of Cape Town, where it is confined to wooded gardens and plantations.

3 Forest Canary *Crithagra scotops*
A small, dark and handsome canary. Upper- and underparts yellow-green, heavily marked with dark streaking. Narrow, bright yellow eyebrow and throat patch present. Male has blackish face, which contrasts with pinkish-horn bill and yellow throat. Female duller overall with greyish face and more heavily streaked underparts. Juvenile duller than female. **Size** 13cm; 12–20g. **Call** Short, high-pitched, warbling song. Contact call is very high-pitched *tseeek*. **Status and Habitat** Essentially a forest species that occurs in forested kloofs, alien thickets and gardens in southern part of the Fynbos Biome. Frequents moist Fynbos habitats in close proximity to its preferred habitat.

4 Cape Siskin *Crithagra totta*
Male has brown back and greyish-brown head and nape. Crown finely streaked with yellow; faint eyebrow present. Underparts lemon-yellow. Black tail has narrow white tip. Each primary has distinctive white tip, resulting in series of white spots on folded wing. Female duller with faint streaking on throat and breast. Juvenile more heavily streaked; lacks white tail and primary tips. **Size** 12cm; 10–16g. **Call** Very vocal. Contact call is regularly repeated *thceep-chup-chup* or variation thereof. **Status and Habitat** Locally common resident with preference for rocky Fynbos habitat. Usually seen in pairs or small groups, rarely forming large flocks. **Endemism** Fynbos Biome.

1 Yellow Canary *Crithagra flaviventris*

The subspecies *C. f. flaviventris* occurs in the Fynbos Biome. Male has olive-yellow upperparts with bright yellow face markings, including frons and long eyebrow. Underparts bright yellow with variable olive shading on breast and flanks. Female very different, brown overall with greenish-yellow rump and lower back. Upperparts and chest streaked brown. Juvenile like female, but more heavily streaked. Grey to horn-coloured bill smaller than that of superficially similar Brimstone Canary, which has greenish (not yellow) frons. **Size** 13cm; 13–20g. **Call** Fast warbling and melodious song. **Status and Habitat** A common resident that occurs throughout the Fynbos Biome but with a distinct preference for low-lying Fynbos, Renosterveld and Strandveld areas. Largely avoids mountain Fynbos.

2 Brimstone Canary *Crithagra sulphurata*

Largest and darkest subspecies (*C. s. sulphurata*) occurs in the Fynbos Biome. Upperparts olive-yellow with fine dark streaking. Distinct eyebrow bright yellow. Breast olive-yellow, contrasting with bright yellow throat. Bill extremely stout, horn. Told from male Yellow Canary by much heavier bill, larger size and greenish frons. **Size** 14cm; 15–23g. **Call** Slow musical mix of warbles and whistles. Contact call is distinctive *tchee-u-wee*. **Status and Habitat** Fairly common resident in southern parts of the Fynbos Biome, but largely absent from more arid northern areas. Found in thicket, riparian and wooded areas.

3 Streaky-headed Seedeater *Crithagra gularis*

A mostly brown canary with a very prominent long and narrow white eyebrow. Upperparts brown without white wing bars. Underparts paler brown, throat white. Rump brown. Bill finer than White-throated Canary or Protea Canary. Juvenile has streaking or blotching, especially on underparts. **Size** 15cm; 12–25g. **Call** Melodious song incorporating *trrreet* contact call. **Status and Habitat** Common resident. Found in diverse array of habitats, with a preference for thickets and riparian areas. Has undergone extensive range extension and is now found throughout the Fynbos Biome.

4 White-throated Canary *Crithagra albogularis*

A large, mostly grey-brown canary with a prominent white throat, chin and pale eyebrow. Bill very large and pale pink to horn. No white bars on wings. Rump yellow to greenish yellow. Female and juvenile slightly duller, especially on rump. **Size** 16cm; 18–38g. **Call** Contact call is piercing *tsuu-eeeee*. Song is typically canary-like, melodious and very varied. Often includes mimicry of other species. **Status and Habitat** Common resident, found throughout the Fynbos Biome, with a preference for drier areas. Largely absent from moist mountain Fynbos habitats. Usually found in pairs or small groups, especially at water points, which they visit regularly.

5 Protea Canary *Crithagra leucoptera* **NT**

A largely brown canary, superficially similar to White-throated Canary. Protea Canary has conspicuous dark patch between bill and white throat, an indistinct eyebrow and two distinct white wing bars. Rump brown, not yellow. Bill large and pale pink to horn. **Size** 15cm; 18–25g. **Call** Contact call is *tree-dili-eeeee*. Song includes various repetitive elements interspersed with mimicry of various species and the contact call. **Status and Habitat** Uncommon and unobtrusive. A true Fynbos endemic found almost exclusively in mountain Fynbos. Inexplicably absent from the Cape Peninsula. Forages on range of seeds, vegetation, fruit and nectar, but favours large *Protea* seeds. **Endemism** Fynbos Biome. **Conservation Status** Near Threatened.

1 Cape Canary *Serinus canicollis*

Male bright yellow-green with large, distinctive, blue-grey nape and mantle. Grey hood runs around to sides of upper breast, occasionally almost forming a complete collar. Face yellow-green with no eyebrow or any other obvious facial markings. Female duller with light streaking on flanks and back. Bill heavy and grey to horn. Juvenile drabber than female with heavily streaked under- and upperparts. Easily separated from juvenile and female Yellow Canary by absence of eyebrow. **Size** 12cm; 12–22g. **Call** Fast warbling high-pitched song. Contact call is distinctive *peeet* or *pee-weee*. **Status and Habitat** A common canary throughout the Fynbos Biome except for the Strandveld of the West Coast, where it is scarce. Can form large flocks. **Endemism** Southern Africa.

Old World buntings   Family Emberizidae

Morphologically similar sparrow-like birds. They have a conical bill and feed on seeds. Two species occur regularly in the Fynbos Biome. The Cinnamon-breasted Bunting (*Emberiza tahapisi*) is occasionally encountered in Fynbos habitats and may become established in future.

2 Lark-like Bunting *Emberiza impetuani*

A quintessential little brown job (LBJ) with no obvious diagnostic features. Best identified by its general size, shape and behaviour. Pale buffy eyebrow evident and an important feature. Upperparts buff to brown. Back, mantle and crown streaked with dark grey. Flight feathers and coverts have dark, central panels. Leading edges of flight feathers rufous, visible as rufous panel in folded wing. Juvenile has mottled breast and buff to pale brown underparts. **Size** 14cm; 13–20g. **Call** Short, high-pitched, canary-like song. The *tuk-tuk* flight call is a good identification feature. **Status and Habitat** A common, nomadic bird of the arid interior, occurring peripherally in the Fynbos Biome. Regular in the Strandveld of the West Coast, particularly in summer.

3 Cape Bunting *Emberiza capensis*

A dapper little bird. Mantle and nape grey-brown, streaked with black. Wing coverts chestnut. Underparts pale grey to buff. Head pattern very bold, with three black and two white stripes. Top of head grey, streaked with black. Throat white or pale grey. Female similar, but face stripes more buff in colour. Juvenile has faintly striped or mottled breast. **Size** 16cm; 17–27g. **Call** Regularly repeated nasal *wer we-wer*. Song is clear *chrip chip chup chip tur-twee*. **Status and Habitat** Common resident. Often very confiding. Found in all Fynbos, Renosterveld and Strandveld types. Scarce in intensive agricultural areas and absent from urban areas.

Mammals

Africa is rightly famous for its mammal fauna. This great diversity of species includes many of the most iconic and spectacular species on the planet. Several are large, diurnal and readily seen, underpinning a massive tourism industry. In contrast, one can spend a full day hiking in pristine mountain Fynbos and see no or only very few mammal species. While the Fynbos Biome does have a variety of interesting mammals, most are secretive and seldom observed.

Africa is home to about 274 indigenous land mammal species. This guide includes 91 species in 28 families (roughly a third of the country count). It excludes species that have been introduced for game farming or tourism purposes as well as those confined to urban and transformed environments. The alien Himalayan Tahr is discussed, as it occurs in the Fynbos on Table Mountain.

ENDEMISM

Most mammal species have large to very large distribution ranges and there are relatively few narrow endemics. Of the 90 indigenous mammal species included in this book, 21 species are endemic to South Africa, five to the Fynbos Biome and five to the greater Cape Floristic Region.

Cape Clawless Otter

Mammal taxa endemic to the Fynbos Biome	
Fynbos Golden Mole	Amblysomus corriae
Boosman's Long-tailed Forest Shrew	Myosorex longicaudatus boosmani
Cape Spiny Mouse	Acomys subspinosus
Cape Marsh Rat	Dasymys capensis
Bontebok	Damaliscus pygargus pygargus
Mammal taxa endemic to the CFR	
Van Zyl's Golden Mole	Cryptochloris zyli
Cape Golden Mole	Chrysochloris asiatica
Grant's Golden Mole	Eremitalpa granti granti
Cape Gerbil	Gerbilliscus afra
Barbour's Rock Mouse	Petromyscus barbouri

BAT ROOSTING SITES

The De Hoop Guano Caves near Bredasdorp are the most well-known cave roosting site in the Fynbos Biome and are estimated to harbour 300,000 bats of five different species: Natal Long-fingered Bat, Temminck's Hairy Bat, Egyptian Slit-faced Bat, Geoffroy's Horseshoe Bat and Cape Horseshoe Bat. Different parts of the cave system are utilised by different species. This site, as the others within South Africa, is of critical conservation significance. Bats assist local farmers by consuming an estimated 100 tons of insects annually. They also offer a great service to the general public, as research has shown that some bats (*Myotis* spp. specifically) can each eat some 600 mosquitoes per hour.

Natal Long-fingered Bats roosting in cave

CONSERVATION CONCERN

In the Fynbos Biome, nine mammal species are classified as threatened and an additional seven as Near Threatened. As such, almost 18% of the mammal species in the Fynbos Biome are considered to be of conservation concern.

Several species of large mammal were historically eradicated from the Fynbos Biome. Many of these are widespread and the extinctions were localised. However, two taxa, the Cape Lion (*Panthera leo melanochaita*) and the Blue Buck (*Hippotragus leucophaeus*) had limited distributions and became globally extinct. Some species that were previously eradicated, such as the Common Hippopotamus, have been reintroduced into protected areas in the Biome. Unfortunately, current protected areas are too small and fragmented for the reintroduction of many other species, such as African Wild Dog (*Lycaon pictus*) and Spotted Hyena (*Crocuta crocuta*).

Mammal species of conservation concern		
Critically Endangered (CR)		
1	Boosman's Long-tailed Forest Shrew	*Myosorex longicaudatus boosmani*
2	Riverine Rabbit	*Bunolagus monticularis*
Endangered (EN)		
3	Van Zyl's Golden Mole	*Cryptochloris zyli*
Vulnerable (VU)		
4	Grant's Golden Mole	*Eremitalpa granti granti*
5	Namibian Long-eared Bat	*Laephotis namibensis*
6	White-tailed Rat	*Mystromys albicaudatus*
7	Cape Marsh Rat	*Dasymys capensis*
8	Leopard	*Panthera pardus*
9	Bontebok	*Damaliscus pygargus pygargus*
Near Threatened (NT)		
10	Fynbos Golden Mole	*Amblysomus corriae*
11	Spectacled Dormouse	*Graphiurus ocularis*
12	Laminate Vlei Rat	*Otomys laminatus*
13	Cape Clawless Otter	*Aonyx capensis*
14	African Striped Weasel	*Poecilogale albinucha*
15	Brown Hyaena	*Parahyaena brunnea*
16	Grey Rhebok	*Pelea capreolus*

The large Cape Dune Mole-rat conducts practically all aspects of its life underground.

LIFE HISTORY

Mammals are secretive and one is generally only aware of a small percentage of the overall species diversity in a given area. Approximately 70% of the mammals in the Fynbos Biome are predominantly nocturnal. The majority of species live a solitary existence, only deviating from this when briefly pairing up to mate and when

Cape Grysbok are able to survive in smaller remnants.

The Cape Fox shelters in burrows during the day.

The Namaqua Rock Mouse is one of the most frequently encountered rodents in the Biome.

Cape Hares are tricky to distinguish from Scrub Hares.

females have dependent young. Some species, such as the Chacma Baboon and many bat species, are however social and live in groups.

Home range size varies greatly in the Fynbos Biome. For the larger carnivores, it can be exceptionally large. Leopard, for example, can have a home range of up to 600km^2 in the Cape Fold Mountains.

Mammals are adapted to survive the fire-driven Fynbos and Renosterveld landscapes they occupy by sheltering in rocky refugia or in burrows. More mobile species, such as antelope, are able to flee the fire front. Once the fire has passed, several mammals continue to survive in the post-fire landscape. In addition to reduced food sources, the lack of vegetation cover renders many species more vulnerable to predation. These direct and indirect mortalities can lead to a reduction in local population sizes. However, populations of rodents and other small mammals rebound quickly as the vegetation regenerates.

No mammal species within the Fynbos Biome are migratory. However, many species of bat undertake local seasonal movements between summer and wintering roosting caves.

IDENTIFYING MAMMALS

Separating different mammal families is generally straightforward, but there are exceptions, such as the different families of insectivorous bat, especially long-fingered bats (Miniopteridae) and vesper bats (Vespertilionidae). Other identification challenges in the Fynbos Biome are posed by the five species of golden mole (Chrysochloridae), five species of shrew (Soricidae) and 21 species of rats and mice (Muridae). And then there is the classic conundrum posed by the two hare species: Cape Hare and Scrub Hare.

Identification challenges are compounded by mammal behaviour and life histories. Many species are exceptionally secretive, live in dense cover and are quick to flee at the slightest disturbance. In addition, most mammals rely largely on scent rather than sound or visual cues to communicate. Humans are largely oblivious to these scent signals and we are therefore often completely oblivious to an animal's presence. Frustratingly with mammals, even when seen well, many of the smaller species require physical measurements or skeletal or dental details to confirm the identification, making in-field identification impossible.

A number of animals are seen only when found dead. This can potentially allow for the identification of species. People are encouraged to photograph any interesting live or dead animal they encounter. For dead small mammals, it is important to get details of the dorsal and ventral sides and, if possible, pictures that show the tail length relative to the head–body length. Some form of size reference is very important.

Resources such as **iNaturalist.org** can assist in confirming identifications. It may however not be possible to identify some animals to species level, even with excellent photographs.

Identification features

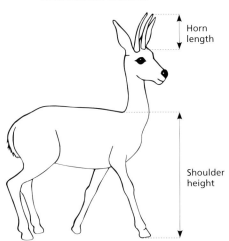
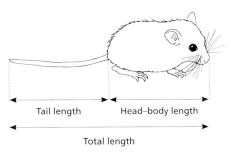

HOOFED MAMMALS: EVEN-TOED OR ODD-TOED?

The Fynbos Biome is home to 18 species of hoofed mammal, also known as ungulates. These animals walk on the tip of their toes. The ancestral five toes and claws have adapted to form hooves for this purpose. Ungulates are divided into two orders: even-toed and odd-toed. In even-toed ungulates, such as hollow-horned ruminants (Bovidae), pigs (Suidae) and hippos (Hippopotamidae), the reduction of weight-bearing toes are to either two or four. In odd-toed ungulates, such as horses (Equidae), the reduction is to either one or three.

Bushpigs are even-toed ungulates.

Zebra are odd-toed ungulates.

Golden moles
Family Chrysochloridae

Short-furred, cylindrical little fossorial insectivores that are extremely difficult to identify to species level. Four heavily clawed digits on forefeet; third digit with largest claw. Often confused with herbivorous mole-rats. Golden moles are smaller, with no visible tail, eyes or ears, and have tiny sharp teeth. Muzzles pink, naked, stubby with hardened tip. They move around just below the surface, leaving tell-tale tunnels above the ground. Beneficial in gardens as they eat pests and aerate the soil. Duthie's Golden Mole (*Chlorotalpa duthieae*) from the southern Cape is confined to forest patches. Five species associated with the Fynbos Biome.

1 Van Zyl's Golden Mole *Cryptochloris zyli* EN

Known from only four specimens. Enigmatic and cryptic. Dorsal coloration slaty-grey with shimmering purple gloss. Underparts duller, marginally paler. Darker than Grant's Golden Mole. Most similar to Cape Golden Mole, but smaller, paler and with better developed first finger on front limbs. **Size** Length: 8cm. **Status and Habitat** Appears to be rare, but undoubtedly under-recorded. Presumably nocturnal and solitary. Recorded from coastal dune belt and adjacent sandy areas from Lambert's Bay and Groenriviermond. **Endemism** CFR (in South Africa). **Conservation Status** Endangered owing to habitat transformation.

2 Cape Golden Mole *Chrysochloris asiatica*

Commonest golden mole in region. Geographical variation in colour and size. Dorsal coloration varies from dark brown to slate-grey with shimmering bronze gloss. Underparts paler and duller. Two white to yellowish patches from nose, along each cheek. Not safely distinguished from Fynbos Golden Mole in the field. **Size** Length: 11cm. **Status and Habitat** Common, but not often encountered. Nocturnal and solitary. Adaptable to diverse habitats, including disturbed areas. Prefers sandier substrates. Ranges from Port Nolloth to Swellendam (possibly even reaching Knysna), inland as far as Kamieskroon and Ceres. **Endemism** CFR (in South Africa).

3 Grant's Golden Mole *Eremitalpa granti granti* VU

Very small and attractive. Dorsal coloration pale silvery-grey with yellow shading and shimmering gloss. Underparts and flanks paler, with more yellowish tone. Cheeks and forehead pale yellow. Only golden mole with well-developed claw on fourth digit of forelimbs. Much paler than Cape and Van Zyl's golden moles. Two subspecies recognised; South African *E. g. granti* likely a separate species. **Size** Length: 8cm. **Status and Habitat** Scarce, solitary and primarily nocturnal in summer. Actively feeds above ground at night. Inhabits loose, sandy substrates, utilising Strandveld in the Fynbos Biome. Found from around Langebaan to Port Nolloth, inland to the Biedouw Valley. **Endemism** Southern Africa; *E. g. granti* endemic to CFR (in South Africa). **Conservation Status** Vulnerable owing to habitat transformation.

4 Fynbos Golden Mole *Amblysomus corriae* NT

Not illustrated. Very similar to Cape Golden Mole, with which it co-occurs in western parts of its range, but appears to prefer moister, richer soils. Two subspecies: *A. c. corriae* (coastal plain from George eastwards) and *A. c. devilliersi* (mountainous areas west of George). Dorsal coloration dark grey with reddish-brown shading on flanks. Reddish colour extends onto belly in *A. c. devilliersi*; belly light grey in *A. c. corriae*. Pale yellowish-brown eye patches often present. Reportedly darker than Hottentot Golden Mole, but ranges not known to overlap. **Status and Habitat** Predominantly nocturnal and solitary. Prefers softer, sandy and loamy soils of Fynbos and forest edges. Occurs in the Cape Fold Mountains from Groot Winterhoek in west to Humansdorp in east. **Size** Length: 12cm. **Endemism** Fynbos Biome. **Conservation Status** Near Threatened owing to habitat transformation.

1 Hottentot Golden Mole *Amblysomus hottentotus*

This species only marginally enters the region in the extreme eastern parts of the Fynbos Biome. Unclear whether range overlaps with Fynbos Golden Mole or any other species. Only the nominate *A. h. hottentotus* occurs in the region. Upperparts usually rich reddish brown with iridescent sheen. Underparts greyish brown and paler. Cheeks pale. Reportedly lighter with more reddish pigments than Fynbos Golden Mole. **Size** Length: 13cm; mass: 75g. **Status and Habitat** Predominantly nocturnal and solitary. Occurs in the Eastern Cape and further afield in South Africa east of the Van Stadens River near Gqeberha. Extent of occurrence in Fynbos habitats not clearly understood. **Endemism** Southern Africa.

Sengis   Family Macroscelididae

Sengis are small, mouse-like mammals with prominent, rounded ears and a distinctly elongated, pointed nose (proboscis) that is very flexible. Previously known as elephant shrews, they are now called sengis as they are not closely related to shrews and only distantly related to elephants. Hind legs and feet slender, much longer than front appendages. Extremely quick and agile, sengis primarily eat invertebrates, especially ants and termites, but also include some vegetable matter in their diet. The Cape Rock Sengi drinks nectar and forages for insects inside flowers, thereby fulfilling a pollination role. Two species occur in the Fynbos Biome.

2 Karoo Round-eared Sengi *Macroscelides proboscideus*

One of the smallest sengis. No white eye-ring around large dark eyes, unlike Cape Rock Sengi. Dorsal coloration yellowish brown to brownish grey, paler on flanks and whitish on underparts. Fur short and soft. Ears large, rounded and erect. Tail slightly longer than head–body length, same colour as upperparts, but darkening towards small black tuft on tip. **Size** Length: 23cm; tail: 12cm; mass: 31–47g. **Status and Habitat** Solitary, crepuscular and nocturnal. Prefers open country with sparse grass cover and/or low shrubs, including alluvial and gravel flats. Occurs in the northern parts of the Fynbos Biome and along the edges with Succulent Karoo. **Endemism** Southern Africa.

3 Cape Rock Sengi *Elephantulus edwardii*

Grey-white eye-ring around large dark eyes distinguishes it from Karoo Round-eared Sengi. Fur soft, fairly short. Upperparts greyish brown in colour, flecked with darker hairs. Colour gradually fades to tawny-grey on flanks and face. Underparts pale grey to white. Ears large, rounded and erect. Warmer brown patches visible behind ears. Tail slightly longer than head–body length, with short dark hair above, white hair below and small black tuft on tip. **Size** Length: 25cm; tail: 13cm; mass: 50g. **Status and Habitat** Widespread and locally common. Predominantly diurnal with some nocturnal activity. Solitary. Occupies rocky environs with large boulders and crevices with varying degrees of vegetation cover. **Endemism** South Africa.

Shrews   Family Soricidae

Small to very small predators. They have a very high metabolic rate and short lifespan, most living for only 1–2 years. Easily separated from mice by their sharp, needle-like teeth, lacking the gnawing incisors of rodents. They also have a more pointed snout and smaller eyes. These fierce little predators are a critical part of the ecosystem. Some species exhibit 'caravanning', where the young are towed along by the female in a line, each individual biting onto the base of the tail of the one in front of them. Five species occur in the Fynbos Biome.

Distinguishing vibrissae in shrews

Shrew identification is challenging, often relying on cranial and dental morphology. In the Fynbos Biome, there are few species and all can be identified to species level with external features. A useful identification feature is the presence of vibrissae (long hairs) on the tail, which separates forest shrews (*Myosorex* spp.) from other genera.

| Forest shrews (*Myosorex*) | Musk and dwarf shrews (*Crocidura* and *Suncus*) |

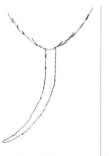

1 Boosman's Long-tailed Forest Shrew
Myosorex longicaudatus boosmani `CR`

This description is for the Fynbos-occurring *M. l. boosmani* from Boosmansbos in the Langeberg Mountains. This subspecies may be split from *M. l. longicaudatus*, which occurs around Knysna. Tail very long (±75% of head–body length) with no vibrissae, two-tone, slightly darker above, may have a prehensile function. Dark slaty-brown above with slightly paler underparts. Limbs dark. Snout broad and pointed. Eyes small and dark. Rounded ears lie flat against head. **Size** Length: 15cm; tail: 6cm. **Status and Habitat** Little known. Restricted to wet mountain Fynbos ecotone with forest patches at high elevations. **Endemism** *M. l. boosmani* is endemic to the Fynbos Biome. **Conservation Status** Critically Endangered owing to tiny known global range.

2 Forest Shrew *Myosorex varius*

A medium-sized shrew with short limbs and conical, elongated, pinkish snout. Darker brown line usually present down centre of snout. Dorsal coloration of short, dense fur variable, but typically dark grey-brown. Underparts paler. Eyes small, beady, dark. Ears rounded, tucked against head. No vibrissae on tail; separated from Long-tailed Forest Shrew by shorter tail (±46% of head–body length). Tail brown, paler on sides, with sparse cover of short hair. head. **Size** Length: 12cm; tail: 4cm; mass: 12–16g. **Status and Habitat** Common. Nocturnal, sometimes diurnal during dry season. Associated with cool, moist microhabitats. Not restricted to forests and found in wide range of habitats. Adaptable and can tolerate disturbance; can occur in larger gardens. **Endemism** Southern Africa.

3 Reddish-grey Musk Shrew *Crocidura cyanea*

A medium-sized shrew. Grey with shades of reddish brown to beige; grizzled appearance. Paler in western parts of range. Underparts and top of feet pale. Tail ±65% of head–body length, two-tone (dark above and pale below), with interspersed longer pale vibrissae. Snout large, conical, pinkish. Eyes small, dark. Ears large, rounded. Resembles Lesser Dwarf Shrew, but larger. Represents a species complex; requires additional research. **Size** Length: 13cm; tail: 5cm; mass: 9g. **Status and Habitat** Fairly common, but usually much less common than Forest Shrew in areas of overlap. Nocturnal, with some diurnal activity. The most widespread of the Fynbos shrew species, with a wider habitat tolerance, including drier environments. Can adapt to disturbed environments such as houses and gardens.

4 Greater Musk Shrew *Crocidura flavescens*

Largest shrew in the region. Fur thick and short, with distinct warm brown hue. Underparts off-white to pale grey, occasionally with shades of yellow. Tail thick, ±50% of head–body length, two-tone (brown above and pale below), with interspersed long vibrissae. Snout conical, with pinkish colour that extends around smallish eyes. Feet pale above. Pugnacious; can be extremely vocal when distressed. Distinct musky smell. Easily identified by large size and cinnamon-brown coloration. **Size** Length: 16cm; tail: 6cm; mass: 27g. **Status and Habitat** Predominantly nocturnal and crepuscular. Prefers higher-rainfall areas. Adaptable to various habitat types, usually in close proximity to water and dense cover. Can sometimes be found under debris on the high-water mark. Most northerly record on the West Coast is Elands Bay. **Endemism** Southern Africa.

5 Lesser Dwarf Shrew *Suncus varilla*

The smallest shrew, and the smallest mammal in the Fynbos Biome. A delicate shrew with warm brownish-grey dorsal coloration, contrasting quite sharply with pale whitish-grey underparts and lower flanks. Limbs pale. Snout conical, pinkish, often with dark line along centre. Tail ±60% of head–body length, two-tone (darker above), with longer vibrissae along length. This species has a large, fragmented distribution and may represent a species complex. **Size** Length: 9cm; tail: 3.3cm; mass: 3g. **Status and Habitat** Common, but not often encountered. Widespread, recorded from diverse habitats, including Fynbos, Strandveld and Renosterveld. Can be active throughout the day.

BATS OF THE FYNBOS BIOME

Bats are the only mammals that have developed the ability of powered flight. They have delicate, leathery wings spanning from elongated fingers to their ankles. Of the 13 bat species present in the Fynbos Biome, 12 are insectivorous and one is fruit-eating.

Cape Serotine Bat

Fruit bats differ from other bats in that they are generally larger, have two wing-claws (as opposed to one in insectivorous bats), no or a very short tail with limited surrounding membranes, large eyes and no tragus (a piece of skin in front of the ear canal that assists with directing sound into the ear). The horseshoe bats are the only insectivorous bats that also lack a tragus.

All species within the Fynbos Biome use echolocation. The elaborate nose-leaves and facial structure of some species aid in this function.

Identification to species level is challenging and most definitively based on skull measurements, dentition, echolocation sonograms and even molecular analysis.

Wind farms are an increasing threat to bats. Species such as Cape Serotine Bat, Lesueur's Hairy Bat, Roberts's Flat-headed Bat and Egyptian Free-tailed Bat seem to be particularly vulnerable.

Field identification features for Fynbos Biome species grouped per family					
Bat family	Species	Facial feature	Interfemoral membrane configuration	Day roosting sites used	Foraging zone*
Fruit bats Pteropodidae	1) Egyptian Fruit Bat (*Rousettus aegyptiacus*)	No nose-leaf structure (simple nose)	• Tail very short, stubby	• Caves • Artificial crevices (e.g. tunnels) • Large congregations • Singly in thick vegetation	• Eats fruit • Large wings
Slit-faced bats Nycteridae	1) Egyptian Slit-faced Bat (*Nycteris thebaica*)	Nose-leaf forms slit	• Tail fully enclosed, bifurcate	• Caves • Mines • Hollow trees • Aardvark burrows • Buildings • Culverts • Single, small groups or occasionally large congregations	• Clutter foragers • Short, rounded wings
Horseshoe bats Rhinolophidae	1) Geoffroy's Horseshoe Bat (*Rhinolophus clivosus*) 2) Cape Horseshoe Bat (*Rhinolophus capensis*)	Nose-leaf forms intricate horseshoe shape No tragus	• Tail fully enclosed • Square	• Caves • Mines and other abandoned artificial underground structures • Culverts (Geoffroy's Horseshoe Bat only) • Buildings (Geoffroy's Horseshoe Bat only) • Small to large congregations	• Clutter foragers • Short, broad wings

Field identification features for Fynbos Biome species grouped per family

Bat family	Species	Facial feature	Interfemoral membrane configuration	Day roosting sites used	Foraging zone*
Long-fingered bats Miniopteridae	1) Natal Long-fingered Bat (*Miniopterus natalensis*) 2) Lesser Long-fingered Bat (*Miniopterus fraterculus*)	No nose-leaf structure (simple nose)	• Tail fully enclosed • Triangular point	• Caves • Mines and other abandoned underground structures • Small to large congregations	• Clutter-edge foragers • Long, narrow wings
Vesper bats Vespertilionidae	1) Namibian Long-eared Bat (*Laephotis namibensis*) 2) Long-tailed Serotine Bat (*Eptesicus hottentotus*) 3) Cape Serotine Bat (*Neoromicia capensis*) 4) Temminck's Hairy Bat (*Myotis tricolor*)	No nose-leaf structure (simple nose)	• Tail fully enclosed • Triangular point	• Caves and mines • Rock crevices • Under exfoliating rocks (Namibian Long-eared Bat only) • Within vegetation (Cape Serotine Bat only) • Under bark (Cape Serotine Bat only) • Buildings • Small to very large congregations	• Clutter-edge foragers • Relatively short, broad wings
Wing-gland or hairy bats Cistugidae	1) Lesueur's Hairy Bat (*Cistugo lesueuri*)	No nose-leaf structure (simple nose; snout sharper than vesper bats)	• Tail fully enclosed • Triangular point	• Rock crevices near water • Roost in small colonies	• Clutter-edge foragers • Short, broad wings
Free-tailed bats Molossidae	1) Roberts's Flat-headed Bat (*Sauromys petrophilus*) 2) Egyptian Free-tailed Bat (*Tadarida aegyptiaca*)	No nose-leaf structure (simple nose)	• ⅓ to ½ of tail free/not enclosed • Tail extends beyond feet	• Rock cracks and crevices • Caves (Egyptian Free-tailed Bat only) • Hollow trees (Egyptian Free-tailed Bat only) • Under bark (Egyptian Free-tailed Bat only) • Buildings, bridges (Egyptian Free-tailed Bat only) • Small to medium-sized congregations	• Open-air foragers • Long, narrow wings

*Foraging zone	Description	Adaptations
Clutter forager	Hunts in and near vegetation or close to the ground and in-between structures.	Echolocation varies between high frequency and long duration or low frequency and short duration. Wing morphology favours short, broad wings for slow, agile flight.
Clutter edge forager	Hunts adjacent to thicker vegetation and structures.	Mixed echolocation signals to differentiate between vegetation and prey, but mostly of average frequency and duration. Wing morphology variable, but wings mostly of average length and width.
Open-air forager	Hunts high above vegetation and away from structures.	Echolocation at low frequencies and of long duration. Wing morphology favours long, narrow wings for speed and agility.

Fruit bats   Family Pteropodidae

Their large size and distinctive appearance make fruit bats easy to identify. They are important pollinators and play a critical role in seed dispersal. One species occurs in the Fynbos Biome.

1 Egyptian Fruit Bat *Rousettus aegyptiacus*

The only fruit-eating bat in the Fynbos Biome, identifiable by its dog-like facial features, large size and very short tail. Dorsal coloration grey-brown to slaty-brown with paler, yellowish collar. Underparts pale warm-grey. Wings dark brown. Eyes large. Ears relatively small. Muzzle long, with no nose-leaves. Forearm with two claws (on first and second finger). Further taxonomic review of genus needed. **Size** Length: 15cm; wingspan: 60cm; forearm: 8.3–9.6cm; mass: 133g. **Status and Habitat** Large colonies roost in caves. Individuals occasionally roost alone in thick vegetation. Mostly forages in Southern Afrotemperate Forest patches or where appropriate fruiting trees have been planted. However, many cave roosting sites are within Fynbos. Will fly large distances to forage.

Slit-faced bats   Family Nycteridae

A characteristic feature is the slit down the front of the muzzle, formed by the nose-leaves. Tip of tail splits to form shallow Y (bifurcate). Tail fully enclosed by interfemoral membrane. Ears large and erect. Broad wings with rounded tips allow for slow, deliberate flight. One species occurs in the Fynbos Biome.

2 Egyptian Slit-faced Bat *Nycteris thebaica*

Coloration variable. Upperparts usually buffy brown to golden orange, always darker than light brown to whitish underparts. Paler in western parts. Ears very large, erect, with finger-like tragus. Wings broad and rounded. Interfemoral membranes extend to tip of tail. **Size** Length: 10cm; wingspan: 24–30cm; forearm: 4.7cm; ear: 3.4cm; tail: 5cm; mass: 10.5g. **Status and Habitat** Common and widespread. Roosts singly or in small groups; large day- and night-roosting congregations can occur. Uses caves for roosting but will also utilise mines, Aardvark burrows, culverts, roofs and hollow trees. Habitat requires some trees or large shrubs.

Horseshoe bats   Family Rhinolophidae

An important feature is the intricate nose-leaf, the bottom part of which resembles a flattened horseshoe shape, slightly raised from the face. Large ears lack tragus. This is the only family within the Fynbos with a square-ending interfemoral membrane. It is extremely difficult to identify these bats to species level and echolocation sonograms are usually required. Two species are associated with the Fynbos Biome. Geoffroy's and Cape Horseshoe bats commonly roost together.

3 Geoffroy's Horseshoe Bat *Rhinolophus clivosus*

The larger of the two Fynbos Biome horseshoe bats. The most reliable morphological difference is the absence of the first upper premolar (present in Cape Horseshoe Bat). Greyish to warm yellowish brown on back. Underparts paler. Ears medium-sized, erect, rounded, with pointed tip and no tragus. Characteristic horseshoe-shaped nose-leaf <9mm in width. Distinct mental groove present in lower lip. Wing membranes pale brown. Indistinguishable from Cape Horseshoe Bat in the field; sonogram required to confirm identification. This taxon requires taxonomic review and may contain cryptic species. **Size** Length: 9.7cm; wingspan: 32cm; forearm: 5.3cm; tail: 2.7–3.8cm; mass: 16.2g. **Status and Habitat** Relatively common; associated with a range of habitats. Generally absent from hot, dry lowlands. Roosts in caves, mines, buildings and culverts in small to very large colonies.

1 Cape Horseshoe Bat *Rhinolophus capensis*

Readily identifiable as a horseshoe bat, but indistinguishable from Geoffroy's Horseshoe Bat in the field and a sonogram is required to confirm the identification. Generally dark brown above with lighter underparts. Wings dark brown. Ears medium-sized, erect, with pointed tips and no tragus. The characteristic horseshoe-shaped nose-leaf <9mm in width. No mental groove on lower lip. First upper premolar present (absent in Geoffroy's). **Size** Length: 8.8cm; wingspan: 32cm; forearm: 4.8–5.2cm; tail: 2.8cm; mass: 11g. **Status and Habitat** Relatively common. Primarily restricted to the Fynbos, Succulent Karoo and Karoo biomes, but in a range of habitats. Roosts in caves and mines in small to very large colonies. Generally avoids roosting in buildings. **Endemism** South Africa.

Long-fingered bats — Family Miniopteridae

Distinguished by significantly elongated second finger bone (phalanx) of third digit, which is approximately three times longer than first phalanx. Long, narrow wings, more than twice their body length, equip these bats for swift and proficient flight in open areas. Simple face without any nose-leaves; skull profile shows raised brain-case. Interfemoral membrane creates distinct triangular point as it extends to tip of tail, similar to vesper bats (Vespertilionidae). Two species occur in the Fynbos Biome. It is very challenging to distinguish between different species and it is only reliably done through DNA analysis, echolocation and skull morphology.

2 Natal Long-fingered Bat *Miniopterus natalensis*

Larger than much rarer Lesser Long-fingered Bat. Best identified by skull and dental morphology. Fur short, thick, slaty-brown above, sometimes with reddish hue. Individual hairs two-toned, paler on tip. Underparts paler, more greyish brown. Nose simple. Small, erect ears with rounded tips. Tragus long with parallel sides and rounded tip. **Size** Length: 11cm; wingspan: 28cm; forearm: 4.5cm; tail: 5.3cm; mass: 10g. **Status and Habitat** Common. Roosts in small to very large numbers in caves or similar structures (including mineshafts). They crowd together in dense clusters. Specific caves are used for hibernation during winter and others as maternity roosts in summer. Found across the Fynbos Biome where there are suitable roosting sites.

3 Lesser Long-fingered Bat *Miniopterus fraterculus*

Very similar to the slightly larger Natal Long-fingered Bat and only safely identified based on skull and dental morphology. Cranium significantly rounded. Muzzle very short, without nose-leaves. Fur soft, long and woolly. Coloration variable. Upperparts russet-brown to nearly black. Underparts paler, grey-brown with darker throat. Ears small and bluntly pointed. Tragus long with parallel sides and rounded tip. May represent a species complex. **Size** Length: 10cm; wingspan: 30cm; forearm: 4.2cm; tail: 5cm; mass: 8g. **Status and Habitat** Appears to be rare; exact distribution in the Fynbos Biome not known. Reputed to occur along the coastal strip, possibly as far west as Cape Town. Dependent on caves or similar structures (including mines) for roosting. Will roost together with Natal Long-fingered Bats, but in much lower numbers.

Vesper bats — Family Vespertilionidae

Tail fully enclosed by interfemoral membranes, forming V-shape towards tip. This feature is shared with long-fingered bats (Miniopteridae) and wing-gland bats (Cistugidae). Simple noses with no nose-leaves. Taxonomy challenging. Identification of many species is best based on analysis of morphological features, echolocation and DNA. Four species enter the Fynbos Biome.

1 Namibian Long-eared Bat *Laephotis namibensis* VU

Distinguished from other Fynbos vesper bats by long ears and large, triangular tragus. Small, with buffy brown dorsal coloration, darker in northern parts of range. Underparts paler. Individual hairs two-tone, with lighter tips. Ears extremely long (2.2–2.5cm), dark brown and held at 45 degree angle to the head. Additional research needed on distinction between this species and De Winton's Long-eared Bat (*L. wintoni*). **Size** Length: 10.5cm; wingspan: ±27cm (for *L. wintoni*); forearm: 3.8cm; tail: 4.4cm; mass: 11g. **Status and Habitat** Apparently rare. Endemic to arid western parts of Namibia with an isolated subpopulation in the Cederberg. Unverified data suggest a wider distribution in the Fynbos. Locally, habitat preference appears to be arid Fynbos in mountainous areas, close to water. Roosts in narrow crevices in cliff faces and under exfoliating rocks. **Endemism** Southern Africa. **Conservation Status** Vulnerable owing to habitat transformation.

2 Long-tailed Serotine Bat *Eptesicus hottentotus*

Larger than Cape Serotine Bat. Colour varies across range, with western populations paler. Upperparts vary from beige and fawn to dark brown. Underparts greyish cream to light brown. Hairs two-tone with lighter tips. Nose simple. Ears medium-sized, dark and set far apart. Tragus knife-shaped. **Size** Length: 11.5cm; wingspan: 35cm; forearm: 5cm; tail: 4.9cm; mass: 16g. **Status and Habitat** Can be common in suitable habitat, but patchily distributed over its wide range. Reportedly less common in South Africa and normally encountered singly or in very small groups (<5 individuals). Primarily associated with mountainous areas with rocky outcrops close to water. Roosts in caves, mines and rock crevices; may use buildings. Distribution linked to roosting site availability.

3 Cape Serotine Bat *Neoromicia capensis*

The most common vesper bat in the region. This small bat is highly variable across its range and further taxonomic research is needed. Where it occurs with similar species, in-field identification is impossible. Identification best based on measurements, echolocation sonograms or dental and skeletal features. Dorsal coloration varies from light to dark brown. Underparts range from greyish brown to off-white. Hair two-tone with lighter tip. Nose simple. Ears medium-sized, dark, round-tipped and set far apart. Tragus short and broad. Top of head dome-shaped. **Size** Length: 8.5cm; wingspan: 24cm; forearm: 3.3cm; tail: 3.2cm; mass: 7g. **Status and Habitat** Very common and widespread. Adapted to a wide range of habitats. Roosts in small numbers (1–3 individuals) under bark or within vegetation. Larger roosts (±100 individuals) in artificial locations such as buildings.

4 Temminck's Hairy Bat *Myotis tricolor*

Separated from other vesper bats by brighter coloration and long, narrow tragus. This small bat has long, shaggy fur with straight ends, different from the curly-ended hair of woolly bats (*Kerivoula*). Dorsal coloration warm copper to orange. Underparts paler. Hairs two-tone, darker at base. Muzzle short, ends in simple nose. Ears medium-sized, triangular and set wide apart. Tragus slender and spear-shaped. Wings moderately broad, uniformly dark brown. **Size** Length: 12cm; wingspan: 28cm; forearm: 5cm; tail: 5cm; mass: 12.5g. **Status and Habitat** Uncommon. Roosts gregariously in moist caves and old mines. Utilises separate summer and winter caves. Widespread, utilising a wide range of habitats but absent from flat, featureless areas and the western coastal plain.

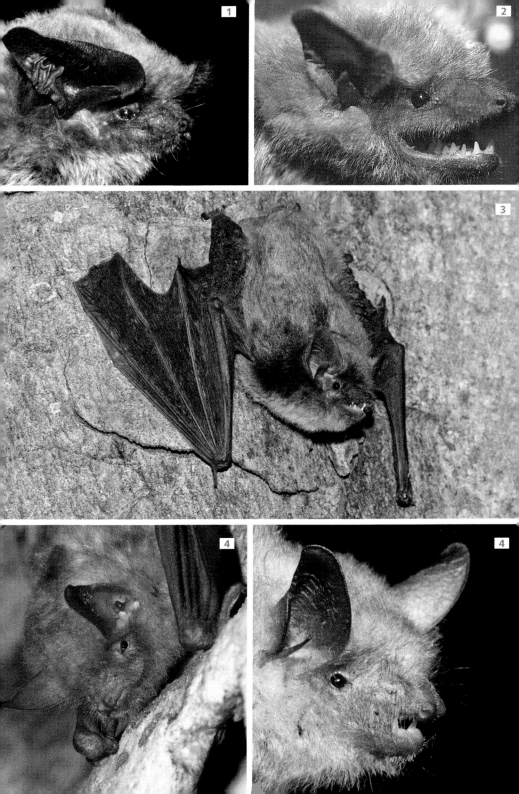

Wing-gland or hairy bats — Family Cistugidae

Originally included in vesper bats (Vespertilionidae). Small bats that lack nose-leaves. Tail fully enclosed by interfemoral membrane, creating triangular point, as with vesper and long-fingered bats (Miniopteridae). A unique feature of this family is the 1–3 glands present on the wings of both sexes. The exact size, shape and location of these glands can vary, and their function is unknown. These bats roost in small colonies. One species occurs in the Fynbos Biome.

1 Lesueur's Hairy Bat *Cistugo lesueuri*

A small bat with long, straight, soft fur and a shaggy overall appearance. Dorsal coloration dull yellow to yellow-beige. Underparts paler yellowish cream. Individual hairs two-tone with darker base. Muzzle slightly longer and more pointed than in vesper bats. Nose simple, without any nose-leaves. Ears medium-sized, with pointed tips. Tragus long and narrow, with rounded point. Wings relatively short, broad and dark brown with one characteristic gland on membrane of each wing. **Size** Length: 9.5cm; wingspan: 23–25cm; forearm: 3.6cm; tail: 4.3cm; mass: 6g. **Status and Habitat** Uncommon and seldom recorded. Associated with rocky hills and koppies. Roosts in rock crevices near water. **Endemism** Southern Africa.

Free-tailed bats — Family Molossidae

Characteristically, a third to half of the tail is 'free' or not enclosed within interfemoral membranes. Most have a dog-like face with a 'wrinkled' muzzle and a simple nose lacking elaborate nose-leaves. The prominent vertical folds on the upper lip give them a bullmastiff-like appearance. They have large ears (roughly equal in length and width) with a small tragus. These bats can crawl forward and backwards efficiently. The only reliable way to distinguish between species is with echolocation spectogram, dentition and DNA analysis. Two species occur in the Fynbos Biome.

2 Roberts's Flat-headed Bat *Sauromys petrophilus*

A small bat with a conspicuously flattened skull, an adaption to roosting in narrow rock cracks. Superficially similar to Egyptian Free-tailed Bat, but distinctly smaller, and large ears do not meet on forehead. Dorsal coloration light greyish brown to brown with slightly paler underparts. Long, narrow wings light brown. Tragus very small; ears lack complex folds. **Size** Length: 10.5cm; wingspan: 26cm; forearm: 4cm; tail: 3.8cm; mass: 9g. **Status and Habitat** Can be locally common in suitable habitat. Limited to western mountainous areas of the Fynbos Biome, particularly the Cederberg, where it's common. Roosts in small colonies in narrow rock cracks and crevices. Forages in open areas, often above or near water.

3 Egyptian Free-tailed Bat *Tadarida aegyptiaca*

Best distinguished from Roberts's Flat-headed Bat by larger size. Large ears meet on forehead. A medium-sized bat, normally dark brown with slightly paler underparts. Long, narrow wings light brown. Has bullmastiff-like appearance owing to wrinkled upper lip. **Size** Length: 11cm; wingspan: 30cm; forearm: 4.8cm; tail: 3.8cm; mass: 15g. **Status and Habitat** Very common and widespread over wide range of habitats. Roosts in small to medium-sized colonies in rock cracks, caves, hollow trees and under bark of dead trees. Also makes use of buildings and the expansion joints in bridges. Closely associated with watercourses in more arid areas.

Hares and rabbits
Family Leporidae

Easily recognised by the long ears on most species, large eyes, short muzzle with small nose, and short, fluffy tail. The bounding or hopping gait is distinctive and the underside of the feet is covered by hair. Females are larger than males. Hares and rabbits differ in several ways. Hares are generally larger, have longer back legs (making them faster runners), longer ears and are less social. When born, hares are fully furred with open eyes (precocial) while rabbits are born hairless, with closed eyes, and are very dependent on parental care (altricial). Hares normally have their young in above-ground scrapes while rabbits make use of dens. When threatened, hares prefer to flee, while rabbits may back their camouflage and hunker down. In-field species identification features between the Cape and Scrub Hare remain debatable and difficult to define. Identification is most accurately based on incisor morphology and skull measurements. The taxonomy of this family is complex and unresolved. Further research is needed on African *Lepus* species and much uncertainty remains. Scrub Hare in particular is very similar to the currently recognised African Savannah Hare (*L. victoriae*) of the north-eastern parts of South Africa, but the exact relationship and respective geographical ranges still need to be defined. Four species are found in the Fynbos Biome.

1 Cape Hare *Lepus capensis*

Smaller of the two local *Lepus* species. Dorsal coloration varies from grey to beige-brown, with grizzled appearance. Pinkish-brown patch on nape (nuchal patch) not as bold buffy orange as in Scrub Hare. Underparts variable. Central belly usually white with pinkish-buff or tan-buff bands on edges. Resulting variable tan-buff bands separate white belly from dorsal coloration. Lighter yellowish markings may be present around nose, on chin and around large eyes. Longish tail white below and black above. Outer side of legs warm buff. **Size** Length: 45–60cm; tail: 7–14cm; mass: 1.4–2.5kg. **Status and Habitat** Common. Solitary and nocturnal, with some diurnal activity. Prefers drier, more open areas. No recent records from the Overberg.

2 Scrub Hare *Lepus saxatilis*

Larger of the two Fynbos-occurring species. Short, dense fur beige-brown and infused with grizzled-grey. Nuchal patch reddish brown, brighter than Cape Hare. Underparts white with no buffy edging between white belly and upperparts. Pale whitish patches on chin, cheeks and around large eyes. Outer sides of limbs greyish brown. Longish tail white below and black above. **Size** Length: 45–65cm; tail: 7–17cm; mass: 1.5–4.5kg. **Status and Habitat** Solitary and nocturnal with limited diurnal activity. Found throughout much of the Fynbos Biome but the eastern edge of range unclear. Prefers habitat with more cover (shrubs), avoiding very open habitats. **Endemism** Southern Africa.

3 Hewitt's Red Rock Rabbit *Pronolagus saundersiae*

An attractive and stocky rabbit. Short, thick fur has warm brown and silver-grizzled appearance. Nuchal patch, rump, bushy tail and lower legs all rufous. Chest and flanks can have warm brown tone with some white on belly. Brownish hues usually present around and above nose. Ears relatively short compared to *Lepus* species. **Size** Length: 43–56cm; tail: 5–11cm; mass: 1.3–2kg. **Status and Habitat** Predominantly nocturnal and solitary. Can be very common. Presence evident from obvious latrine sites. Will bask in the early mornings or late afternoons. Widespread with disjunct distribution owing to dependence on rocky environments with grass and shrub cover for shelter and food. **Endemism** Southern Africa.

Distinguishing features of the four Fynbos Biome lagomorphs

Species	Morphological features	Habitat
Cape Hare *Lepus capensis*	Tail: White below, black above. Ears: Long (110–140mm) with black markings on tips. Ventral and flank coloration: Belly completely white in middle. Tan-buff bands on flanks separating dorsal and ventral coloration. Leg colour: Outer side of legs (especially front legs) warm buff. Nuchal patch: Pale buff or pinkish brown, sometimes inconspicuous. Adult skull length: Smaller of the two *Lepus* species at 81.5–91.1mm.* Upper principal incisors: Narrow, 2.3–2.8mm each, squarish in cross-section and simple, shallow enamel groove filled with cement.*	Most abundant lagomorph in South Africa. Most commonly encountered hare in drier, open habitats. Preference for short, open grassy habitat and lightly wooded areas. Sympatric with Scrub Hare in most of range.
Scrub Hare *Lepus saxatilis*	Tail: White below, black above. Ears: Long (100–150mm) with black markings on tips. Ventral and flank coloration: Ventral parts white with no buff bands separating ventral and dorsal coloration. Leg colour: Outer side of legs greyish brown. Nuchal patch: Rich buffy orange, usually conspicuous. Adult skull length: Larger of the two *Lepus* species, 85.6–106mm.* Upper principal incisors: Broader and more robust, 2.7–3.5mm each, slightly wedge-shaped and rectangular in cross-section with variable and more elaborate, deeper enamel groove filled with cement.*	Absent from forests, desert and open grasslands. Less abundant in arid areas than Cape Hare. Preference for more wooded thickets and shrubby habitats but will venture into grassland edges and agricultural fields with some bush encroachment.
Hewitt's Red Rock Rabbit *Pronolagus saundersiae*	Tail: Dark red-brown, uniformly coloured. Ears: Shortest (63–106mm).	Mountainous and rocky habitats with grasses and shrubs.
Riverine Rabbit *Bunolagus monticularis*	Tail: Uniformly coloured dark, warm, grey-brown. Ears: Long (109–124mm). Facial markings: White ring around eye, dark line on lower jaw with white below.	Riverine scrub of seasonal river systems and fertile plains of the Karoo and arid Renosterveld.

* T.J. Robinson (1982), Key to South African Leporidae (Mammalia: Lagomorpha), *South African Journal of Zoology*, 17:4, 220–222, DOI:10.1080/02541858.1982.11447806

1 Riverine Rabbit *Bunolagus monticularis* `CR`
A flagship species for riverine habitats in the Karoo. Unique, very attractive and docile. Silvery-grizzled fur has tones of warm brown, especially on flanks and underparts. Nuchal patch rufous-brown with similar colour on legs. Facial pattern distinct: thin white eye-ring present; small white patches below nose; striking black line runs from nose along lower jawline. Line bordered below by broad white line. Ears relatively long and erect. Tail short, fluffy and dark brown. **Size** Length: 52cm; tail: 9cm; mass: 1.5–1.9kg. **Status and Habitat** Rare, solitary and nocturnal. Dependent on soft, deep soils for burrowing. Primarily associated with dense vegetation in semi-arid areas. Originally only known from seasonal river systems in central Karoo, but recently found to be more widespread. Marginal in the Fynbos Biome, known to occur in arid Renosterveld. **Endemism** South Africa. **Conservation Status** Critically Endangered owing to habitat transformation from agricultural activities.

RODENT FAMILIES OF THE FYNBOS BIOME

Four rodent families occur in the Fynbos Biome: Dormice, mole-rats, porcupines, and rats and mice. Most rodents are herbivores with teeth specifically adapted to gnawing and grinding. Characteristically, their incisors grow continually, being worn down during feeding and gnawing. Rodents are widespread, extremely successful and adaptable. The diversity of form and function has allowed them to occupy diverse niches and habitats. While the majority are terrestrial, some are fossorial, arboreal or semi-aquatic. They have a short life expectancy, but are prolific breeders. As such, populations are able to respond quickly to environmental changes such as seasonal wet spells. While usually vilified by humans, rodents are critically

Brants's Climbing Mouse

important to the sustainability and health of ecosystems. As an example, some are essential pollinators and seed dispersers in the Fynbos Biome. Introduced alien rodents, however, have significant negative ecological and economic impacts.

Dormice   Family Gliridae

Sometimes confused with squirrels owing to their furry tail. Dormice are however nocturnal (all squirrels in South Africa are diurnal) and much smaller. They are adept climbers and have excellent hearing. They are omnivores but uniquely lack a cecum (part of the gut used for fermenting plant material). In this they differ from all other rodents. One species is found in the Fynbos Biome. The Woodland Dormouse *(Graphiurus murinus)* also enters the CFR but, being primarily arboreal, is associated with riverine and other thicket areas.

2 Spectacled Dormouse *Graphiurus ocularis* `NT`
An easily identified, large, attractive rodent. The distinctive fluffy tail is slightly shorter than head–body length and covered in long white-tipped hair. Fur thick, soft, silvery-grey above. Underparts and top of feet white. Eyes large and dark. Broad black line extends across sides of face. Cheeks and lips white. Top of head grizzled grey. Nose and tip of muzzle pink. Bold white at base of each rounded ear. **Size** Length: 25cm; tail: 10cm; mass: 80g. **Status and Habitat** Uncommon, nocturnal resident in rugged sandstone formations. Also utilises buildings and other human-made structures in remote natural areas. **Endemism** South Africa. **Conservation Status** Near Threatened.

Mole-rats   Family Bathyergidae

Regularly confused with the insectivorous golden moles (Chrysochloridae), however mole-rats are rodents and feed solely on plant matter with their very prominent incisors. Furthermore, mole-rats are larger, with a visible tail and eyes. Creates distinct mounds (mole hills) through burrowing. The family is endemic to Africa. Three species are found in the Fynbos.

1 Cape Dune Mole-rat *Bathyergus suillus*

The world's largest truly fossorial mammal. Soft fur on stout, cylindrical body. Legs short. Buffy beige to grey above, with paler flanks and greyish belly. Slight variation in coloration from west (lighter) to east (darker). Paler patches around eyes, ears and throat. Some show variable white spot on forehead. Eyes very small. Ear pinnae absent. Snout naked, pink and pig-like. Prominent upper incisors heavily grooved, unlike other mole-rats. Large, curved claws on forefeet equip it for digging. Male larger than female. **Size** Length: 32cm; tail: 5cm; mass: 885g (infrequently exceed 2kg). **Status and Habitat** Solitary. Common in loose, sandy substrates. Favours coastal dune and sandy flats. Absent from rocky mountain slopes. **Endemism** CFR (in South Africa).

2 Common (African) Mole-rat *Cryptomys hottentotus*

Short-legged, tubular; distinguished from other mole-rats in the region by small size and uniform coloration. Soft fur fawn to brown or sooty grey with no distinctive markings. Belly coloration paler, buff or light brown. Eyes small. Ear pinnae absent. Claws on feet not enlarged; digging primarily done with smooth, prominent incisors. **Size** Length: 15cm; tail: 2cm; mass: 100–150g. **Status and Habitat** Common, but seldom seen. Lives in colonies throughout much of Fynbos Biome. Utilises diverse habitats, including heavier soils than other two Fynbos mole-rats. **Endemism** Southern Africa.

3 Cape Mole-rat *Georychus capensis*

Distinctive black-and-white facial markings. Tubular body and short legs covered with soft buffy to warm-brown fur. Underparts paler. Attractive black to dark brown mask-like markings on head and face contrast with white muzzle and white patches around ear openings. Narrow white rings around small eyes. Some show white spot in centre of head. Feet pink, with fine white hair. Tail short, covered with long white hair. Claws less pronounced than those of Cape Dune Mole-rat, as prominent, smooth incisors are primarily used for digging. **Size** Length: 20cm; tail: 3cm; mass: 180g. **Status and Habitat** Relatively common, preferring sandy substrates. Isolated populations in KwaZulu-Natal and Mpumalanga (as well as some Western Cape subpopulations) may constitute separate species. Solitary. **Endemism** South Africa.

Porcupines   Family Hystricidae

Unmistakable, large, stocky, terrestrial animals covered in cylindrical, bicoloured quills. Slow-moving, relying heavily on quills for self-defence. They form monogamous pairs and shelter in burrows, caves, rock crevices or even human-made structures.

4 Cape Porcupine *Hystrix africaeaustralis*

Africa's largest rodent. Heavyset with rounded head, massive nose, short ears and small black eyes. Covered in coarse, long, black hair; interspersed with long, bicoloured, cylindrical quills on dorsal side. Crest of long hairs from head to upper back. Crest and quills erected when agitated or threatened. White bar across chest curves up to side of neck. Short limbs, clawed paws with naked pads. **Size** Length: 75–100cm; tail: 10–15cm; mass: 10–24kg. **Status and Habitat** Nocturnal, common and widespread. Utilises variety of habitats. Eats a range of bulbs, roots, tubers and tree bark. Known to eat carrion on occasion and chew on bone to obtain phosphorus and calcium (osteophagy).

Porcupine quills are modified hair. These quills are not projectile, nor poisonous, but can inflict significant injuries. Being hollow, they create an impressive rattling noise.

Rats and mice

Family Muridae

Rats and mice are highly adaptable and inhabit almost all terrestrial habitat niches. Twenty-one species occur with the Fynbos Biome. While the introduced alien rodents are significant pests, it is incorrect to paint our entire, remarkable and important, rodent fauna with the same brush. They form an integral part of the natural environment. Several rodent species are important pollinators and many perform a critical role in the distribution and burying of the seeds of Fynbos plants.

In-field identification aid

When identifying a rat or mouse species in the field, determining the specimen's tail length relative to its head–body length is a good starting point. This table presents three tail length categories, along with a summary of other key aspects, such as shape, coloration and habitat.

Tail length	Possible identification	Other key aspects
Shorter than head–body length (HB) / <50% of total length (TL)	White-tailed Rat (*Mystromys albicaudatus*)	• Nocturnal • Hamster-like • Tail short, smooth, white • Grey to brownish grey above
	Pouched Mouse (*Saccostomus campestris*)	• Nocturnal • Hamster-like • Grey to brown above • Tail thin, very short (⅓ of TL) • Sandy substrates in more arid areas
	Krebs's Fat Mouse (*Steatomys krebsii*)	• Nocturnal • Tail short (½ of HB) • Sandy substrates
	Cape Short-tailed Gerbil (*Desmodillus auricularis*)	• Nocturnal • Thickset, medium-sized gerbil • White patches at base of ears • Shortest tail of all gerbils (80% of HB) • Hard substrates in arid areas
	Cape Marsh Rat (*Dasymys capensis*)	• Crepuscular and diurnal • Very rare • Similar to vlei rats, with longer tail (86% of HB) • Glossy sheen to coat • Good-condition vegetation close to wetlands and rivers
	Pygmy Mouse (*Mus minutoides*)	• Nocturnal • Diminutive size • Belly white • Small white patch below ears • Tail ±80% of HB
	Brants's Whistling Rat (*Parotomys brantsii*)	• Crepuscular and diurnal • Whistling alarm call standing on hind legs close to burrow • Dry, deep, sandy habitats
	South African Vlei Rat (*Otomys irroratus*)	• Diurnal and crepuscular • Ears large, generally covered by long hair • Tail dark above, 60% of HB • Three upper molars >8.8mm; 4–7 laminae on third upper molar • Hind feet >25mm • Well-vegetated moist habitats
	Robert's Vlei Rat (*Otomys karoensis*)	• Crepuscular and diurnal • Smallest vlei rat • Tail pale, ±75% of HB • Dense (particularly restio-dominated) vegetation in rocky habitat • Three upper molars <8.8mm; 4–7 laminae on third upper molar • Hind feet <25mm
	Laminate Vlei Rat (*Otomys laminatus*)	• Crepuscular and diurnal • Largest vlei rat • Tail hairy, ±50% of HB • Moist mountain Fynbos (restio-dominated) • 9–10 laminae on third upper molar

Bush Karoo Rat   Pygmy Mouse

Tail length	Possible identification	Other key aspects
Generally equal to head–body length / ±50% of total length	Cape Gerbil (*Gerbilliscus afra*)	• Nocturnal • Large gerbil • Hind limbs much larger than forelimbs • Communal in sandy substrates, burrows very obvious
	Cape Spiny Mouse (*Acomys subspinosus*)	• Nocturnal • Bristle-like spines, especially on back and rump • Good-condition Fynbos habitat • Rocky areas
	Four-striped Grass Mouse (*Rhabdomys pumilio*)	• Diurnal • Four dark stripes down back
	Southern Multimammate Mouse (*Mastomys coucha*)	• Nocturnal • 12 pairs of nipples with whitish hair around each • Belly grey • Rapid colonisers after disturbance
	Bush Karoo Rat (*Otomys unisulcatus*)	• Diurnal • Large domed stick nests • Arid and semi-arid habitat with good vegetation cover
Longer than head–body length / >50% of total length	Grey Climbing Mouse (*Dendromus melanotis*)	• Nocturnal • Tail long, semi-prehensile • Dark stripe down grey back • Upperparts greyish
	Brants's Climbing Mouse (*Dendromus mesomelas*)	• Nocturnal • Tail long, semi-prehensile • Upperparts brownish (with or without dark stripe)
	Pygmy Hairy-footed Gerbil (*Gerbilliscus paeba*)	• Nocturnal • Small, slender gerbil • Hair underneath front part of large feet • Smaller than Cape Gerbil and longer hair on tail tip
	Namaqua Rock Mouse (*Micaelamys namaquensis*)	• Nocturnal • Common • Small colonies • Rocky habitats • Dry vegetation collected at crevice entrances
	Verreaux's White-footed Mouse (*Myomyscus verreauxii*)	• Nocturnal • Similar to Southern Multimammate Mouse, but differs in longer tail, whiter underparts and fewer mammary glands • Good-condition Fynbos habitat
	Barbour's Rock Mouse (*Petromyscus barbouri*)	• Nocturnal • Small, smaller than Pygmy Rock Mouse • Arid, inland, rocky environs • Dark brownish-grey upperparts
	Pygmy Rock Mouse (*Petromyscus collinus*)	• Nocturnal • Small size with large ears and whiskers • Arid, inland, rocky environs • Yellowish-beige to light brown upperparts

1 White-tailed Rat *Mystromys albicaudatus* VU

A docile, hamster-like rodent, very rarely encountered. Ears large and round. Eyes big. Smooth, short tail (<half of head–body length) white. Upperparts soft, grey to brownish grey; underparts greyish white. Top of feet white. **Size** Length: 16–24cm; tail: 6–7cm; mass: 75–130g. **Status and Habitat** Nocturnal, terrestrial and secretive. Rare across its range. Localised in the Fynbos Biome; recorded from a wide variety of sites. Probably under-recorded. **Endemism** Southern Africa. **Conservation Status** Vulnerable owing to habitat degradation and transformation.

2 Pouched Mouse *Saccostomus campestris*

A compact rodent that superficially resembles a hamster. Rotund, heavyset, with short limbs. Soft fur generally grey to brown above, with sharply contrasting white underparts. Cheek pouches for food storage. Top of feet white. Tail very short (<third of total length), pink, unscaled and covered with long sparse hairs. **Size** Length: 15–26cm; tail: 5cm; mass: 45g. **Status and Habitat** Nocturnal, solitary and terrestrial. Widespread and found in various habitats throughout southern Africa, most commonly on sandy substrates. Marginal in the Fynbos Biome and most likely to be encountered in the more arid areas and in the ecotone with the Succulent Karoo.

3 Krebs's Fat Mouse *Steatomys krebsii*

A dumpy, attractive rodent with soft fur. Dorsal coloration ranges from buffy brown to grey. Underparts and top of feet white. Shortish tail weakly bicoloured (pinkish brown on top, paler below) and slightly longer than half of head–body length. There are several disjunct populations of this species across its extensive range, one of which appears to be limited to the CFR. Taxonomic review of these various populations is likely to result in additional species being described. **Size** Length: 13cm; tail: 5cm; mass: 24g. **Status and Habitat** Infrequently encountered, nocturnal and terrestrial, living singly or in pairs. Within the Fynbos Biome it is limited to sandy substrates, but occurs throughout the biome.

4 Grey Climbing Mouse *Dendromus melanotis*

Climbing mice are dainty rodents, easily identified by their long, semi-prehensile tail and distinct, dark vertebral stripe. Grey Climbing Mouse has characteristic grey or brownish-grey upperparts, not reddish brown as with Brants's Climbing Mouse. Underparts white to pale grey. Ears relatively large, with white patch at base. Some have dark patch on forehead, which is separate from dark vertebral stripe. Hind feet long and prominent. Tail substantially longer than head–body length. **Size** Length: 15cm; tail: 8cm; mass: 4–15g. **Status and Habitat** Nocturnal and semi-arboreal, climbing up to 2m high in vegetation. Nests above ground in dense vegetation or in burrows. Most abundant climbing mouse, but not frequently encountered. Predominantly associated with grassland and wetland habitat. Found throughout the Fynbos Biome, including degraded habitats, even in ploughed fields.

5 Brants's Climbing Mouse *Dendromus mesomelas*

Slightly larger than Grey Climbing Mouse; upperparts reddish brown, not grey or brownish grey. Variable dark vertebral stripe usually present. Extremely long, thin tail semi-prehensile and utilised when climbing. Underparts pale buff with whitish belly. **Size** Length: 17cm; tail: 10cm; mass: 9–14g. **Status and Habitat** Nocturnal. Probably fairly common but rarely encountered. Utilises densely vegetated habitats and is often associated with wetlands. Less abundant and more localised than Grey Climbing Mouse. Not known to utilise transformed areas. Has been found in weaver (*Ploceus* spp.) nests within reedbeds.

1 **Cape Gerbil** *Gerbilliscus afra*

Largest and most abundant gerbil species in the Fynbos Biome. Distinguished from Hairy-footed Gerbil by naked soles of hind feet and its larger size. Long, thick fur grey-beige to reddish brown with grizzled appearance. Underparts white. Eyes large. Ears long and erect. Tail ≥ head–body length and uniform in colour, usually paler than upperparts. Hind limbs much larger than forelimbs. **Size** Length: 30cm; tail: 15cm; mass: 100g. **Status and Habitat** Nocturnal and communal. Found on sandy substrates where it can be locally abundant. Numbers fluctuate widely in response to environmental conditions. Readily utilises transformed habitat, such as agricultural areas, where it is sometimes considered a pest. Western Barn Owls have proven very effective as bio-control agents. **Endemism** CFR (in South Africa).

2 **Pygmy Hairy-footed Gerbil** *Gerbilliscus paeba*

A small, slender gerbil with hair underneath the front part of its large feet. Smaller than Cape Gerbil, with notably longer hair on tail tip. Dorsal coloration variable, but usually a shade of pale orange-brown interspersed with darker brown hairs. Underparts white. Tail paler than upperparts and much longer than head–body length. Eyes large and prominent. Further taxonomic interrogation of the four South African subspecies of Pygmy Hairy-footed Gerbil is needed. **Size** Length: 20cm; tail: 11cm; mass: 25g. **Status and Habitat** A common, nocturnal, open-habitat specialist. Associated with sandy substrates and found in sand Fynbos, alluvium Fynbos and Strandveld habitat types. Most abundant in the arid and western part of the Fynbos Biome and absent from moist mountain Fynbos and much of the southern coastal plain.

3 **Cape Short-tailed Gerbil** *Desmodillus auricularis*

Stocky, relatively short-snouted gerbil. The only gerbil with a tail shorter than its body (±80% of head–body length). Also separated from other gerbils by white patches at base of ears. Upperpart coloration extremely variable, even at same locality: can be bright buffy orange to greyish brown above. Underparts always white. Ears small and rounded. Front half of soles and underside of toes hairy. Tail has no terminal tuft. **Size** Length: 20cm; tail: 9cm; mass: 53g. **Status and Habitat** A common, nocturnal species that favours hard substrates in arid areas. Prefers open habitats with little cover and can tolerate disturbed areas. Recorded as far south as Saldanha on the West Coast. Absent from the Cape Fold Mountains and the southern Cape coastal areas.

4 **Cape Spiny Mouse** *Acomys subspinosus*

This Fynbos endemic is considered a keystone species owing to its importance as a pollinator and seed distributer (through scatter-hoarding). Readily identified by its bristle-like hair, which forms spines, most developed on lower back and rump. Dorsal coloration greyish brown, with grizzled appearance. Flanks slightly paler with rufous tone. Abrupt change between brownish flanks and white underparts. No distinct face markings. Tail ≤ head–body length. **Size** Length: 17cm; tail: 8cm; mass: 22g. **Status and Habitat** Nocturnal. Widespread, but not commonly encountered. Associated with rocky areas within good-condition Fynbos habitats. **Endemism** Fynbos Biome.

5 **Namaqua Rock Mouse** *Micaelamys namaquensis*

A robust rodent with variable coloration. Upperparts usually reddish brown to yellowish beige. Numerous dark-tipped hairs in fur produce grizzled appearance. Face often with greyish tones. Underparts white with some bright buff or greyish hues on flanks. Eyes and ears relatively large. Tail variable in length but always longer than head–body length, has scaly appearance and sparse covering of short, pale hair. Widespread, with up to 16 previously described subspecies. May constitute a species complex. **Size** Length: 26cm; tail: 15cm; mass: 50g. **Status and Habitat** Nocturnal, common, and rupicolous, living in small colonies. Utilises range of rocky outcrops in diverse habitats. Collections of dry vegetation in rock crevices is a good indication of their presence. May frequent human structures in remote areas but are mostly associated with natural, rocky habitats. Important pollinators and seed dispersers.

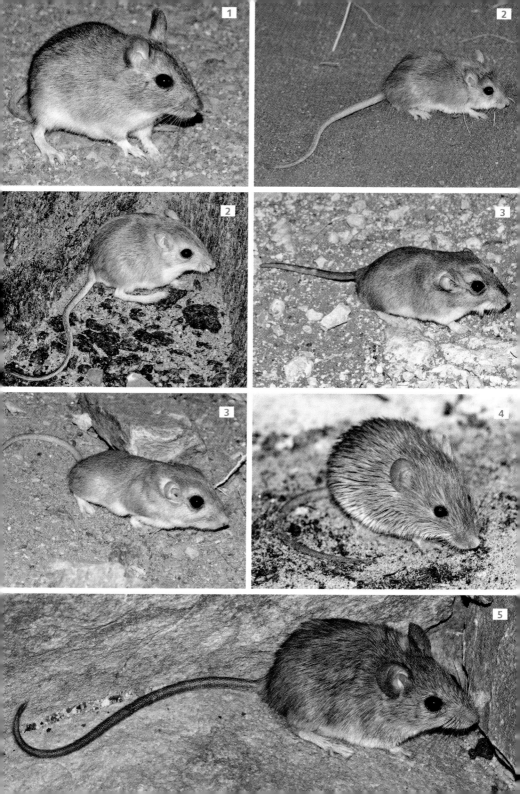

1 Cape Marsh Rat *Dasymys capensis* **VU**

Enigmatic and rarely encountered. Long considered a subspecies of African Marsh Rat (*Dasymys incomtus*) but now recognised as a distinct species. This compact rodent resembles vlei rats (*Otomys*) but has a longer tail. Fur long, soft and shaggy, with glossy sheen. Upperparts reddish brown to dark greyish brown. Underparts dull grey. Tail slightly shorter than head–body length. **Size** Length: 28.5cm; tail: 13cm; mass: 110g. **Status and Habitat** Presumably crepuscular and diurnal. Inhabits good-condition wetland habitat. Currently known from few scattered localities from Wolseley to Knysna, along the southern Cape Fold Mountains. Adept swimmers. **Conservation Status** Vulnerable owing to ongoing wetland degradation and loss. **Endemism** Fynbos Biome.

2 Four-striped Grass Mouse *Rhabdomys pumilio*

Common, frequently seen and attractive. Four longitudinal, dark brown stripes down back distinctive. Dorsal coloration variable but primarily shades of brown and grey with darker flecking. Underparts whitish. Ears reddish brown and round. Tail two-tone (darker above than below), equal to or slightly shorter than head–body length. **Size** Length: 18–26cm; tail: 8–13cm; mass: 30–85g. **Status and Habitat** Abundant, diurnal and crepuscular. Frequently encountered. Adaptable and tolerant of transformed habitats such as agricultural and semi-urban environments. Plays an important role as pollinators and seed distributers. **Endemism** CFR (in South Africa).

3 Pygmy Mouse *Mus minutoides*

Very small. Dorsal coloration ranges from brownish buff to grey. Hairs have fine black tips, giving back a grizzled appearance. Fewer dark-tipped hairs on flanks, which are more buffy orange. Distinct transition to white underparts. Ears rounded with small white patches at base. Tail ±80% of head–body length. The ubiquitous House Mouse (*Mus musculus*) is closely associated with human dwellings and can be differentiated by its brown or greyish (not white) belly, lack of white ear spots and longer tail (> head–body length). Taxonomic revision of the genus *Mus* is likely to result in the description of additional species. **Size** Length: 11cm; tail: 5cm; mass: 6g. **Status and Habitat** Abundant, nocturnal habitat generalist. Widespread throughout the Fynbos Biome and can adapt to transformed habitats, but not found in suburbia.

4 Southern Multimammate Mouse *Mastomys coucha*

Large number of mammary glands on female (up to 12 pairs) is a distinctive feature. Two very similar species occur in South Africa; their respective distribution ranges need to be clearly defined. Only Southern Multimammate Mouse believed to enter the Fynbos Biome. Coloration variable, upperparts ranging from grey to buffy-brown with paler flanks. Juvenile darker grey. Individual hairs darker towards base. Underparts dark to pale grey with whitish hair around each nipple. Tail finely scaled, variable in length but generally equal to or slightly shorter than head–body length. Very similar to Verreaux's White-footed Mouse but has a shorter tail, darker underparts and female has far more mammary glands. **Size** Length 20cm; tail 10cm; mass 40g. **Status and Habitat** Nocturnal and terrestrial. Habitat generalist that enters the Fynbos Biome in the east as far west as about Swellendam. **Endemism** Southern Africa.

5 Verreaux's White-footed Mouse *Myomyscus verreauxii*

Distinguished from Southern Multimammate Mouse by longer tail, whiter underparts and fewer mammary glands (five pairs only) on female. Dorsal coloration grey to buffy brown, paler on flanks and gradually becoming whitish on belly. Fur around and particularly in front of eyes often darker grey. Indistinct sooty band may run from base of ears onto muzzle. Finely scaled tail longer than head–body length (120–135%). Tail two-tone, brownish above and paler below. Feet white. **Size** Length: 25cm; tail: 14cm; mass: 40g. **Status and Habitat** Nocturnal and terrestrial. Probably locally fairly common but seldom recorded. Associated with good-condition Fynbos, as well as forest edges, riverine thickets and damp, grassy areas. Important pollinators, especially for ground proteas. **Endemism** CFR (in South Africa).

No photo of the Cape Marsh Rat exists.
This African Marsh Rat looks very similar.

1 Brants's Whistling Rat *Parotomys brantsii*

The shrill, whistling call reveals its presence and assists with identification. Usually calls in close proximity to burrows and when standing on hind legs. Whistling rats are very closely related to vlei rats (*Otomys*). Stocky rodent with soft fur. Dorsal coloration variable but generally pale yellowish grey to yellow-brown. Colour gradually fades over flanks and grades into uniformly pale greyish-white underparts. Eyes and ears large. Muzzle has distinct rounded profile. Tail shorter than head–body length (±60%). **Size** Length: 18–24cm; tail: 10cm; mass: 100–155g. **Status and Habitat** Crepuscular and diurnal. Colonial, living in individual burrows in close proximity to one another. Dry, deep, sandy habitats of the Nama- and Succulent Karoo, but can also be found in Strandveld along the West Coast. **Endemism** Southern Africa.

2 South African Vlei Rat *Otomys irroratus*

Extremely difficult to separate from other vlei rat species, requiring molar and hind foot measurements. Separated from Robert's Vlei Rat by three upper molars (the molar series) being longer than 8.8mm and hind feet being longer than 25mm. Separated from Laminate Vlei Rat by fewer (4–7) laminae on third upper molar. Robust rodent with long, soft coat; dark slaty-grey with variable brownish hues and grizzled appearance. Rusty tones often present on face and muzzle. Flanks paler, gradually merging with pale grey underparts. Tail dark brown above, paler below, ±60% of head–body length. **Size** Length: 24cm; tail: 9cm; mass: 120g. **Status and Habitat** Common, widespread, diurnal and semi-gregarious. The most frequently encountered vlei rat associated with dense vegetation in the Fynbos Biome. It prefers grassy, wetland or riverine habitat with good vegetation cover. Also occasionally found in relatively dry but dense habitats. **Endemism** South Africa.

3 Robert's Vlei Rat *Otomys karoensis*

Not illustrated – skull only. Also known as Fynbos Vlei Rat. Extremely difficult to separate from other vlei rat species. Distinguished from South African Vlei Rat by three upper molars (the molar series) being shorter than 8.8mm and hind feet being shorter than 25mm. Separated from Laminate Vlei Rat by fewer (4–7) laminae on third upper molar. Generally smaller than Laminate Vlei Rat and more buffy and less grey than South African Vlei Rat. Stocky rodent with grizzled buffy-brown dorsal colour. Flanks slightly paler, gradually becoming light grey on underparts. Throat and feet whitish. Short tail less than half of total length and appears to be paler than in South African Vlei Rat. **Size** Length: 25cm; tail: 9cm; mass: 95g. **Status and Habitat** Diurnal and crepuscular. Terrestrial and common in suitable habitat. Associated with dense vegetation cover and rocky slopes, especially in restio-dominated areas. It generally occurs in drier habitat than South African Vlei Rat. **Endemism** South Africa.

4 Laminate Vlei Rat *Otomys laminatus* **NT**

Not illustrated – skull only. Largest and heaviest of the four Fynbos *Otomys*. Very similar to South African Vlei Rat and Robert's Vlei Rat. The only *Otomys* species that has 9 or 10 laminae on third upper molar. Stocky, with soft, shaggy fur. Upperparts dark buffy brown to reddish brown. Underparts and throat pale yellowish. Tail short (± half of head–body length), thickly haired and two-tone (dark above, lighter below). **Size** Length: 30cm; tail: 10cm; mass: 190g. **Status and Habitat** Diurnal and crepuscular. Uncommon, localised and rarely encountered. Terrestrial and restricted to mountain Fynbos. Known to occur in moist grassland and coastal forest in other parts of its range. Known to occur in restio-dominated mountain Fynbos wetlands near Paarl, in the Kogelberg and on the Cape Peninsula. **Endemism** South Africa. **Conservation Status** Near Threatened owing to restricted range, small population size and on-going threats to wetlands and fragmentation of suitable habitat.

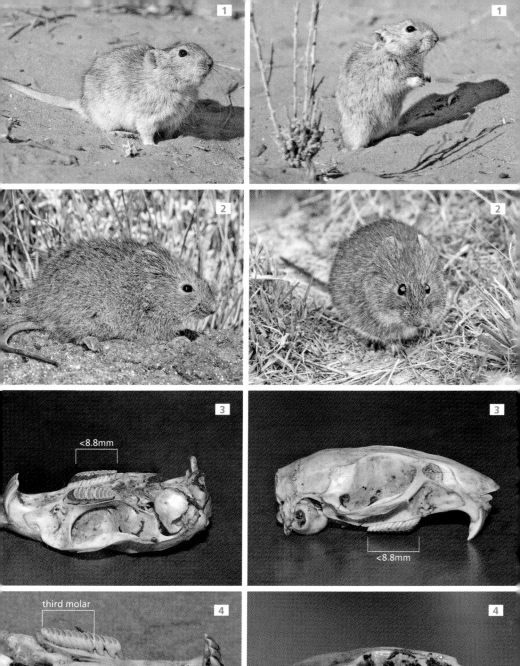

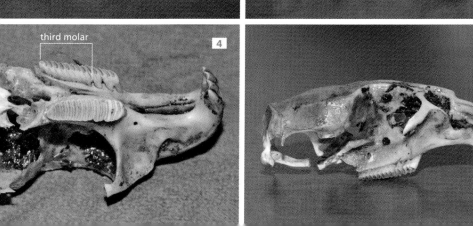

1 Bush Karoo Rat *Otomys unisulcatus*

Stocky rodent with compact appearance. Dorsal coloration ashy brown, fur interspersed with black hairs. Underparts pale buffy. Tail approximately equal to head–body length; pale brownish, darker above. The only local *Otomys* to have ungrooved lower incisors. Constructs large, conspicuous, dome-shaped nests of dry twigs and sticks. Nests can be over 2m in diameter and usually at base of shrub. There are burrows under the nests. **Size** Length: 24cm; tail: 9.5cm; mass: 125g. **Status and Habitat** Diurnal. Lives in small groups of up to eight. Abundant in suitable habitat. Favours habitats that do not burn or have a more infrequent fire cycle, such as open coastal Strandveld habitats and arid rocky areas. Terrestrial, but will climb up to 1m to feed in bushes. Differs from other local *Otomys* species in its preference for arid and semi-arid habitats. **Endemism** Southern Africa.

2 Barbour's Rock Mouse *Petromyscus barbouri*

Little known. Smaller and darker grey than Pygmy Rock Mouse. A small rodent with dark brownish-grey upperparts that are finely flecked with pale brown. Dorsal colour grades gradually into paler grey belly. Ears rounded and large. Whiskers long and prominent. Tail longer than head–body length, dark grey and paler below. **Size** Length: 16cm; tail: 8cm; mass: 16g. **Status and Habitat** Rupicolous and rarely encountered. Nocturnal and solitary. A Succulent Karoo species that enters the Fynbos Biome along the arid interior western edge. **Endemism** CFR (in South Africa).

3 Pygmy Rock Mouse *Petromyscus collinus*

Similar to Barbour's Rock Mouse and best distinguished from that species by its larger size and paler upperparts. A small rodent with fine, silky, yellowish-beige to light brown fur. Large rounded ears and long prominent whiskers. Tail longer than head–body length with sparse hair cover and scaly appearance. Juvenile greyer. **Size** Length: 19cm; tail: 10cm; mass: 20g. **Status and Habitat** Nocturnal and rupicolous. Secretive and rarely encountered. Adapted to arid and rocky habitats. Primarily known from the Nama- and Succulent Karoo, just entering the interior arid edges of the Fynbos Biome. Known to occur in the Groot Swartberg area.

Old World monkeys   Family Cercopithecidae

These primates have forward-facing eyes, good colour vision, a relatively poor sense of smell, dextrous hands, flat nails rather than claws, and a large brain. Opportunistic, very adaptable omnivores. Their barks, grunts and roars are important in the complex social structure of troops. One species occurs in the Fynbos Biome. The widespread Vervet Monkey (*Chlorocebus pygerythrus*) occurs in the well-wooded areas of the eastern side of the CFR.

4 Chacma Baboon *Papio ursinus*

The largest non-human primate in South Africa. Unmistakable. Fur shaggy, shades of grey-brown, often with grizzled appearance. Bare areas on dog-like muzzle black, as are top of the hands and feet. Eyes relatively small and set in the front of the skull. Rounded ears are flat against head. Tail approximately equal to head–body length and projects upwards for first third, then sharply downwards for the remainder. Female significantly smaller than male. **Size** Length: 100–160cm; tail: 50–85cm; mass: 12–45kg. **Status and Habitat** Common, diurnal and gregarious. Highly adaptable; found in diverse range of habitats, but needs cliffs or large trees to roost at night. Generally absent from featureless, flat areas in the lowlands.

CARNIVORES OF THE FYNBOS BIOME

There are 18 carnivore species in the Fynbos Biome, with several species having become locally extinct. Carnivores fulfil a very important ecological role. They form a critical part of the food chain and are important in controlling the populations of potential pest species. Many species are important seed dispersal agents and some local species have been recorded feeding on nectar, thereby providing a pollination function for some Fynbos plants.

Canids   Family Canidae

Classic dog-like appearance, with a prominent muzzle, large pointed ears, broad chest, long legs and bushy tail. Many of the smaller species are nocturnal while the larger, social species tend to be diurnal. As with many predators, larger species are regularly in conflict with humans. Three species still occur in the Fynbos Biome. The African Wild Dog (*Lycaon pictus*) is locally extinct.

1 Cape Fox *Vulpes chama*

The only 'true' fox (*Vulpes* sp.) in southern Africa. Small, with a warm, sandy dorsal coloration and grizzled silver-grey on back and flanks. Front of legs, chest, throat and lower parts of muzzle pale buff. Eyes large and dark. Ears big and erect, rich tawny colour behind. Underparts pale buff. Long, bushy tail ends in dark tip. Call is high-pitched yelp, uttered at night. **Size** Length: 86–97cm; tail: 29–39cm; shoulder height: 30cm; mass: 2.5–4kg. **Status and Habitat** Predominantly nocturnal and solitary. Common, but abundance lower where Black-backed Jackal is present. Prefers sparsely vegetated arid and semi-arid habitats. Occurs across the Fynbos Biome but more prevalent in lowlands, where it also utilises agricultural areas.

2 Bat-eared Fox *Otocyon megalotis*

Easily distinguished from Cape Fox by black legs, sooty markings on face and, most notably, the significantly large ears. Dorsal coloration tawny beige. Numerous longer, white-tipped black guard hairs produce grizzled appearance. Legs and tail tip black. Variable sooty to black shading around eyes and top of muzzle, forming T-shaped pattern on face. Back of enormous ears dark, black towards tips. The distinctive ears are used to detect subterranean insects and other small prey items. **Size** Length: 75–90cm; tail: 23–34cm; height: 30cm; mass: 3–5kg. **Status and Habitat** Nocturnal and social, occurring in family groups of 2–6 individuals. Common and widespread in open scrubland and readily uses farmlands. Prefers arid areas with short vegetation and bare ground. Extremely vulnerable to being hit by vehicles at night.

3 Black-backed Jackal *Lupulella mesomelas*

Largest of the three Fynbos Biome canid species. Dorsal coloration rich rufous- to orange-brown, with distinct dark saddle on back. Saddle broadest at shoulders, black, densely interspersed with silver hair throughout. Ears large and erect. Belly white, as are the chest, throat and lower parts of long muzzle. Long tail predominantly black, variably grizzled. Territorial call is distinctive series of plaintive howls. **Size** Length: 71–130cm; tail: 26–40cm; height: 30–48cm; mass: 6–12kg. **Status and Habitat** Mostly nocturnal, solitary and cunning. Common, but shy and very secretive where persecuted. Opportunistic generalist with wide habitat tolerance. Widespread throughout Biome, favouring drier, open environments, but will make use of densely vegetated areas.

Mustelids   Family Mustelidae

Mustelids are small to medium-sized carnivores with an elongated body and short legs. Although all carnivores have anal scent glands, these are enlarged in Mustelidae. As such, mustelids can all produce a unique, powerful smell, with Striped Polecat and African Striped Weasel able to eject their pungent secretions towards a perceived threat. Several species have a distinctive black-and-white coloration, which serves as a warning to potential predators (aposematic coloration). Four species are found in the Fynbos Biome.

1 Cape Clawless Otter *Aonyx capensis* NT

Large, stocky, semi-aquatic and the only otter in the Fynbos Biome. Short fur brown to dark chocolate-brown. Underparts slightly paler; throat, chest and lower portions of face off-white to pale cream. Muzzle short and rounded, with large, flat nose. Ears small and rounded. Five clawless, stubby digits on each foot with partial webbing on hind feet. Thick, long tail used for swimming. **Size** Length: 110–130cm; tail: 50cm; shoulder height: 35cm; mass: 10–17kg. **Status and Habitat** Common and widespread. Closely associated with a variety of permanent and temporary water bodies as well as the coastline. Must have access to fresh water for drinking where utilising the coast for foraging. Active during day or night, peak activity periods early morning and late afternoon. **Conservation Status** Near Threatened, primarily owing to degradation of aquatic environments.

2 Honey Badger *Mellivora capensis*

Famously tenacious and incredibly brave. Medium-sized, sturdy and muscular with fairly short legs and relatively short tail. Coat coarse, distinctly patterned. Underparts, lower flanks and tail black, contrasting sharply with silvery-grey to white upperparts, which run from top of head to base of tail. White back usually variably grizzled, outer edges palest, often appearing as two white stripes on upper flanks. Eyes and ears small. Impressive claws for digging. Growls and grunts readily when annoyed, challenged or while foraging. **Size** Length: 90–100cm; tail: 20–24cm; height: 30cm; mass: 8–14kg. **Status and Habitat** Mainly nocturnal, but regularly seen during day. Solitary and widespread, occurring at low densities. Home ranges extensive. Adaptable and able to utilise a wide range of habitats. Found throughout Fynbos Biome, particularly favouring the coastal lowlands.

3 African Striped Weasel *Poecilogale albinucha* NT

Also known as Snake Weasel owing to its extremely thin and elongated shape. Short, coarse, black fur, with four broad white to yellowish longitudinal bands down back. Bands merge at base of tail and on nape to form uniform white crown. Tail hair long, white with black base, resulting in grizzled appearance. Eyes and ears small. Assumed to spend much time underground. Small enough to utilise rodent burrows. **Size** Length: 40–50cm; tail: 12–16cm; height: 5–7cm; mass: 220–350g. **Status and Habitat** Solitary, rare and secretive. Predominantly nocturnal. Utilises Fynbos, Strandveld and Renosterveld habitats. Also recorded from pine plantations and agricultural areas. **Conservation Status** Near Threatened owing to habitat loss and harvesting for traditional medicine.

4 Striped Polecat *Ictonyx striatus*

Differs from African Striped Weasel by larger size, longer hair and three distinct white spots on the face. Crown not uniformly white. Soft, silky coat black with four broad white stripes, which run from head along back to base of tail. Variable spot in centre of forehead; larger white patches below each ear. Relatively large, rounded ears with white tips. Tail variably white and black. **Size** Length: 57–67cm; tail: 26cm; height: 10–15cm; mass: 0.6–1.4kg. **Status and Habitat** Nocturnal and solitary. Common, but seldom seen. Found across Fynbos Biome, from sea level to mountainous habitats. Very adaptable and widespread, even persisting in agricultural areas. Prone to being hit by cars at night.

Mongooses
Family Herpestidae

Generally slender, small mammals with short legs. Known for their speed and agility. They have pointed facial features, small, round ears closely pressed to the head, and a long bushy tail. Mongooses occupy a diverse range of habitats. Significant predators and some species perform an important role in controlling rodent populations. Four species occur in the Fynbos Biome.

1 Cape Grey Mongoose *Herpestes pulverulentus*

The most frequently seen mongoose in the Fynbos Biome. Also known as Small Grey Mongoose. Dorsal coloration light to slate-grey with intense grizzled patterning visible at close range. Ventral parts like upperparts, but not grizzled. Shorter hair on legs and muzzle appear darker than dorsal coloration. Tail long, 85–90% of head–body length. Easily separated from Large Grey Mongoose by significantly smaller size and absence of dark tail tip. **Size** Length: 55–76cm; tail: 20–34cm; mass: 0.5–1.25kg. **Status and Habitat** Diurnal, solitary, widespread and common. Adaptable and found in diverse habitats across the Fynbos Biome, where it utilises dense vegetation and rocky areas for shelter. Avoids very open areas. **Endemism** Southern Africa.

2 Large Grey Mongoose *Herpestes ichneumon*

Significantly larger than Cape Grey Mongoose, with very long, black-tipped tail. Upperparts grey overall. Dense covering of long, banded, black-and-white guard hairs result in grizzled appearance. Guard hairs progressively longer on flanks and hindquarters. Underparts variable shades of grey with warmer tones. Long tail exceeds head–body length and tapers towards black tufted tip. Legs relatively short and darker than body. **Size** Length: 100–112cm; tail: 45–58cm; mass: 2.5–4kg. **Status and Habitat** Diurnal. Mainly solitary, but occasionally seen in small groups. Usually associated with riparian areas and wetland edges. Largely confined to coastal lowlands. Can be quite common in certain areas such as the Overberg. Becoming more common close to Cape Town and spreading further up the West Coast in recent years.

3 Water Mongoose *Atilax paludinosus*

Large, powerful mongoose associated with aquatic habitats. Dense, shaggy coat usually dark chocolate-brown, but can vary from russet-brown to nearly black. Dense covering of long, coarse guard hairs, which are dark, glossy and often banded, creating a grizzled appearance. Lower half of large nose characteristically pinkish. Long, splayed, clawed toes leave distinct tracks in wet soil. **Size** Length: 80–100cm; tail: 30–40cm; mass: 2.5–4.2kg. **Status and Habitat** Nocturnal and crepuscular. Solitary, shy and secretive. Common in suitable habitat. Closely associated with seasonal and perennial wetlands, estuaries and other water bodies. Readily utilises artificial wetlands and degraded urban waterways. Found across the Fynbos Biome where there is suitable cover and riparian habitat.

4 Yellow Mongoose *Cynictis penicillata*

The only pale mongoose in the Fynbos Biome. Short fur ranges from sandy yellow to ochre. Coats of Fynbos Biome animals are densely interspersed with pale grey hairs, especially on head and neck. Ventral coloration, including chest, throat and chin, slightly paler. Long tail ends in white tip. Alert appearance and demeanour, frequently standing on hind legs to survey surrounds. **Size** Length: 40–60cm; tail: 18–25cm; mass: 450–900g. **Status and Habitat** Predominantly diurnal with limited nocturnal activity. Solitary, bold and adaptable. Prefers drier open habitats. Readily utilises heavily impacted agricultural areas. Common and widespread, but avoids rocky, mountainous habitats and densely vegetated areas.

Genets and civets   Family Viverridae

Small to medium-sized carnivores with an elongated, slender body, long tail and short legs. Like cats (Felidae) they have retractable claws. Two species occur in the Fynbos Biome. Further genetic assessment is needed to clarify whether the subspecies of Small-spotted Genet (*Genetta genetta felina*) relevant to the Biome represents a separate species, namely Feline Genet (*G. felina*).

1 Small-spotted Genet *Genetta genetta*

Distinguished from Cape Genet by whitish tail tip, smaller dark spots and crest of longer hair along backbone, which can be raised when alarmed. Upperparts vary from light sandy grey to off-white, with relatively small, uniformly dark spots, which are roughly orientated in longitudinal lines. Underparts off-white to pale grey with yellowish tinge. Bold facial pattern with black chin and black bands on either side of muzzle. Large white spots below eyes. White to greyish spots also present above eyes and on either side of nose. Distinct ringed tail approximately equal to head–body length, with 8–10 lighter bands, usually ends in pale tip. **Size** Length: 86–100cm; tail: 40–50cm; mass: 1.5–2.5kg. **Status and Habitat** Nocturnal, solitary and secretive. Common and widespread. Favours well-vegetated and/or rocky areas. Able to tolerate partially degraded areas.

2 Cape Genet *Genetta tigrina*

Similar to Small-spotted Genet but distinguished by black tail tip, larger spots (often with chestnut-brown centres) and less obvious crest along back. Pale fawn to light grey above, with black to russet-coloured spots in roughly longitudinal lines. Underparts light greyish white. Bold facial markings similar to but often less pronounced than Small-spotted Genet; chin pale. Distinct, ringed tail has 7–9 lighter bands, ending in dark tip and approximately equal to head–body length. **Size** Length: 85–110cm; tail: 40–50cm; mass: 1.5–3.2kg. **Status and Habitat** Nocturnal, solitary and common. The two genet species are sympatric throughout most of the Fynbos Biome, but Cape Genet prefers more mesic and wooded areas. **Endemism** Southern Africa.

Hyaenas and aardwolf   Family Hyaenidae

Medium-sized to large. While generally dog-like in appearance and behaviour, evolutionary origins are closer to cats (Felidae) and civets (Viverridae). A characteristic feature is the slanted back. The shoulders are significantly higher than the rump owing to the longer front legs. Spotted Hyaena (*Crocuta crocuta*) was once abundant in the Fynbos Biome, but was regionally extinct by 1934. Two species persist in the Fynbos Biome.

3 Brown Hyaena *Parahyaena brunnea* **NT**

Large and very distinctive, with a markedly shaggy appearance. Front legs notably longer than hind legs. Mostly dark brown, mottled with lighter brown. Mantle paler tan-brown. Legs pale brown to buff with irregular black bands. Tail short, dark and shaggy. Muzzle bare and uniformly dark. Ears large, erect, pointed, constricted at base. When agitated, it raises an impressive mane that runs from nape to tail. **Size** Length: 130–160cm; tail: 18–260cm; height: 80cm; mass: 35–50kg. **Status and Habitat** Solitary, nocturnal, rare and secretive. Favours arid habitats. Historically widely distributed across the Western Cape, but range significantly reduced. A small population persists around Anysberg Nature Reserve with other scattered records, potentially indicating the recolonisation of some areas. **Conservation Status** Near Threatened owing to persecution.

1 Aardwolf *Proteles cristatus*

This small member of the Hyaenidae is a true insectivore and the only member of the family with five (rather than four) toes on each foot. Upperparts pale tan to yellowish with black vertical stripes across body. Long mane along middle of slanted back is erected when agitated. Legs banded. Fluffy tail predominantly dark; last third of long tail hairs black, first two-thirds off-white. When agitated this hair is also erected and tail appears much paler. Muzzle, area around eyes and feet black. Ears large and erect. **Size** Length: 84–100cm; tail: 20–28cm; height: 47cm; mass: 7–10kg. **Status and Habitat** Nocturnal, solitary and shy. Adapted to diverse habitats; favouring more arid environs where termites are abundant. Tolerant of some disturbance as long as termites are present. Not common in Fynbos Biome but recorded from more arid open areas.

Cats   Family Felidae

They range from small to large, with a a sleek muscular build, distinctive rounded head, flattish face, large eyes and whiskers. With the exception of the Cheetah (*Acinonyx jubatus*), all species have retractable claws. Felids require the highest protein content in their diet of all carnivores. All species have declined in range and abundance and they are amongst the most threatened mammal families globally. Lion (*Panthera leo*), Serval (*Leptailurus serval*) and Cheetah all historically occurred in the Fynbos Biome but are now locally extinct. This included a distinct subspecies of lion, the Cape Lion (*P. l. melanochaita*), which is now globally extinct.

2 African Wild Cat *Felis silvestris*

Very similar to the domestic cat, with which it frequently hybridises. However, the rich, red-brown colour behind the ears, as well as the longer legs, is distinct in pure specimens. Dorsal colour varies across large range, but generally warm beige-brown to grey. Faint dark vertical stripes sometimes visible on body. Pale eyes with vertical pupils. Indistinct darker facial marks may be present. Pronounced black banding on legs. Hair on bottom of feet black. Long tail with four or five dark bands and a dark tip. Underparts lighter than body, often more buffy. **Size** Length: 85–96cm; tail: 25–36cm; height: 35cm; mass: 4.9kg (male), 3.7kg (female). **Status and Habitat** Nocturnal and solitary. Fairly common. Wide habitat tolerance but requires some vegetation cover. Tolerates degraded habitat.

3 Caracal *Caracal caracal*

A medium-sized, compact and very attractive cat. Hind legs marginally longer than front, resulting in rump being slightly higher than shoulders. Dorsal coloration reddish brown to bright rufous. Fur short and dense. Underparts whitish with faint darker blotching. Long erect ears distinctive; black behind and pointed with tufts of long black hair on tips. White markings around eyes, nose and mouth. Black markings accentuate facial features. Tail short, unmarked and same colour as back. **Size** Length: 99–127cm; tail: 18–34cm; shoulder height: 40–45cm; mass: 7–19kg. **Status and Habitat** Predominantly nocturnal. Common, widespread and very adaptable. Can tolerate degraded environments.

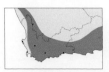

1 Leopard *Panthera pardus* VU

Large, spotted and distinctive. Variably sized black spots on limbs, flanks, hindquarters and head. Spots gradually turn into rosettes on rest of body. Patterning unique to each individual. Basal colour of upperparts pale yellowish beige to orange-buff. Underparts white. Long tail more than 50% of head–body length, same colour as back above, white below, with large dark spots. Tip of tail pure white below. Ears short and round. While leopards from the Fynbos Biome are significantly smaller than their northern counterparts, they are not genetically distinct. **Size** Length: 1.7m; tail: 68cm; mass: 31kg (male), 21kg (female). **Status and Habitat** Nocturnal, solitary, secretive and rarely encountered. Wide habitat tolerance but dependent on adequate cover. In the Fynbos Biome, primarily persists in mountainous areas. Extremely adaptable; would historically have utilised all available habitats within Biome. **Conservation Status** Regional status Vulnerable owing to persecution, hunting and habitat transformation.

Aardvark   Family Orycteropodidae

A monotypic family endemic to Africa. The Aardvark is an ecosystem engineer and a keystone species. At least 39 species of vertebrates have been found to utilise Aardvark burrows, including Forest Shrew, South African Shelduck, Egyptian Slit-faced Bat, Puffadder and various rodents. The validity of the 18 described subspecies is uncertain, and more research is needed.

2 Aardvark *Orycteropus afer*

Wonderfully bizarre. Large, barrel-shaped, heavyset and muscular, with rounded back, thick short legs, and long, heavy, tapering tail. Elongated pig-like snout very distinctive. Donkey-like ears long, tubular, erect. Sparse, coarse hair dark, showing pinkish-grey to tan skin. Overall colour tends to match substrate where it occurs. Legs hairier than body. Four digits on front feet and five on the back. Claws on front feet long, spatulate and used for digging. **Size** Length: 1.4–1.8m; tail: 45–60cm; mass: 40–70kg. **Status and Habitat** Solitary and predominantly nocturnal. Diurnal activity rare, mostly in times of drought. Fairly common but seldom seen. Wide habitat tolerance, but dependent on sufficient volumes of the ant and termite species they feed on. Widespread in Biome but absent from extremely rocky areas and steep slopes in mountain Fynbos.

Hyraxes   Family Procaviidae

Small, dumpy, tailless animals. Gregarious and herbivorous. Hyraxes have conical, tusk-like upper incisors used for grazing and browsing. They are important prey items for a host of predators. One species occurs in the Fynbos Biome.

3 Rock Hyrax *Procavia capensis*

Rotund and compact, with no tail. Thick, short fur predominantly grizzled brown to grey-brown; some individuals quite buffy. Scattered, elongated tactile hair present across body. Underparts paler, but not white. Patch of longer black hair in centre of back covers dorsal gland. Paler patches present above eyes, around lips and behind ears. Muzzle short, pointed. Eyes large; ears small and rounded. Legs short with padded feet and rounded digits. May constitute a species complex. **Size** Length: 40–60cm; height: 15–22cm; mass: 2.5–5kg. **Status and Habitat** Gregarious. Diurnal, but will forage on warm, bright nights. Widespread in diverse habitats with rocky outcrops. Adaptable to transformed environments including culverts, stone walls and erosion gullies. Skittish, barks alarm calls at perceived threats. Tame at busy tourist sites. Latrine sites are good indicator of their presence.

Horses and relatives

Family Equidae

Typically 'horse-like'; large, big-headed and long-necked. Long, slender legs, each with single hoof. Face elongated, with large ears. The Mountain Zebra is the only species naturally associated with the Fynbos Biome, although some land owners have stocked extralimital Plains Zebra (*Equus quagga*).

1 Cape Mountain Zebra *Equus zebra zebra*

Two subspecies of mountain zebra are recognised; the Cape Mountain Zebra (*E. z. zebra*) is found in the Fynbos Biome. The presence of a dewlap distinguishes mountain zebras from other zebras. Patterning highly distinctive: white with dense series of black bars across entire body. No two individuals have the same pattern. No shadow stripes (diffuse brown stripes between black stripes). Belly white with black centre stripe. Distinct gridiron pattern on rump above tail. Tip of muzzle warm brown. Nose and lips black. Short, erect, dense mane runs from between ears to shoulders. **Size** Length: 2.7m; tail: 40cm; shoulder height: 1.3m; mass: 250–260kg. **Status and Habitat** Social and diurnal. Prefers hills, mountain slopes and plateaus. Nearly extirpated in the 1950s, but population numbers recovered owing to sound management. Historical distribution across much of Fynbos Biome; reintroduced to various protected areas and private farms. **Endemism** South Africa.

Pigs

Family Suidae

These distinctive mammals have adapted to a wide range of habitats. They are omnivorous and fulfil an important seed dispersal function, especially in forested habitats. All species enjoy a good wallow in mud. One species is found in the Fynbos Biome.

2 Bushpig *Potamochoerus larvatus*

Large and robust. Has typical 'pig-like' elongated snout, which is blunt-ended and used for rooting around in soil. Very long, coarse hair variable in colour. Generally warm brown to grey-brown with darker shading. Greyish-white facial hair and pale grizzled mane along spine to mid-back. Large ears pointed and covered with shorter pale hair. Thin tail ending in a tassel of dark hair. Juvenile attractively patterned: brown with pale yellowish, longitudinal stripes. **Size** Length: 1.3–1.7m; tail: 38cm; height: 55–88cm; mass: 60–80kg. **Status and Habitat** Social, predominantly nocturnal and seldom seen. Relatively widespread, preferring dense vegetation such as thickets and riverine vegetation. Occurs along southern parts of the Biome as far west as Bot River. Utilises Fynbos and forested areas, as well as agricultural lands and pine plantations.

Hippopotamuses

Family Hippopotamidae

Hippos are iconic and one of Africa's most instantly recognisable and charismatic animals. This fascinating African endemic family contains only two species. They are amphibious.

3 Common Hippopotamus *Hippopotamus amphibius*

Unmistakable. Massive, with a rotund shape, short legs, large rectangular head and short tail. Smooth skin slaty-grey with pinkish hue. Underparts more pinkish. Sparse, coarse hairs on body. Muzzle broad, angular; massive gape with prominent canines. Nostrils and eyes on top of head; breaking water surface while rest of head and body submerged. Stubby tail tip edged in coarse hair. **Size** Length: 3.4–4.2m; tail: 30–50cm; height: 1.5m; mass: 1,000–2,000kg. **Status and Habitat** Semi-aquatic, gregarious and highly territorial. Most active at night. Requires suitable aquatic habitat (perennial rivers, vleis, dams or estuaries) with sufficient grazing. Historically widespread but extirpated from the Fynbos Biome. Access to fresh drinking water important when utilising saline habitats such as estuaries. Reintroduced to a few protected areas and private farms in the Biome.

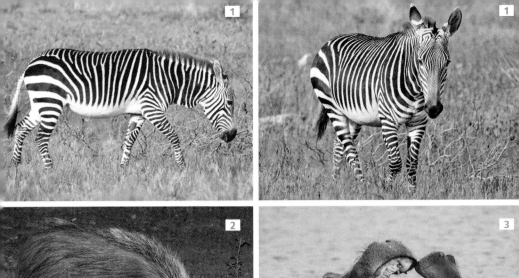

Hollow-horned ruminants
Family Bovidae

Diverse in size and form, though all have sturdy hooves and males develop permanent unbranched, hollow horns with a bony centre. Females also have horns in some species. Occupying a wide range of habitats, bovids have different feeding strategies. They can be grazers, browsers, mixed feeders and/or frugivorous. They play an important role in shaping plant communities. Ten species are found naturally in the Fynbos Biome, while the game-farming industry has introduced several extralimital species.

1 Common Eland *Tragelaphus oryx*

The largest antelope in the world. Upperparts beige to caramel; legs paler. Can show shades of steel-grey, particularly on neck, and most notable in older animals. Short, dark mane runs along back of neck. Long, thin tail ends in tuft of long dark hair. Both sexes have dewlaps and straight, twisted horns. Bulls much larger, with thicker horns and distinct patch of longer, dark hair on forehead (inset). Older males develop very large dewlaps. **Size** Length: 2.2–4.2m; tail: 60cm; shoulder height: 1.5–1.7m; mass: 450–700kg; horn length: 60cm. **Status and Habitat** Diurnal. Occurs in herds and utilises a wide range of habitats. Historically common and widespread. In the Fynbos Biome, occurs in numerous protected areas and on private farms where reintroduced.

2 Greater Kudu *Tragelaphus strepsiceros*

Stately, large, with short, brownish-grey coat and 6–10 thin, white vertical stripes across body. Mane runs along back, merging with longer hair on relatively short tail. Bulls larger, more robust, greyer in colour and with long, distinctive, spiralled horns. Horn development can be used to age males. Bulls also have distinctive strip of longer hair down centre of throat. **Size** Length: 2.3–2.9m; tail: 43cm; shoulder height: 1.2–1.5m; mass: 165–250kg; horn length: 1.2m. **Status and Habitat** Relatively common, forming small herds. Largely crepuscular but completely nocturnal where hunted. Historically absent from much of the low shrublands of the Fynbos Biome. Enters the Fynbos Biome on the edges of the Succulent Karoo, especially where there are riverine thickets. Widely introduced and able to move at will owing to impressive jumping abilities. Becoming established on the West Coast south of Langebaan owing to introductions.

3 Southern Bushbuck *Tragelaphus sylvaticus*

A secretive, medium-sized antelope. Dorsal coloration varies greatly; reddish brown to grey-brown or slaty-brown. Adult male darker chocolate-brown; female and juvenile brighter reddish brown. Dark blaze on muzzle runs from forehead to nose. Variable white spots between and below eyes, around lips, on flanks and rump. White bands on throat and chest. Short, bushy tail dark above and white below. Male larger, with medium-sized, relatively straight horns with twist in middle, and crest of longer hair down back, raised when alarmed. **Size** Length: 1.3–1.66m; tail: 20cm; shoulder height: 70–80cm; mass: 30–45kg; horn length: 26cm. **Status and Habitat** Primarily nocturnal. Usually solitary, but occasionally in pairs or small groups of females with young. Common in suitable thick vegetation along southern coastal areas of the Fynbos Biome. Occurs as far west as Hermanus.

1 Grey Rhebok *Pelea capreolus* NT

A slender antelope with thick, short, woolly fur. Grey, with light shades of fawn on head, neck and legs. Long, thin face has whitish tip to muzzle, large black nose and eyes. Distinctive ears very long, thin and erect. Tail short, woolly and white underneath. Belly white. Male marginally larger than female and has erect, straight, narrow horns. **Size** Length: 1.1–1.3m; tail: 10cm; shoulder height: 75cm; mass: 20kg; horn length: 20cm. **Status and Habitat** Diurnal, forming small herds. Prefers rocky hillsides and mountain slopes within the Fynbos Biome. Regularly seen on agricultural fields, particularly in the Overberg. **Endemism** Southern Africa. **Conservation Status** Near Threatened owing to a decrease in population size, most likely attributed to poaching and predator pressure.

2 Red Hartebeest *Alcelaphus buselaphus*

Large and distinct, unlike any other species in the Fynbos Biome. Slanted profile; hindquarters lower than shoulders. Upperparts rich, reddish caramel, fading slightly on flanks. Pale patch on rump from the base of tail to top of hindquarters. Tail long, dark and tufted. Black coloration on all legs. Head long, with black blaze and brown bar between eyes. Both sexes have horns; male horns more thickset. Bases of horns close together on top of head; narrowly splayed, ridged and curve forward before bending sharply backwards. **Size** Length: 2.3m; tail: 47cm; shoulder height: 1.25m; mass: 120–150kg; horn length: 52cm. **Habitat** Gregarious and diurnal. Historically widespread but locally extirpated. Reintroduced to various protected areas and private farms in the Biome. Adaptable and utilises a diverse range of habitats.

3 Bontebok *Damaliscus pygargus pygargus* VU

A beautiful Fynbos Biome endemic. Considered a subspecies of *Damaliscus pygargus* along with Blesbok (*D. p. phillipsi*). Warm chocolate-brown on head and neck, fading to soft cinnamon on saddle and darkening to dark brown on flanks, rump and upper legs. Belly, base of tail, buttocks as well as inner and lower legs white. Characteristic uninterrupted white blaze on face from base of horns to nose. Both sexes have ridged horns that splay outwards and curve backwards. Calves uniform warm fawn with white on cheeks, throat, belly and around eyes. **Size** Length: 1.7–2m; tail: 30–45cm; shoulder height: 90cm; mass: 62kg; horn length: 38cm. **Status and Habitat** Overberg coastal plain endemic. Nearly extirpated owing to indiscriminate hunting. Saved by the actions of farmers; now widely reintroduced to various protected areas and private farms beyond the original distribution. **Endemism** Fynbos Biome. **Conservation Status** Vulnerable owing to hybridisation risk with Blesbok and limited remaining habitat.

4 Klipspringer *Oreotragus oreotragus*

Tan-brown to greyish with grizzled appearance. Head usually richer buff than rest of body; facial area often greyish. Underparts slightly paler. Pale greyish-white coloration on chin, around nose and occasionally around eyes. Two prominent glands visible below inner corner of each eye. Tail very short. Horns on male only, short, parallel, straight, ridged at base. Female slightly larger. Walks on flattened hoof tips, an adaption for gripping rocky surfaces. Unique hair hollow and flattened for optimal insulation. **Size** Length: 80–100cm; tail: 8cm; shoulder height: 50–60cm; mass: 10–13kg; horn length: 8cm. **Status and Habitat** Diurnal, in pairs or small family groups. Widespread and common in suitable habitat from sea-level to high altitudes. Restricted to mountainous and rocky outcrops, hills or gorges; absent from flat areas lacking structure.

Male Red-wing Starling plucking hair for nesting material

1 Steenbok *Raphicerus campestris*

Small and dainty, with reddish-fawn fur dorsally and white underparts. White buttocks clearly visible when fleeing. White around lips, below chin and around eyes. Large subocular glands on inner corners of large eyes. Horns on male only, short, sharp, parallel, ridged at base. **Size** Length: 75–90cm; tail: 5cm; shoulder height: 50m; mass: 11kg; horn length: 9cm. **Status and Habitat** Widespread, common and largely diurnal. Usually solitary. Favours open areas. Generally absent from thick vegetated areas such as dense moist Fynbos. Occurs throughout drier, more open areas of the Biome. Will utilise areas with very sparse vegetation cover, including agricultural fields. This habit of utilising open fields means that it is more easily and regularly seen than other small antelope.

2 Cape Grysbok *Raphicerus melanotis*

Distinguished from Steenbok by white flecking in coat and lack of white underparts. Has distinct preference for dense vegetation cover and seen far less frequently than Steenbok. Small and delicate, with distinctly rounded back and slanted hindquarters. Coloration warm orange-brown, interspersed with white hair. Paler greyish areas around eyes, nose and lips. Conspicuous subocular glands present below inner corner of each large eye. Male develops short, straight, smooth horns. **Size** Length: 72–81cm; tail: 5.5cm; shoulder height: 54cm; mass: 10kg; horn length: 8cm. **Status and Habitat** Predominantly nocturnal and cryptic. Solitary. Relatively common within restricted range. Primarily associated with the CFR and found across the Fynbos Biome, favouring areas with required dense vegetation cover. Will enter agricultural areas in close proximity to suitable cover. Able to persist in small urban sites, but vulnerable to predation by dogs. **Endemism** South Africa.

3 Common Duiker *Sylvicapra grimmia*

Also known as Grey or Bush Duiker. Sturdy and small, but significantly bigger than Cape Grysbok and Steenbok. Grey-brown to reddish brown. Inner flanks and lower belly white to greyish. Distinct black stripe down muzzle. Black lines on forelegs and sometimes hind legs. Bushy tail, black above and white below. Distinct long, conical tuft of hair usually present on top of head. Paler rings around eyes. Large subocular glands form prominent, dark lines below eyes. Male develops short, straight, sharp horns. Female generally larger. **Size** Length: 90–135cm; tail: 10–22cm; shoulder height: 50cm; mass: 18–21kg; horn length: 11cm. **Status and Habitat** Solitary, crepuscular and nocturnal. Widespread and common, found throughout Fynbos Biome in areas with sufficient vegetation cover. Will enter agricultural fields, utilising the fringes with sufficient natural vegetation or tall crops.

4 Himalayan Tahr *Hemitragus jemlahicus* Ⓐ

Medium-sized, stocky, goat-like animal with dense, shaggy coat. Both sexes with short strongly recurved horns; very thick at base. Legs relatively short and head smallish in relation to body. Coat shades of light to warm or dark brown. Hind-quarters and legs usually darker. Adults have dark face. Adult male has impressive shaggy mane around neck and shoulders, extending down top of front legs. Juvenile more uniformly pale. **Size** Length: 1.2–1.7m; tail: 9–12cm; shoulder height: 0.6–1m; mass: 135–180kg. **Status and Habitat** Native to the Himalayas. Small population established on the northern part of the Cape Peninsula from two escaped zoo animals in 1930s. Confined to rocky areas, including exposed cliffs. Occurs in small mixed herds; older males mainly solitary. **Conservation Status** Alien. Must be eradicated to protect the sensitive Table Mountain ecology.

GLOSSARY

Allopatric: Pertaining to a particular species of which the geographical distribution does not overlap with that of another, usually closely related species.

Altricial: Pertaining to a young animal hatched or born in an undeveloped state and in need of parental care and feeding.

Annual: Occurring once a year. In this context can refer to lifespan of some species that only live for one year.

Aquatic: Pertaining to an animal or plant that predominantly lives in water.

Arboreal: Pertaining to an animal that predominantly lives in or frequents trees.

Biodiversity: The biological diversity on Earth, including genetic, species and ecosystem level variations, as well as the evolutionary and ecological processes that maintain this diversity.

Biome: A consolidated or fragmented ecological unit of similar ecosystems, fauna and flora communities and complexes, that share climatic factors and soil types. Recognised biomes in South Africa include: Fynbos, Succulent Karoo, Nama-Karoo, Albany Thicket, Forest, Savanna, Grassland, Desert and Indian Ocean Coastal Belt.

Cape Floristic Region (CFR): The only floristic region within the Cape Floristic Kingdom and a globally unique collection of vegetation components (biomes). This region is located on the south-western tip of Africa and consists of an original core area (consisting of the Fynbos Biome, Afrotemperate Forest Biome and Albany Thicket Biome) which has been expanded to the Greater CFR, including the Succulent Karoo Biome.

Caudal autotomy: Self-amputation of a tail as a behavioural adaptation of some animals that voluntarily shed or discard their tail, or part thereof, as a self-defence mechanism. The tail is regenerated afterwards.

Cere: The normally bare, fleshy patch around the nostrils at the base of the bill of some bird species.

Class: A major taxonomic rank in biological classification of organisms, between phylum and order.

Conservation status: Threat status of a particular species based on an assessment of its risk of extinction if the current threats remain in place.

Ecosystem: A grouping of living and non-living components, their interactions, the structure it takes and the ecological processes that maintain it, that form a functional ecological unit.

Ecosystem engineer: Any species that creates, meaningfully modifies, maintains or destroys a habitat. Their activities are very important in maintaining a healthy ecosystem as it can effect change to the species richness and landscape-level heterogeneity of an area.

Endemic / endemism: Endemic refers to a species that is restricted to a specific geographical area and occurs nowhere else. Endemism is the occurrence of endemic species.

Envenomation: The injection of venom into another organism, usually through a bite or a sting.

Family: The taxonomic group between order and genus, consisting of one or more genera sharing a common attribute and that has evolved from the same ancestor.

Fauna: The animals of a particular region, habitat or geological period.

Flora: The plants of a particular region, habitat or geological period.

Fossorial: Pertaining to an animal that lives primarily underground. Such animals are specifically adapted to this fossorial lifestyle and are efficient burrowers.

Fynbos Biome: One of the biomes contained within the CFR. This globally unique biome consists of three vegetation complexes, namely Fynbos, Strandveld and Renosterveld, which all contain numerous finer-scale vegetation type units.

Gape: The fleshy area at the base of a bird's bill where the upper and lower mandibles meet. Generally conspicuous in juvenile birds.

Genus: The taxonomic group between family and species, consisting of one or more species that are structurally and phylogenetically related.

Geophyte: A perennial plant that includes an underground storage organ for food and water, and propagates through underground buds. Commonly referred to as 'bulbs'.

Guard hairs: Long, coarse hair forming the outer fur and can be seen rising above the thicker layer of under-fur.

Habitat: An area occupied by a species or group of species as a result of the particular environmental conditions that exist in this area.

Home range: The geographical area where an animal spends all of its time and that contains all the resourced that animal needs to survive and reproduce.

Indigenous: Refers to something that originated or naturally occurs within a specific area.

Karroid habitat: Habitat that consists primarily of the small-leaved, succulent, dwarf shrubland vegetation characteristic of the Karoo biomes.

Keystone species: A species that is critical to an ecosystem. In its absence, the particular ecosystem will be significantly altered or could even cease to exist.

Mesic: Describes an environment or habitat with a moderate moisture content.

Monotypic: Having only one type or representative. Relevant to a taxonomic grouping, for example a monotypic genus contains only one species.

Mucronate: Ending in a short, sharp point.

Order: The taxonomic group between class and family, consisting of one or more families sharing a set of similar characteristics.

Oviparous: Pertaining to an animal with the ability to produce young through eggs that hatch after they have been laid.

Palearctic: A biogeographical area consisting of Europe, the part of Asia north of the Himalayas, the northern and central parts of the Arabian Peninsula and the part of Africa north of the Sahara. One of the eight biogeographic realms of ecozones of Earth.

Perennial: Lasting or existing for a long period of time. Also referring to plants or animals that live for several years.

Phylogeny: The evolutionary history of an organism or a group of organisms.

Pollinators: Organisms that assist in transferring pollen from the male part of the flower (stamens) to the female part of the same or another flower (stigma). This pollen transfer ensures the fertilisation of the plant and the production of fruit, seeds and young plants.

Population: A number of organisms of the same species that live and interbreed in a particular geographical area.

Precocial: Pertaining to a young animal hatched or born in a developed state and able to feed itself almost immediately.

Protected Areas: Area that are protected by law and managed primarily for biodiversity conservation.

Reintroduction: The action of putting a plant or animal back into a former habitat.

Rictal bristles: The term 'rictus' refers to the gape. These bristles were thought to function as a 'net' assisting a bird to capture insects in flight. The actual role of these bristles is now being debated and they may not actually help physically with prey capture but rather perform a sensory function.

Rupicolous: Pertaining to an animal that lives on rocks or in rocky environments.

Scatter-hoarding: Animal behaviour whereby food is hidden in various scattered locations during times of surplus for future use when food is less readily available.

South Africa: The geographical range consisting only of the Republic of South Africa, excluding Lesotho and Swaziland.

Southern Africa: The geographical range that includes South Africa and neighbouring countries of Lesotho, Eswatini, Namibia, Botswana, Zimbabwe and the portion of Mozambique south of the Zambezi River.

Species: The lowest taxonomic group below genus, consisting of similar organisms that are capable of interbreeding.

Species complex: A group of closely related organisms that are so similar in appearance that the boundaries between them are often unclear.

Subspecies: A taxonomic rank below species level which represents one or more populations of a species that show variation in morphological characteristics.

Sympatric: Describing a situation where two or more compared species have overlapping geographical rages.

Taxon: A taxonomic grouping of any rank, such as subspecies, species or family.

Taxonomy: The science concerned with classification resulting in the hierarchical order arranging various organisms into successive levels of biological classification, consisting of Domain, Kingdom, Phylum, Class, Order, Family, Genus and lastly Species.

Terrestrial: Pertaining to an animal that predominantly lives on land, as opposed to living in water, trees or underground.

Tragus: An important feature in many bat species and consisting of a piece of skin in front of the ear canal that assists in directing sounds into the ear.

Vibrissae: Long, stiff hairs on mammals (normally on the face, such as whiskers) or coarse, bristle-like feathers around the gape of certain bird species.

Viviparous / viviparity: Pertaining to the ability of an animal to give live birth to offspring that has developed within the maternal body due to the retention of the fertilised eggs in the oviducts.

EXCLUDED BIRD SPECIES

The following species have been recorded in the region, but are not considered 'true' Fynbos Biome birds. As such, they are not featured in the species accounts.

Key				
Vagrant	V	Locally Extinct		LE
Alien	A	Introduced		I
Wetlands / rivers	1	Grassland		6
Coastline	2	Agricultural areas		7
Woodland	3	Thickets		8
Forest / forest edge	4	Succulent Karoo		9
Gardens	5	Suburbia		10

Avocet, Pied 1, 2
Barbet, Black-collared 3, 4, 5
Barbet, Crested V
Bateleur V
Batis, Pririt 9
Bee-eater, Blue-cheeked V
Bee-eater, Little V
Bee-eater, Olive V
Bee-eater, Southern Carmine V
Bee-eater, Swallow-tailed V
Bee-eater, White-fronted V
Bee-eater, White-throated V
Bishop, Yellow-crowned V
Bittern, Dwarf V
Bittern, Eurasian LE
Bittern, Little 1
Blackcap, Bush V
Blackcap, Eurasian V
Booby, Brown V
Booby, Red-footed V
Brownbul, Terrestrial 4
Bulbul, African Red-eyed 5, 9
Bulbul, Dark-capped V
Bunting, Cinnamon-breasted 3, 6, 9
Bunting, Golden-breasted 3
Bushshrike, Grey-headed V
Bushshrike, Olive 4, 8
Bustard, Kori V
Bustard, Ludwig's 9
Buzzard, Crested Honey V
Buzzard, European Honey 3
Buzzard, Forest 3, 4
Buzzard, Red-necked V
Camaroptera, Green-backed 4

Canary, Black-headed 7, 9
Canary, Black-throated V
Chaffinch, Common A, 3, 5
Chat, Ant-eating 7, 9
Chat, Karoo 9
Chat, Tractrac 9
Cisticola, Wing-snapping 6, 7
Coot, Red-knobbed 1
Cormorant, Bank 2
Cormorant, Cape 2
Cormorant, Crowned 2
Cormorant, Reed 1
Cormorant, White-breasted 1, 2
Courser, Bronze-winged V
Courser, Burchell's 7
Courser, Double-banded 9
Courser, Temminck's V
Crake, African V
Crake, Baillon's 1
Crake, Black 1
Crake, Corn V
Crake, Little V
Crake, Spotted V
Crane, Wattled 1
Crow, House A, 10
Cuckoo, African V
Cuckoo, African Emerald 4
Cuckoo, Black 3, 4
Cuckoo, Common V
Cuckoo, Great Spotted V
Cuckoo, Jacobin 3, 8
Cuckoo, Red-chested 4, 5
Cuckooshrike, Black 4, 8
Cuckooshrike, Grey 4
Curlew, Eurasian 1, 2
Darter, African 1
Dove, Lemon 4
Dove, Rock 10
Dove, Tambourine 4, 8
Drongo, Fork-tailed 3, 5, 8

Duck, Fulvous Whistling 1
Duck, Knob-billed V
Duck, Maccoa 1
Duck, White-backed 1
Duck, White-faced Whistling 1
Dunlin V
Eagle, African Fish 1
Eagle, African Hawk V
Eagle, Black-chested Snake 3
Eagle, Brown Snake 3
Eagle, Crowned 4
Eagle, Lesser Spotted V
Eagle, Long-crested 3, 4
Eagle, Steppe V
Eagle, Tawny V
Eagle, Wahlberg's V
Egret, Great 1
Egret, Little 1
Egret, Snowy V
Egret, Yellow-billed (Intermediate) 1
Eremomela, Karoo 9
Eremomela, Yellow-bellied 3, 8
Falcon, Amur 6, 7
Falcon, Eleonora's V
Falcon, Red-footed V
Falcon, Sooty V
Finch, Red-headed I, 5
Finfoot, African 1
Firefinch, African 3, 8
Firefinch, Red-billed 8, 9
Flamingo, Greater 1
Flamingo, Lesser 1
Flufftail, Buff-spotted 4, 8
Flycatcher, African Dusky 4, 5

Flycatcher, African Paradise 3, 4
Flycatcher, Blue-mantled Crested 3, 4
Flycatcher, European Pied V
Flycatcher, Spotted 3
Frigatebird, Great V
Gallinule, Allen's V
Gallinule, Purple V
Gannet, Australasian V
Gannet, Cape 2
Godwit, Bar-tailed 2, 3
Godwit, Black-tailed V
Godwit, Hudsonian V
Goose, Spur-winged 1
Goshawk, African 3, 4
Goshawk, Gabar 3
Grebe, Black-necked 1
Grebe, Great Crested 1
Grebe, Little 1
Greenshank, Common 1, 2
Gull (Common), Black-headed V
Gull, Franklin's V
Gull, Grey-headed 1, 2
Gull, Hartlaub's 1, 2
Gull, Kelp 2, 7
Gull, Lesser Black-backed V
Gull, Sabine's 2
Hamerkop 1
Harrier, Montagu's V
Harrier, Pallid V
Harrier, Western Marsh V
Hawk, African Cuckoo 3, 4
Heron, Black V
Heron, Black-crowned Night 1

INDEX TO SCIENTIFIC NAMES

INDEX TO COMMON NAMES

PICTURE CREDITS

AF = Albert Froneman/Images of Africa, AS = stock.adobe.com, AT = Andrew Turner, CW = Cathy Withers-Clarke,
DR = Dominic Rollinson, JG = John Graham, JM = Jacques van der Merwe, MB = Mike Buckham, MP = Matthew Prophet,
NvR = Natio van Rooyen, PR = Peter Ryan, ST = Stefan Theron, TH = Trevor Hardaker

7 **bottom**: © CW – AS
13 **heuweltjies**: Tony Rebelo
14 **middle**: MP
16 **clearing**: JM, **bottom** TH
17 **bottom**: JM
27 **4 right**: AT
69 **2 both**: Marius Burger
71 **3**: AT
73 **2 left**: Marius Burger
75 **3**: AT
85 **2 left**, **2 bottom** and
3 bottom: AT
99 **1 left**: Krystal Tolley,
1 right: Marius Burger
121 **1 both**: Mike Fabricius,
3 right: AT
122 **bottom**: MP
124 **bottom**: MB
129 **1 left**: JG, **1 right**: AF,
3 right and **4 right**: NvR
131 **3 right**: JG, **4 left**: PR,

133 **2 both**, and **3 left**: JG,
3 right: Luke Verburgt,
4 right: © Dewald – AS
135 **1 left**: Justin Rhys Nicolau,
1 right: Kevin Shaw,
3 right: © Alta Oosthuizen – AS
139 **4 left**: PR
141 **2 left**: MP, **3 middle**: PR,
4 left: ST, **4 right**: JG
143 **4 left**: TH, **4 right**: MP
145 **1 left** and **4 left**: JG,
1 right and **2 right**: DR,
4 right: TH
147 **2 both**: MB, **4 left**: MP,
4 right NvR
149 **2**: ST, **4 both**: TH
151 **3 right**: JG
153 **1 left** and **4 left**: JG,
1 right: DR, **3 left**: TH, **3
right**: PR

155 **2 right**: DR, **2 right**: TH,
3 right: PR
157 **1 left**: JG, **1 right**: Adam
Riley, **2 right**: MB
159 **4 inset**: NvR
161 **1 left**: © PACO COMO – AS,
1 right: JG, **2 middle**: Howard
Langley, **2 left**: PR
163 **1 left**: Howard Langley,
3 right: MP
169 **3 left**: JG, **3 right**: PR
173 **4**: PR
177 **2 left**: © Christian
Décout – AS
194 **1 left**: AF
209 **bushpig**: Bernard duPont,
zebra: Roger de la Harpe – AS
211 **1 left**: Jennifer Jarvis
215 **1**: Nico Dippenaar
221 **3**: Ara Monadjem
223 **1**, **2** and **4 right**: David

Jacobs, **4 left**: Ara Monadjem
225 **1 both**: Trevor Morgan,
2 both: David Jacobs
229 **1**: Margaret Hardaker
239 **1**: Neville Pillay
243 **2**: Chris and Mathilde Stuart
245 **2 right**: MP
247 **3**: Devonpike at English
Wikipedia, Public domain,
via Wikimedia Commons,
4: Jukani Wildlife Sanctuary,
South Africa
249 **2**: Magriet Brink
251 **2**: JH, **3 right**: TH
255 **1 top and right**: Steenbras
Nature Reserve team, **1 left**:
© The Cape Leopard Trust, **2
left**: PIXATERRA – AS, **2 right**:
simoneemanphoto – AS
257 **2 left**: Bernard duPont
263 **4**: Rob Tarr